T0331345

Contemporary public administration scholars are paying more attention to evidence-based policy, while largely neglecting the greater polarization of political systems recently characterizing North America and the European Union. *Public Policy, Governance and Polarization: Making Governance Work*, edited by Jesuit and Williams, takes the readers into the causes, nature, and consequences of ideological polarization, determining the extent to which it might inhibit evidence-based policy formulation and be an obstacle to public engagement-based styles of policy making.

Denita Cepiku, *Professor of Global Public Management, University of Rome Tor Vergata, Italy*

Public Policy, Governance and Polarization: Making Governance Work provides a workable definition of "polarization" in politics and the production of public policy. The co-authors use comparative case studies from the United States, Canada, and Europe as a means of better understanding the causes and effects of political polarization. These analyses assert that political polarization is here to stay and will likely grow even more pronounced in the coming years. Consequently, public administrators must learn how to work with and manage polarization.

Nicholas Bauroth, *Associate Professor of Political Science at North Dakota State University, USA*

Public Policy, Governance and Polarization

Polarization is widely diagnosed as a major cause of the decline of evidence-based policy making and public engagement-based styles of policy making. It creates an environment where hardened partisan viewpoints on major policy questions are less amenable to negotiation, compromise or change. Polarization is not a temporary situation – it is the "new normal."

Public Policy, Governance and Polarization seeks to provide a theoretical foundation for scholars and policy makers who need to understand the powerful and often disruptive forces that have arisen in Europe and North America over the past decade. Academics and practitioners need to better understand this growing trend and to find ways in which it may be managed so that policy solutions to these threats may be developed and implemented.

Researchers and future policymakers in fields such as public administration, public management and public policy need to recognise how institutional design, corporatist interest group systems and different pedagogical approaches may help them understand, discuss and work beyond policy polarization. Edited by two leading political science scholars, this book aims to begin that process.

David K. Jesuit is a Professor and Chairperson of the Department of Political Science and Public Administration at Central Michigan University (CMU), USA.

Russell Alan Williams is an Associate Professor of Political Science at Memorial University, Canada.

Routledge Critical Studies in Public Management
Edited by Stephen Osborne

The study and practice of public management has undergone profound changes across the world. Over the last quarter century, we have seen:

- increasing criticism of public administration as the over-arching framework for the provision of public services;
- the rise (and critical appraisal) of the 'New Public Management' as an emergent paradigm for the provision of public services;
- the transformation of the 'public sector' into the cross-sectoral provision of public services; and
- the growth of the governance of inter-organizational relationships as an essential element in the provision of public services.

In reality these trends have not so much replaced each other as elided or co-existed together – the public policy process has not gone away as a legitimate topic of study, intra-organizational management continues to be essential to the efficient provision of public services, whilst the governance of inter-organizational and inter-sectoral relationships is now essential to the effective provision of these services.

Further, whilst the study of public management has been enriched by the contribution of a range of insights from the "mainstream" management literature it has also contributed to this literature in such areas as networks and inter-organizational collaboration, innovation and stakeholder theory.

This series is dedicated to presenting and critiquing this important body of theory and empirical study. It will publish books that both explore and evaluate the emergent and developing nature of public administration, management and governance (in theory and practice) and examine the relationship with and contribution to the over-arching disciplines of management and organizational sociology.

Books in the series will be of interest to academics and researchers in this field, students undertaking advanced studies of it as part of their undergraduate or postgraduate degree and reflective policy makers and practitioners.

Public Policy, Governance and Polarization

Making Governance Work

Edited by
David K. Jesuit and
Russell Alan Williams

Routledge
Taylor & Francis Group

LONDON AND NEW YORK

First published 2018 by Routledge

2 Park Square, Milton Park, Abingdon, Oxfordshire OX14 4RN
52 Vanderbilt Avenue, New York, NY 10017

Routledge is an imprint of the Taylor & Francis Group, an informa business

First issued in paperback 2019

British Library Cataloguing in Publication Data
A catalogue record for this book is available from the British Library

Library of Congress Cataloging in Publication Data
Names: Jesuit, David K., editor. | Williams, Russell Alan, 1970– editor.
Title: Public policy, governance and polarization: making governance
work / [edited by] David K. Jesuit and Russell Alan Williams.
Description: Abingdon, Oxon; New York, NY: Routledge, 2017. |
Includes bibliographical references and index. |
Identifiers: LCCN 2017005943 (print) | LCCN 2017022852 (ebook) |
ISBN 9781315560342 (eBook) | ISBN 9781138675933
(hardback: alk. paper)
Subjects: LCSH: Policy sciences. | Polarization (Social sciences)
Classification: LCC H97 (ebook) | LCC H97.P793 2017 (print) |
DDC 320.6–dc23
LC record available at https://lccn.loc.gov/2017005943

ISBN: 978-1-138-67593-3 (hbk)
ISBN: 978-0-367-87835-1 (pbk)

Typeset in Times New Roman
by Wearset Ltd, Boldon, Tyne and Wear

Contents

An example of polarization: the climate change debate   85

 4 Consensual environmental policy in the Anthropocene:
    governing what humanity hath wrought   87
    WALTER F. BABER AND ROBERT V. BARTLETT

 5 Polarized climate debate? Institutions and structure in
    subnational policymaking   106
    RUSSELL WILLIAMS AND SUSAN MORRISSEY WYSE

 6 Polarized business interests: EU climate policy-making
    during the "Great Recession"   126
    RAFFAEL HANSCHMANN

PART III
Potential remedies to polarized policymaking   157

 7 Comparative national energy policies and climate change
    actions in countries with divided and unified governments:
    reflections, projections and opportunities for improved
    pedagogy   159
    THOMAS ROHRER AND PAMELA S. GATES

 8 Exploring the mediating effects of institutions on polarization
    and political conflict: evidence from Michigan cities   174
    NATHAN GRASSE, THOMAS GREITENS, DAVID JESUIT,
    AND LAWRENCE SYCH

 9 Political polarization, fiscal stress and financing public
    universities: a comparative analysis of the Ontario and
    Michigan public policy experience   186
    LAWRENCE SYCH AND MARCY TAYLOR

10 The silence is deafening: a look into financial services sector
    policymaking in Canada   208
    IAN ROBERGE

    Conclusion: managing polarization to make governance work 224
    DAVID K. JESUIT AND RUSSELL ALAN WILLIAMS

    Index   228

Figures

Tables

Contributors

Walter F. Baber, Professor in the Graduate Center for Public Policy and Administration at California State University, USA.

Robert V. Bartlett, Professor, Department Chair and Gund Chair of the Liberal Arts, Department of Political Science, University of Vermont, USA.

Jeremiah J. Castle, Post-doctoral Fellow, Central Michigan University, Mount Pleasant, Michigan, USA.

Charles Conteh, Graduate Program Director, Associate Professor, Public Policy and Management, Department of Political Science, Brock University, St. Catharines, Canada.

Lindsay Flynn, Assistant Professor, Department of Political Science, Wheaton College, USA.

Pamela S. Gates, Professor of English and Dean of the College of Humanities and Social and Behavioral Sciences, Central Michigan University, USA.

Nathan Grasse, Associate Professor, School of Public Policy and Administration, Carleton University, Canada.

Thomas Greitens, Associate Professor and Director of the Master of Public Administration Program, Central Michigan University, USA.

Raffael Hanschmann, Doctoral Researcher, Department of Economics and Social Sciences, University of Potsdam, Germany.

David K. Jesuit, Professor, Political Science and Public Administration, Central Michigan University, USA.

Piotr R. Paradowski, Data Expert and Research Associate, LIS Cross-National Data Center, Luxembourg.

Ian Roberge, Department Chair and Associate Professor, Political Science Department, Collège Glendon, Université York, Canada.

Thomas Rohrer, Director, Great Lakes Institute for Sustainable Systems, Central Michigan University, USA.

Daniel M. Shea, Director of the Goldfarb Center for Public Affairs and Civic Engagement and Professor of Government, Colby College, USA.

J. Cherie Strachan, Associate Professor, Political Science and Public Administration, Central Michigan University, USA.

Lawrence Sych, Professor, Political Science and Public Administration, Central Michigan University, USA.

Marcy Taylor, Professor of English, Assistant Dean of the College of Humanities and Social and Behavioral Sciences, Central Michigan University, USA.

Russell Alan Williams, Associate Professor, Memorial University Department of Political Science, Memorial University, Canada.

Michael R. Wolf, Associate Professor of Political Science, Indiana University and Purdue University-Indianapolis, USA.

Susan Morrissey Wyse, Faculty of Environmental Studies, York University, Canada.

Preface

This volume represents the continued intellectual collaboration of scholars and practitioners under the auspices of the Transnational Initiative on Governance Research and Education Network, or "TIGRE Net." This international group of scholars, students and field specialists is dedicated to identifying the opportunities and challenges public managers confront in the global economy, and to providing them with the strategies and skills necessary to overcome obstacles to domestic, cross-border and international coordination. Outputs from the TIGRE Net include several academic conferences and workshops, which have been supported by a grant from the Canadian Social Science and Humanities Research Council (SSHRC) and academic partners in the US, Italy and Canada. Research from these events has been published in a number of academic outlets, including journals such as the *International Journal of Public Administration* (IJPA) and the *International Journal of Public Sector Management* (IJPSM). Previous edited collections have included *Making Multilevel Governance Work: Lessons from Europe and North America* (2012), published by CRC Press, and *Governance and Public Management: Strategic Foundations for Volatile Times* (2014), published by Routledge. Core partners of TIGRE Net include universities in the US (Central Michigan University and California State-Long Beach), Italy (the University of Rome "Tor Vergata" and the University of Macerata) and Canada (York University, Toronto and Brock University, St. Catharines).

Introduction and overview

Polarization explained and applied

*Jeremiah J. Castle, David K. Jesuit and
Russell Alan Williams*

For some time now, the study of American politics has been dominated by concerns about "polarization" and the extent to which political views on key public policy challenges have diverged and hardened along partisan lines. Indeed, Pew Research Center (2014) called polarization the "defining feature of 21st century American politics, both among the public and elected officials." While the problem has been diagnosed for some time (Poole and Rosenthal 1984), the consensus is that the polarization has intensified over the last two decades (Layman et al. 2006). Fueled by globalization and increasing economic uncertainty, self-selection in media sources, the arrival of social media and personal information bubbles, and changes in party organization and financing (explanations are myriad), the concern is that political polarization presents additional challenges to policymakers at multiple levels of governmental authority, presenting complex political disputes that impede the policy process and thus inhibit resolution of pressing policy problems.

Indeed, much of the concern is that polarization is a particularly pernicious obstacle to policymaking in policy areas presenting the greatest challenges to modern governance. The hardening of ideological positions is hampering governments' ability to manage everything from economic stagnation, growing income inequality, ineffective financial regulation, immigration reform, and climate change. While the core lesson of the study of public policy for decades has been the crucial importance of successfully managing the political arena in order to accomplish policy objectives (Kingdon 1995; Cairney 2016), polarization in American politics vastly complicates modern government.

While arguments about the role of polarization in modern political life have developed more slowly outside of the US, particularly if specific policy areas (such as climate change) are set aside, there is increasing recognition that the dynamics driving polarization are not uniquely "American." For example, while there has always been evidence of similar political dynamics in Europe, Canada and elsewhere, the more recent rise of populism, and the particular fault lines over policy issues such as group and migrant rights, multiculturalism, and "Brexit" has increased concern about the role of polarization in governance. As such, we seek to further our understanding of political polarization, how it operates across a variety of settings and how it impacts policymaking so that strategies and recommendations for overcoming this dilemma, and "making governance work," may be developed.

For our purposes, it is important to recognize the extent to which "polarization" is widely diagnosed as a principle cause of the decline of evidence-based policymaking and as an obstacle to contemporary public engagement-based styles of policymaking. Polarization is seen to create an environment where hardened partisan viewpoints on major policy questions are less amenable to negotiation, compromise or change given the availability of new information. Significantly, polarization adds an additional challenge to policymaking in already complex multi-level governance settings where actors have multiple points of entry to impact decision making. The federal systems of Canada and the US, and the multi-level governance dynamic of the European Union, present complex political challenges in which responding to perceived problems requires negotiation and compromise across governments. Polarization can impede this policy style and thus inhibit resolution of numerous problems.

This edited volume explores the challenges of developing and implementing public policies that address such fundamental problems in an era characterized by growing political polarization, as evidenced by populist "protest" political movements in numerous countries in North America and Western Europe. Previous research, as well as conference and workshop experiences with practitioners from several countries, has highlighted the importance of successfully managing the political arena in order to accomplish policy objectives. As such, we seek to further our understanding of political polarization so that strategies and recommendations for making governance work may be developed.

Defining polarization

While many people have a general feeling that politics is becoming more "polarized" both in the US and abroad, defining exactly what we mean by polarization is a difficult and controversial matter. Early on in the polarization literature, scholars recognized that polarization is a multidimensional concept involving both the bifurcation of opinion and the relative distance between opinions (DiMaggio et al. 1996). In other words, for polarization to be present, the public must be increasingly divided into two opposing camps with few moderates or independents refusing to "take sides." In addition, there must be a relatively large degree of ideological distance between those parties. For example, two parties that are located just to the left and just to the right of the median voter are not polarized, but two parties that are located on the far right and far left are. Although defining a multidimensional concept like polarization is difficult, we adopt a working definition of polarization as, "the increasing division of a population into two (or more) opposing camps that are ideologically distant from one another." In our usage, we posit a continuum that ranges from no polarization, as implied by Wilson's (1887) notion of bureaucratic rationalism, to civil war, where two or more sides are so deeply divided that violence is considered a legitimate means of resolving political differences. Such extremes are uncommon (or nonexistent in the former case).

As will be shown in the chapters that follow, we find evidence to support the notion that polarization threatens political systems' ability to resolve policy dilemmas. While the range of political settings examined in this volume make it impossible to test at what point polarization renders governance unworkable, undermining the basis for evidence-based problem solving, it is important to recognize that there is a distinction between politicization, which reflects what we consider to be a healthy state of affairs within a democratic political system, and polarization as we employ the term. The former implies that the preferences and beliefs of voters and political party elites are roughly at a historical or global average on an ideological scale, whether that is a simple traditional left–right index or something more complex (and accurate). Polarization, meanwhile, refers to a situation where the ideological gap is wider than ordinarily exists within a particular polity. The chapter by Roberge in this volume, as well as our concluding chapter, engages this discussion in greater detail.

Polarization over time and across units

Polarization may be treated as a temporal concept, focusing on a particular case over time. One frequently hears, for example, that the US has become more ideologically divided in recent years than it was previously. There is, in fact, evidence indicating that polarization has been growing in the US.

It is also possible to view polarization from a cross-sectional perspective, as the chapters of this volume do. Namely, the ideological gap between major parties or factions contesting power is wider in some communities, whether they are countries, cities or states, than others. Regardless of whether one chooses to examine the concept across time or across settings, the central objective of this edited volume is to determine the extent to which ideological polarization might inhibit policy formulation and implementation, and the mechanisms by which it occurs. In order to accomplish this task, we first offer a brief overview of the literature on polarization in the US, which has been frequently cited as an example of a highly polarized political system. After this brief review, we outline the remainder of the volume.

Political polarization in American politics

Within the literature, there is little debate over the general assertion that politics in the US has become more polarized. However, scholars' opinions vary widely on the causes, nature, and consequences of that polarization. Below, we summarize the literature on polarization in the US. First, we consider each of the three major political institutions in the US, highlighting cases of polarization in each. Second, we review the spirited debate over whether the general public has become more polarized. Finally, we discuss the implications of polarization for public policy. Ultimately, we find evidence that the polarization in US political institutions is sufficient to create significant obstacles for the making of public policy. If the general public is indeed becoming more polarized, those obstacles will only increase in the future.

Polarization and institutions in the US

Among political observers, there is little doubt that Congress has become more polarized since the 1980s. Recent decades have seen rising partisan rancor at Capitol Hill, including particularly nasty fights over the Iran–Contra investigation, the budget battle between Speaker Newt Gingrich and the Clinton administration, the impeachment of Bill Clinton, healthcare reform (culminating in the passage of the Affordable Care Act), and the debt ceiling (Mann and Ornstein 2006, 2012). Although it is less recognized than the issue-based polarization, academics have persuasively shown that Congress is becoming more polarized on procedural matters as well (Theriault 2008).

The academic debate on Congressional polarization mostly focuses on the themes of causes and consequences. A major development in the field was Poole and Rosenthal's (1997) development of NOMINATE, a mathematical summary of how a legislator had voted on every roll call vote taken in Congress. Poole and Rosenthal (1997) argue that Congressional voting can be effectively summarized by a single dimension that represents a left–right ideological divide. Their work shows persuasively that party polarization in Congress began to rise in the 1970s and has continued increasing since.

One consequence of polarization is increasing gridlock. Binder (2003, 2015) shows that legislative gridlock has increased dramatically from the 1950s to the present. In particular, the 112th Congress (2011–2012) over-performed predicted legislative gridlock given the makeup of Congress (Binder 2015). While gridlock is always a potential institutional risk in American government given the division of powers, the point is that the steady upward trajectory in gridlock is a product of polarization and it directly reduces progress on salient issues such as healthcare, immigration, the environment, and homeland security.

Signs of polarization are increasingly apparent in the executive branch as well. Given the legislative gridlock in Congress, presidents have increasingly turned to executive orders to achieve some of their policy preferences (Howell 2003; Cooper 2014). The dual trends of polarized policy and increasing use of executive orders are apparent in many policy areas, including the treatment of abortion. For example, the "Mexico City" law that prevents government-funded NGOs from providing abortions was instituted by the Reagan administration, rescinded by the Clinton administration, reinstituted by George W. Bush, and again revoked by Barack Obama.[1]

The polarization and mistrust that characterize Congress and the presidency is increasingly apparent in the judiciary too. In the 1960s and 1970s, conservatives were outraged by a series of cases including *Griswold* v. *Connecticut* (1965) and *Roe* v. *Wade* (1973) that, they believed, signaled justices were increasingly "legislating from the bench." In response, conservative legal thinkers formulated originalism, an interpretive philosophy that stresses that law must be interpreted in response to the intent of those who wrote the laws. Outraged liberals argued that such a philosophy ignored the fact that the Constitution was a "living document" in which old words might apply to new situations. This debate was carried out both in legal scholarship and in court decisions across the country.

The recognition of the courts' influence on policy has led to increasingly divisive fights for judicial nominations. After seeing first-hand how political views could result in the defeat of a nominee during the acrimonious hearings for Robert Bork's candidacy for the Supreme Court, nominees responded by speaking mostly in vague legalese during hearings. The acrimony extends to lower court nominations as well, with Republicans repeatedly refusing to consider Barack Obama's judicial nominees, leading to the Senate engaging the "nuclear option" (eliminating the filibuster when considering judicial nominees). In short, the signs of polarization are apparent throughout the three branches of American government.

Polarization at the mass level

At the mass level, there is considerably more debate over whether Americans are polarized. In one of the first major investigations of the question, sociologist James Davison Hunter (1991) argued that the previous Protestant v. Catholic division between the parties had been replaced by a new division based on religious orthodoxy. In his account, modernity was causing culturally orthodox individuals from a variety of faith traditions to join together to oppose cultural progressives. Hunter's thesis found national relevance in the wake of Patrick Buchanan's speech at the 1992 Republican National Convention, in which the conservative firebrand declared that: "There is a religious war going on in this country, a cultural war as critical to the kind of nation we shall be as the Cold War itself, for this war is for the soul of America" (quoted in Fiorina et al. 2010: 1).

While Hunter's account resonated with the conventional wisdom of political observers, social scientists have questioned whether it accurately characterizes the average American. Morris Fiorina et al. (2010) argue that the mass public has not become more polarized, in the sense that many Americans continue to identify as independent and there remains a strong moderate "center" in the American ideological distribution. Rather, Fiorina et al. (2010) contend that Americans have become more consistently ideologically "sorted" into the parties since the 1960s, with liberals increasingly identifying with the Democratic Party and conservatives increasingly identifying with the Republican Party, thereby creating the illusion of polarization. Critics including Abramowitz and Saunders (2008) have argued that Fiorina et al. overstate the level of agreement, and they use different data to show that Americans are polarized (or, at least, highly sorted) along the lines of party, geography, and religion. Furthermore, more recent data from the Pew Research Center (2014) suggests that the number of moderates in the political landscape is decreasing. On Pew's 10-point issue scale, the percentage of Americans with consistently liberal views has risen from 3 percent in 1994 to 12 percent in 2004, while the percentage with consistently conservative views has risen from 7 percent to 9 percent. While far from a complete bifurcation, this recent data suggests that polarization in the mass public is increasing over time.

The consequences of polarization

Given the state of political scientists' understanding of polarization, it is likely to have tremendous consequences for American public policy. As the two major parties' agendas become more polarized, the minority party's incentive to generate gridlock rather than allow victories for the majority becomes more pronounced. This gridlock creates periods of policy stagnation followed by periods of policy innovation. For example, the minimum wage illustrates this dynamic, stagnating for decades (creating, in effect, a decline in spending power) followed by a sudden raise when political conditions make it difficult for the minority party to maintain its protest (McCarty et al. 2008).

Furthermore, in order to achieve policy innovation, Congress may increasingly rely on "unorthodox lawmaking" to overcome this gridlock (Sinclair 2011). The legislative strategies falling into this category are within the boundaries of the legislative process, but may have a polarizing effect on Congress. For example, during the passage of the Affordable Care Act, the Democrats overcame the lack of a filibuster-proof majority in the Senate by having the House pass the Senate's version of the bill and then amending the bill using the budget reconciliation process. While the move was undoubtedly legal, it left many Republicans in Congress feeling bullied by the legislative process, robbing Congress of any remaining legislative reciprocity and good will.

Another important consequence of polarization may be a decline in citizen trust of government (King 1997; Hetherington 2005). For example, in Hibbing and Theiss-Morse's (1995, 2002) account, the American public behaves according to the old adage, "you shouldn't watch the making of sausage or legislation." Public battles over legislative procedures and public policy, such as the acrimonious battle over healthcare reform in 2010, generate resentment and frustration on the part of a public that struggles to understand the institutional and behavioral sources of disagreement in Congress. This declining trust in government and policy may have a cyclical effect, causing members of the public to elect outsider politicians who pledge to "clean up Washington." Once these outsiders become a part of Congress, they engage in divisive rhetoric and self-serving obstructionist politics, generating even more frustration among the public (Brady and Theriault 2001).

Finally, if the general public is indeed growing more polarized, it may signal that many of the issues addressed in this volume will only continue to worsen. Political science has shown that each of the three branches of government are to some extent responsive to the American public. If elections continue to resemble the back-and-forth battles of 2008, 2010, 2012, 2014, and 2016, institutions may

find themselves under increasing pressure to handle divided government and repeated changes in power.

As noted earlier, the literature on polarization in other national settings is not as well developed. In Europe, Canada, and elsewhere, while there has been considerable discussion of the extent to which some form of "polarization" might be inhibiting effective governance, this work lacks the focused (and detailed) examination seen in the US. There is also some sense that scholars focused on other national settings have come "late to the game" on polarization, only recognizing the extent to which some sort of ideological and partisan realignment may be undermining evidence-based policymaking in recent years. What is notable for our purpose is that, when seen across other settings, political polarization manifests itself differently, given differing institutional arrangements. The diverse group of scholars that have contributed to this volume thus offer us some preliminary ways to think about polarization comparatively as a cross-national problem for policymakers.

Path of the volume

Given the enormous consequences of polarization, understanding its causes, consequences, and potential solutions is of utmost importance to understanding governance. Therefore, the remainder of this volume is organized into three parts that explore key topics in the study of the relationship between polarization and public policy and administration in greater depth.

Part I includes contributions from scholars who explore the origins of political polarization, including globalization, growing inequality, and the media. In Chapter 1, Conteh argues that economic restructuring, deindustrialization, and the transition to the "knowledge-driven" economy has created a potent environment for polarization in most urban regions in Canada and the United States. Through a comparative cross border comparison, he examines the structures and processes of urban governance, and how coalitions navigate what are "crowded" policy environments nested within complicated multilevel governance settings. In particular, he compares the challenges of managing divergent discourses and conflicting interests in industrial restructuring in two mid-sized city regions in Canada and the US (the Niagara and Rochester regions). His findings suggest that the potential for polarizing policy ideas, that might make it impossible for cities to respond to these challenges, can be managed and points to some key lessons from these two examples that offer some cause for optimism.

Wolf et al. (Chapter 2), meanwhile, find that polarization is deeply embedded in geographic and demographic trends in the US such that compromise is seen as a weakness in an intensely partisan political environment. Relying on a series of national public opinion surveys conducted by the authors, they conclude that Americans' self-selected exposure to partisan media, candidates' increasing ability to micro-target voters during electoral campaigns, and Americans' increasingly homogeneous social networks cultivate a general public unwilling to support ideological compromises.

In Chapter 3, Flynn and Paradowski also find that polarization of the general public within countries can be linked to structural causes. They use statistical matching methods to integrate electoral and wealth surveys in order to explore the relationship between income, wealth, and voters' ideological preferences in the US, Germany, and Sweden. This is especially salient as these countries, along with most advanced market capitalist economy countries, have witnessed growth in income and wealth inequality, exacerbated by the financial crisis in 2008. Flynn and Paradowski conclude that while greater levels of both wealth and income are associated with a greater likelihood of voting for a conservative party in the US, only income is associated with voting preferences in Germany. Little support is found for economic voting in Sweden, despite increasing levels of wealth and income inequality. The implication is that, depending on the political and economic context within a country, trends in income and wealth inequality promote greater polarization. This may, in turn, lead to the adoption of policies that widen this gap even further. Thus Chapters 2 and 3 offer somewhat pessimistic conclusions about the prospects of compromise.

Part II includes a set of chapters that examine an illustrative policy challenge that has been subject to polarized debate: climate change. Some may consider Chapter 4 to be normative. Here, Bartlett and Baber argue that humankind's search for the governing consensus that is required to protect the environmental preconditions of its own existence may be the most daunting challenge humans will ever face. They identify five core analytical problems of "earth system governance" that must be overcome in order for humanity to survive and discuss consensus oriented solutions to them that have emerged from the environmental governance experiences of a global cross section of humanity. Their argument highlights the extent to which effective governance in climate policy requires discourses far removed from what is often seen as the polarized positions taken by partisans.

In Chapter 5, Russell Williams and Susan Morrissey Wyse offer a case study examination of the issues raised by Bartlett and Baber in Chapter 4. They examine Canada's engagement in the global greenhouse gas reduction regime, arguing that Canada, often regarded as a climate policy "pariah" after its withdrawal from the Kyoto Protocol, faces a very difficult set of choices in meeting the commitments negotiated in the Paris Process. While public debate about anthropocentric climate change is not as polarized as it is in other "foot-dragging" jurisdictions (e.g., Australia and the US), unfortunately climate policy is effectively polarized. Canadian federalism, which has resulted in individual provinces having responsibility for emission reductions, has created the space for widely divergent approaches, undermining the potential for an effective national strategy. While this promises to complicate Canada's participation in the Paris Process, and Canadian international environmental policy in general, the key point is that polarization here is institutionally-driven given the differences in regional economies, rather than a reflection of the kind of partisan polarization seen elsewhere. It nonetheless greatly complicates governance in the sector.

In the final chapter in this part (Chapter 6), Raffael Hanschmann, also examines polarization and its impact on environmental policy, here environmental policymaking in the European Union after the recent economic, fiscal, and debt crisis. He demonstrates that the crisis opened up previously latent cleavages over the regulation of automobile emissions, reinforced by the protectionist behavior of Member States' governments, leading to less ambitious policy outputs. The chapter contributes to the volume by improving the understanding of how exactly economic hardships polarize policymaking, unveiling the causal links between the crisis, actor behavior, and policy outputs. Like Williams and Wyse's contribution, polarization and a hardening of policy positions has contributed to the difficulties of policymaking in this sector even in the absence of the kind of clear partisan realignment observed in the US.

While the first and second parts of the volume focus on the problem of polarization, the third and final part includes chapters that develop potential solutions to polarized policymaking, ranging from institutional design to pedagogies and financing in higher education.

In Chapter 7, Rohrer and Gates offer case studies of climate change policy in three countries: the US, Denmark, and the People's Republic of China. This allows them to compare countries with divided governments, countries with multi-party coalition governments, and those having undivided or authoritarian governments. From this comparison of the role of political settings in shaping environmental debates, they ultimately propose a new pedagogy for improving public education about climate change, to ensure an educated populace on this critical global issue.

Grasse et al. (Chapter 8) attempt to identify the types of institutional arrangements that mediate polarized political conflicts. They do so by exploring political conflict in city councils in Michigan, assessing the degree to which polarization and other variables drive political conflict, as well as the extent to which the city's institutional structures can serve to limit it. In order to assess institutional structures, they examine factors such as the nature of elections (partisan/nonpartisan), the presence of a strong mayor or city manager, and reliance on district or at-large elections. Grasse et al. also control for other potential explanations for conflict to determine the influence of polarization on political conflict. They conclude that institutions can, in fact, somewhat ameliorate the effects of polarization.

In Chapter 9, Sych and Taylor examine the influence of legislative polarization at state and provincial levels in Michigan and Ontario on their respective policies for financing higher education. They identify and analyze trends across several common measures of financial condition during the 2003–2014 fiscal years in order to assess the nature of responsive budgetary actions and determine how such actions are rhetorically presented to their stakeholders within a federal system beset by polarization and fiscal stress. A policy narrative framework with a rhetorical analysis complements the analysis of university financial condition. Finally, Sych and Taylor explore the consequences this polarization has on universities in these territories and conclude with a set of recommendations.

Ian Roberge provides the final substantive chapter in this volume (Chapter 10). In some ways, it is a very fitting concluding chapter to this part, as well as those that preceded it, as he challenges the claims of the contributors, including the co-editors. Namely, this chapter considers the ways by which polarization, or what he characterizes as "politicization" might actually improve policymaking and presents the well-established argument in public administration that bureaucracy can limit democracy. From this perspective politicization can be argued to reflect a thriving democratic policy environment. The opposite of polarization is technocratic governance, which is thought to provide for a more efficient policy process and eventually a more effective policy. Policymaking in technocratic governance, however, takes place behind closed doors, without public input and with little scrutiny or accountability. Roberge offers a comparative analysis of financial services sector policymaking in the US and Canada to support these conclusions. This chapter, therefore, brings us back to the debate we raised earlier in the Introduction: To what extent is polarization a challenge to effective governance in the twenty-first century and what strategies might help to manage the extent to which polarization can contribute to gridlock and ineffective policy responses? For Roberge, polarization need not be a crisis; in some circumstances it may be part of the solution to longstanding policy problems.

There are several central lessons we would like readers to take away from the following chapters. First, political polarization is not likely to diminish in the coming years. Our chapters suggest that the demographic and economic trends that underlie the growing ideological divide, such as globalization, economic restructuring, and economic inequality, will not just disappear. These structural changes create the potential for increasingly divergent views about the role of government in society. Moreover, the mainstream media, including the increased use of social media, as well as decentralized decision-making structures, have the potential to exacerbate this potential for polarization.

Second, in terms of specific policy challenges, some will not be well managed in a polarized environment – some issues require shared values and policy commitments. For example, climate change, which features prominently in this volume, is not a policy area in which diverse responses and discordant beliefs about the need for action will "work." To date, the objective threats posed by global climate change have not been sufficient to support the style of governance needed in this sector. Polarization is producing ineffective policy responses undermining our ability to make governance work.

This brings us to our final point. Namely, polarization can be managed. Reformed institutional structures that depoliticize issues and tools such as strategic planning have been effectively used by policymakers and public administrators to facilitate consensus. These themes will be explored in more detail in our concluding chapter. In the meantime, we hope that readers will find the following chapters provide insights into the causes, consequences, and possible solutions to political polarization.

Note

1 The White House Office of Policy Development, "US Policy Statement for the International Conference on Population," *Population and Development Review* 10 (1984), 574–579; William Clinton, January 22, 1993, "Memorandum for the Acting Administrator of the Agency for International Development, Subject: AID Family Planning Grants/Mexico City Policy," accessed April 20, 2011, http://clinton6.nara.gov; George W. Bush, 22 January 2001, "Memorandum for the Administrator of the United States Agency for International Development, Subject: Restoration of the Mexico City Policy," accessed April 20, 2011, http://georgewbush-whitehouse.archives.gov; Barack Obama, January 23, 2009, "Mexico City Policy and Assistance for Voluntary Population Planning," accessed April 20, 2011, www.whitehouse.gov.

Bibliography

Abramowitz, Alan I. and Kyle L. Saunders. 2008. "Is polarization a myth?" *The Journal of Politics* 70(2): 542–555.

Binder, Sarah A. 2003. *Stalemate: Causes and consequences of legislative gridlock.* Washington, DC: Brookings Institution Press.

Binder, Sarah. 2015. "The dysfunctional congress." *Annual Review of Political Science* 18: 85–101.

Brady, David W. and Sean M. Theriault. 2001. "A reassessment of who's to blame: A positive case for the public evaluation of Congress." In John R. Hibbing and Elizabeth Theiss-Morse, eds., *What is it about government that Americans dislike?* New York: Cambridge University Press, pp. 175–192.

Cairney, Paul. 2016. *The politics of evidence-based policymaking.* London: Palgrave Pivot.

Cooper, Phillip J. 2014. *By order of the president: The use and abuse of executive direct action,* 2nd edn. Lawrence, KS: University Press of Kansas.

DiMaggio, Paul, John Evans, and Bethany Bryson. 1996. "Have American's social attitudes become more polarized?" *American Journal of Sociology* 102(3): 690–755.

Fiorina, Morris, Samuel J. Abrams, and Jeremy C. Pope. 2010. *Culture war? The myth of a polarized America,* 3rd edn. New York: Pearson Longman.

Hetherington, Marc J. 2005. *Why trust matters: Declining political trust and the demise of American liberalism.* Princeton, NJ: Princeton University Press.

Hibbing, John R. and Elizabeth Theiss-Morse. 1995. *Congress as public enemy: Public attitudes toward American political institutions.* New York: Cambridge University Press.

Hibbing, John R. and Elizabeth Theiss-Morse. 2002. *Stealth democracy: Americans' beliefs about how government should work.* New York: Cambridge University Press.

Howell, William G. 2003. *Power without persuasion: The politics of direct presidential action.* Princeton, NJ: Princeton University Press.

Hunter, James Davison. 1991. *Culture wars: The struggle to control the family, art, education, law, and politics in America.* New York: Basic Books.

King, Anthony Stephen. 1997. *Running scared: Why America's politicians campaign too much and govern too little.* Glencoe, IL: Free Press.

Kingdon, John W. (1995). *Agendas, alternatives, and public policies.* New York: Harper-Collins.

Layman, Geoffrey C., Thomas M. Carsey, and Juliana Menasce Horowitz. 2006. "Party polarization in American politics: Characteristics, causes, and consequences." *Annual Review of Political Science* 9: 83–110.

Mann, Thomas E., and Norman J. Ornstein. 2006. *The broken branch: How Congress is failing America and how to get it back on track*. Oxford: Oxford University Press.

Mann, Thomas E., and Norman J. Ornstein. 2012. *It's even worse than it looks: How the American constitutional system collided with the new politics of extremism*. New York: Basic Books.

McCarty, Nolan, Keith T. Poole, and Howard Rosenthal. 2008. *Polarized America: The dance of ideology and unequal riches*. Cambridge, MA: MIT Press.

Pew Research Center. 2014, June 12. "7 things to know about polarization in America."

Poole, Keith T. and Howard Rosenthal. 1984. "The polarization of American politics." *Journal of Politics* 46(4): 1061–1079.

Poole, Keith T. and Howard Rosenthal. 1997. *Congress: A political-economic history of roll call voting*. New York: Oxford University Press.

Sinclair, Barbara. 2011. *Unorthodox lawmaking: New legislative processes in the US Congress*. Washington, DC: CQ Press.

Theriault, Sean M. 2008. *Party polarization in Congress*. New York: Cambridge University Press.

Wilson, Woodrow. (1887). "The study of administration." *Political Science Quarterly* 2(2): 197–222.

Part I

Polarized mass publics and electoral politics

1 Concerted action in complex environments

A comparison of industrial restructuring in mid-sized city-regions in Canada and the United States

Charles Conteh

Introduction

This chapter examines the structures and processes of navigating through political polarization in crowded policy environments that are nested within multiple tiers of jurisdiction. In particular, the discussion compares the challenges and prospects of managing divergent discourses and conflicting interests in industrial restructuring in two mid-sized city-regions in Canada and the United States, namely the Niagara and Rochester regions, respectively. The broader context of the two cases consists of the growing problems of industrial decline, economic stagnation, rising income inequality and persistent (if not increasing) pockets of poverty plaguing a growing number of mid-sized cities in North America. The key implication of these latest trends is that managing the political arena of urban spaces is now more than ever fraught with contestations as simmering socioeconomic tensions boil to the top of political discourse. The discussion analyzes how the two cases managed their tensions, and concludes with some practical and theoretical lessons for advancing our understanding of managing political polarization for more effective governance.

Polarization refers to the prevalence of intransigent divergent political, ideational, material and social schisms among key actors, with the potential to derail the institutions of governance and entrap policy discourses in a vicious cycle of vitriolic exchanges and loss of compromise. It should be noted that differences of opinion and the debates and contestations that follow such differences are an intrinsic part of the democratic ethos. However, when such conflicts become pathological, symptoms such as ideological intransigence and loss of interest in sound evidence start to cripple effective governance. These pathologies are the real causes for concern for scholars and practitioners alike (DiMaggio et al., 1996; Baldassarri and Gelman, 2008). There is an increasing trend in Canada and the United States in particular toward ideological mudslinging and vitriolic rhetoric that often indulges in demonizing opponents rather than relying on reason and evidence to guide public deliberation in policy choices (McCarty et al., 2006; Mann and Ornstein, 2012). In such an atmosphere of ideological trench warfare, the real victims are the age-old virtues of negotiation and compromise in navigating change and solving socioeconomic problems. The concept of "polarization" is thus a growing subject of interest in many research traditions within political science.

Polarizing fissures can manifest themselves along ideological lines, most formally expressed through party platforms and hyperbolic rhetoric. But they are more pervasive than that. In societies around the world, polarization can take ethnic, racial, religious and other sociocultural forms. In North America, these fissures have often manifested themselves through the lenses of class and race, with political parties and their fringe constituencies serving as the most visible platforms and conduits for expressing these tensions. At the local level, however, these tensions and divides are observed less as party clashes and more as conflicts among individuals and groups about the socioeconomic destiny of cities and how to allocate resources to combat economic stagnation, income inequality and chronic poverty. The crippling schisms of polarization in the policy discourses of city-regions are often exacerbated by the complexity of multi-tiered jurisdictions in which actors are drawn not only from across various sectors but also from various levels of government. Given the focus of the extant literature on political polarization at the national level, there is a lack of understanding of the manifestations of political polarization at the local level and how they are managed. Our focus in this discussion, therefore, is to address this vacuum in the literature. Attention is duly given to the nature of political contestation and attempts at resolution of differences among a constellation of actors within city-regions.

The term "city-region" is used in this discussion to denote a metropolitan area and its surrounding hinterland. City-regions would often consist of one or two relatively large cities forming a conurbation or urban zone along with a number of smaller towns and rural areas sharing resources such as one or more central business districts, a network of transport systems, a common labour market and certain natural attractions or amenities like waterfronts and conservation areas. A city-region does not presuppose a single administrative unit. Such entities tend to be characterized by multiple administrative districts like municipalities. However, to enhance the administrative efficiency of managing common resources and economic interdependency most city-regions in Canada and the United States have over the years developed regional administrative arrangements aimed at enabling such geographic zones to function as a single unit.

The discussion is premised on the fact that most of the socioeconomic challenges of the twenty-first century are most evidently concentrated in mid-sized cities (Conference Board of Canada, 2014; Scott and Storper, 2015). Over the past two decades, global economic integration, technological change and emerging competition from newly industrializing economies have reshaped the world's economic landscapes (Waits, 2000; Blakely and Leigh, 2010). The result is an unprecedented structural shift in economies, not unlike the shift from an agro-based to factory economy in the late 1800s or the shift to mass production in the mid-1900s (Atkinson and Correa, 2007; Kresl and Singh, 2012; World Economic Forum, 2013). Global economic integration is creating new opportunities and threats for nations and cities around the world (Bhagwati, 2004; Greenspan, 2007; Wiarda, 2007). From industrial decline to environmental degradation, and all of the social malaise in between, cities across the world have witnessed unprecedented challenges in an age of post-industrial restructuring and the reconfiguration of the world's economic geography. Plant closures have decimated mid-sized cities' downtown cores and deepened the plight of income inequality and economic marginalization. Globalization has thus imposed new forms of polarization and divergence within and among cities (Young, 2012; Conference Board of Canada, 2013; Conteh, 2013).

The key question addressed in this chapter is as follows: How are city-regions mobilizing key local resources and actors from public, private and non-profit institutions to engage in concerted action and address the local socioeconomic challenges of global economic restructuring? The chapter is structured as follows. The next section develops the conceptual framework that guides the empirical section of the discussion. This conceptual framework provides a lens for analyzing the institutional infrastructure underpinning the management of polarized and contentious policy environments. The two subsequent sections of the chapter examine the key features of concerted action (or lack thereof) in the two cases. The concluding discussion raises a number of practical lessons and theoretical implications for overcoming polarization and pursuing concerted action in multi-actor policy environments.

The multi-actor implementation framework

The integrated conceptual framework developed in this section consists of combined insights from implementation theory, organization theory and the governance literature, and will be referred to as the multi-actor implementation framework. The goal is to combine the analytical strengths of these three distinct but parallel research traditions in order to contribute to our understanding of the prospects and challenges of concerted action in polarized policy environments. The rest of the discussion in this section briefly introduces the relevant elements of implementation research, organization theory and the governance literature for our present discussion, and then integrates these perspectives into a single framework. The chapter will then apply the integrated framework in our examination of concerted action in the Niagara and Rochester city-regions.

The term "implementation" as a popular concept in contemporary discourse among scholars of public policy dates back to the work of Pressman and Wildavsky (1973) in the early 1970s. Policy implementation research provides the essential link between political and economic analysis of policy implementation and the organizational or institutional analysis of public administration (Hjern and Hull, 1987). As policy implementation processes became influenced by structural changes in public administration toward decentralization, devolution of responsibilities, partnerships and restructuring of accountability relationships in service delivery, policy implementation research increasingly reflects these trends (Kettl, 2000; Pal, 2006; O'Toole, 2007). The result is an attempt by scholars to understand how policies are being implemented in concert with non-state actors in cooperative or contentious partnership arrangements (Kernaghan et al., 2000).

As a reflection of the transitions toward complex and contested multi-actor policy processes, one notices the emergent focus of implementation research on issues of polarization and concerted action among multiple actors from various loci and levels (O'Toole, 2000; Hill and Hupe, 2003; Lindquist, 2006). In federal systems, for instance, the different levels of policy action consist of federal, provincial or state and municipal jurisdictions and their agencies. The loci of policy action often consist of constellations of ideational and interest coalitions within and outside the state within a policy subsystem.

Organization theory also offers certain elements that can facilitate understanding of concerted policy action in polarized policy subsystems. From the standpoint of this literature, governance can thus be understood as a process involving a series of interactions among public agencies on the one hand, and between public agencies and organized target groups within the community and the private sector on the other (Sinclair, 2001; Schofield, 2004). Organization theory's long tradition of examining the interactions between organizations and their external environment is particularly relevant for our discussion (Thompson, 1967; Denhardt and Denhardt, 2003). Portions of this literature referred to as open-systems analysis focus on understanding the relationship between public organizations and their strategic (or external) environment (Wamsley and Zald, 1973; Denhardt, 2004; Tompkins, 2005). As Jreisat (2002) succinctly put it, the open-systems approach broke fundamentally from the machine models (closed-systems) view of policy implementation, focusing instead on complex and contentious relations between organizations and the broader political context within which they operate. In particular, organization theory has been grappling with the need to re-examine policy intervention by public agencies as a highly complex process in which they engage other organizations (including community and private sector organizations), often as partners rather than subordinates. Kettl (2000) provides a compelling summation of the above-mentioned trends in his observation that organization theory, in particular, and public administration, in general, are revisiting and adjusting the discipline of public policy and public management's analytical approach to allow for the view that agencies are adaptive organisms that respond to often contentious political and technical change in their environment in order to survive and be effective.

The governance literature's concern with the dialectics of horizontal engagement between public agencies and non-state organizations is also relevant for the discussion in this chapter. Insights from governance theory, for instance, have accounted for the actions and strategies of organized target groups and other societal interests in less hierarchical policy settings (Agranoff and McGuire, 1998; Kooiman, 2000; Peters and Pierre, 2000; Rhodes, 2000). Although the concept of governance has escaped a clear definition, in the context of advanced democracies it generally refers to a wide variety of self-sustaining networks through which the state engages in sharing power and administrative responsibility with non-state policy actors. Governance literature embraces a broad range of perspectives, from those that identify a dominant public sector constrained by a constellation of organized societal actors within a relatively complicated policy subsystem (Peters, 2001) to those that perceive highly complex, contested and polarized systems in which adaptive abilities are required of all members within a network (including public agencies). This adaptive process through polarization and turbulence has been described as "co-evolution" (Teisman et al., 2009).

Some of the major analytical frameworks in the governance literature include network governance (Keast et al., 2004), governance networks (Kooiman, 2003; Pierre and Peters, 2005) and collaborative management (Agranoff and McGuire, 2003). These broad analytical frameworks overlap in many ways, and have been further grouped under themes such as multi-level governance (Hill and Hupe, 2002; Cepiku et al., 2013), transition management (Kooiman, 2003; Loorbach, 2007) and complex adaptive systems (Teisman and Klijn, 2008; Tesiman et al., 2009).

The governance literature views policy processes as characterized by variations of state–society relations, with the latter in turn consisting of societal groups mobilized by principles of self-governance pursuing various forms of joint action with public organizations. Some scholars of governance refer to this as third-sector engagement in co-production (Kooiman, 2000; Peters and Pierre, 2000; Rhodes, 2000; Agranoff and McGuire, 2003). The governance literature, therefore, seeks to identify the nature of the interaction between public organizations (as necessary agents of policy implementation) and other organized entities outside the state, often focusing on the contentious front lines of service delivery.

Integrating the perspectives

The central concern shared by policy implementation research, organization theory and the governance literature is to understand how government organizations interact with their external environment in pursuing concerted actions within polarized and contentious policy environments. A common thread flowing from this shared concern is the need to re-conceptualize power and authority among public and non-state organizations in the policy environment (Rothstein, 2007).

In attempting to integrate the insights from the aforementioned analytical traditions, it is important to identify the distinct element of each perspective. Implementation research has long sought to advance insights into the relationships between various levels of government. One constant challenge in this regard has been the polarizing tensions between frontline agencies and their head offices. In federal systems such as Canada's, for instance, these tensions take on a particularly poignant character in the form of intergovernmental jurisdictional rivalries and frustrated efforts at joint action (Simeon, 2006).

Organization theory adds to this by suggesting that the success of policy implementation is a function not merely of the government's intraorganizational integrity and technical expertise, but also of its adaptation to the imperatives of its external environment. This perspective calls our attention to the willingness or ability of organizations to reorganize their culture, operations and, even, structural features in ways that may involve sharing authority and power, as well as developing a culture of compromise and learning. How public agencies seek to adjust their mission to reflect the changing values and interests of the local environment thus becomes an important consideration in overcoming polarization.

The governance literature, for its part, calls our attention to the emergent phenomenon of third-sector engagement in co-production. In the governance literature, the institutional and ideational forces underlying the shift towards horizontal management can be understood as causing a transition toward an emphasis on coordination and striking compromises as a key function of organizational competence. The expectations and demands of organized actors outside the public sector imply that the external environment is not just a set of variables to be manipulated by public agencies. Building legitimacy for effective policy intervention requires public agencies to identify the main actors within the field and their specific demands, and then seek ways to coordinate the various bases of power.

Thus, through the lens of an integrated framework, one can make a key proposition: the political legitimacy and coordinating capacity of public agencies are indispensable ingredients of concerted policy action in polarized policy environments. Interorganizational interactions in this context are both cooperative and conflictual as public agencies navigate through various levels of constitutional and policy jurisdictions, while at the same time striving to gain legitimacy and positive feedback from non-state policy stakeholders. Structured hierarchies are confronted with the need to adjust their processes to the imperatives of horizontal management in order to maintain system stability, resolve polarizing tensions, manage change and deepen the impact of their policy intervention.

In conclusion, the multi-actor implementation framework views governance as encompassing diverse expressions of interorganizational cooperation among public agencies on the one hand, and between state agencies and organized societal interests on the other. These interorganizational co-operative efforts can be seen as strategic networks of concerted action involving intergovernmental cooperation among agencies with similar mandates from different levels of government, and state–society partnerships incorporating non-state actors. This framework provides a lens for analyzing the case studies in the next two sections.

The case of Niagara, Ontario

The Niagara city-region, like other major regions in Canada, has been struggling to revitalize its local economy after massive industrial restructuring (including plant relocation and downsizing) in the automobile and similar manufacturing industries. The region's manufacturing sector has been particularly affected by intense global competition from low-cost jurisdictions and environmentally loose regimes in the emerging markets of developing countries. Niagara's other challenges include: slow population growth, aging population and mass youth exodus; a lower than average number of post-secondary graduates; low relative earnings, high property taxes; and no interregional transportation network (Niagara Community Observatory, 2015). The region lost almost 8,000 manufacturing jobs between 1996 and 2005. The median income is $23,400 – taking last place on a list of 11 census metropolitan areas in Ontario. Employment growth is less than 1 percent per year, compared to an Ontario average of 17.5 percent (Niagara Workforce Planning Board, 2010).

In the face of its changing economic fortunes, the Niagara region has been subject to increasing political and economic pressures from a wide range of domestic actors, especially the private sector, to respond to the new threats from international competition and demographic shifts in the region. But other interests like anti-poverty and environmental groups have also been quite keen to exploit the window of the crisis to insert their voices into the discourse about the region's future. Over the past decade, Niagara has started to consult with a large swathe of its community with the aim of working together around the themes of growth and prosperity (Niagara Region, 2009). Out of these consultations have emerged a number of Economic Growth Strategies, with the first dating back to 2005. However, the consultation that led to the 2005 Growth Strategy revealed the deep polarization that existed in the region. Divergent visions of the region's future emerged from the debates with deep ideational intransigence that thinly masked the clash of material interests among key actors. Environmental groups insisted on preserving the Niagara region as "green belt" whereas business groups such as the Greater Niagara Chamber of Commerce saw a future for an advanced manufacturing cluster in the region. There was also a sense of growing inequality and rising poverty that added fervour to the social tensions that formed the backdrop to the consultations. Even though a Growth Plan was eventually published, the intransigence among environmental, anti-poverty and business interests derailed any meaningful implementation of the Plan.

Added to this crippling polarization in the broader context of Niagara's effort at regional economic adaptation and reinvention was the province of Ontario's 25-year Growth Plan for the Greater Golden Horseshoe region (released in 2006) (Government of Ontario, 2006). Under the government of Ontario's Places to Grow Act of 2005, the Growth Plan for Golden Horseshoe has a number of aims to revitalize major cities and smaller communities to become vibrant and convenient centres of environmentally-friendly growth and development. The Growth Plan also projects 25 centers (or cities) in the region as urban growth centres and economic generators. The significance of the Growth Plan is that it signals that the Ontario government sees a role for itself as active leader within the policy space of municipalities. This development meant potential tensions between assertive cities and the province as the former perceive the latter as intrusive and micro-managerial. The Ontario government's initiative illustrates an endemic current of confrontation and contestation in the multilevel dynamics of Canada's federal system. Amidst these growing jurisdictional tensions, however, was recognition that industrial restructuring requires joint policy initiatives consisting of resources and agencies from various levels of government.

The latest strategic plan (2012) of the Niagara region has been marked by a more positive environment of constructive discourse. Like the 2005 Plan, it is the result of broad and extensive consultation with regional stakeholders such as Niagara's governments, businesses and environmental and community activists. An important element in arriving at this relatively inclusive growth strategy was a deliberate shift in attitude by the region that could mean less polarization and conflict between the regional authority and its constituent municipalities. The region reframed its mandate from directly delivering programs and directing outcomes to horizontally facilitating joint interventions with municipalities as well as coordinating more closely with non-state actors to empower the latter. Another key feature of the region's attempt to defuse the increasingly antagonistic discourse of environmental and anti-poverty groups was to adopt the narrative of the "compassionate" and "ecologically responsible" region in the formulation of its growth strategy. However, a predominant feature of resource allocation in the implementation of the Growth Strategy was a focus on supporting traditional industries and nurturing new ones (Niagara Knowledge Exchange, 2013). Thus, while the rhetoric of consultation and policy development was adjusted to co-opt social and environmental groups, the institutional context of resource allocation was an exclusive policy engagement between the region and the private sector (Conteh, 2013).

Another element of the region's navigation through polarization in pursuit of concerted action is the institutional reconfiguration of its economic development governance arrangements (Niagara Community Observatory, 2015). The Niagara Economic Development Corporation (NEDC – a now defunct semi-autonomous corporation) was the first agency that embarked on an ambitious drive to address the region's economic woes (Niagara Region, 2009). Its mandate was to promote Niagara on a global scale and work in partnership with the region's 12 municipalities to provide services that encourage investment in and travel to the region, along with business support services to attract, maintain and increase jobs in the region. However, the NEDC largely failed in engaging the region's 12 municipalities and their respective economic development offices (EDOs). This failure itself reflected age-old fissures in the local politics of a two-tier governing structure. The four largest cities in the region simply refused to surrender their distinct EDOs to a centralized authority at the regional level, which serves as the upper tier in the region's two-tier system of local government. The persistence of this tension eventually led to the demise of the NEDC. It was replaced by a less autonomous economic development department, the Niagara Economic Development Department (NEDD), housed within the regional administrative departmental structure. This new institutional arrangement was seen by the larger cities as a way of curbing the excessive powers and ambitions of the now defunct NEDC.

Despite its relatively modest mandate, the NEDD is empowered to serve as the main conduit through which the joint policy actions of economic development agencies operating in the region are channeled. It is mandated to work closely with the 12 local area municipalities and other partners in the region as well as from the provincial and federal government in pursuit of the region's economic development aspirations. Compared to its predecessor, the NEDD has been careful to court the goodwill and support of municipal EDOs in its plans and deliberations. The NEDD also invests considerably in cultivating partnerships with private sector associations, post-secondary institutions and agencies from various levels of government to provide the typical range of business support services, such as registration, financing, marketing and the like. For instance, the NEDD's strategic engagement includes a range of other actors from the federal and provincial governments working in the region in pursuit of the goal of economic reinvention (Niagara Chamber of Commerce, 2013). The federal government's main agency of economic development in southern Ontario (where Niagara is located) is the Federal Economic Development Agency for Southern Ontario (FedDev). FedDev often either directly funds projects or works through its Community Futures Development Corporations (CFDCs), three of which operate in Niagara. The main provincial organizations responsible for economic development, and with which the NEDD shares a similar policy mandate, are the Ministry of Economic Development, Employment and Infrastructure (MEDEI) and the Ministry of Research and Innovation (MRI). Other actors in the region are a constellation of municipal Small Business Enterprise Centres (SBECs) and EDOs.

Moreover, the boundaries of the local public sector have become more porous under the NEDD as non-state actors such as post-secondary institutions exercise greater policy influence as knowledge generators in innovation driven local economies. For example, organizations such as Innovate Niagara, the Chambers of Commerce, Business Improvement Areas (BIAs), Brock University, Niagara College, Collège Boréalis, BioLinc, Niagara College Innovation Centre, Rankin Technology Centre and Vineland Research Centre are some of the principal non-state actors within the local policy subsystem of Niagara's economic development ambitions. Thus, more fluid processes of multilevel governance and state–society relations have replaced the rigid formal structures of federalism. Also, complex networks of horizontality are emerging in place of the neat constitutional boundaries that separate the state from society.

The relative success of the NEDD's operations thus far is a reflection of its recognition that governance is a function not merely of an organization's expertise and resources but also of its adaptation to the demands and sensitivities of actors in its external environment. Unlike a decade ago when the institutions of governance were entrapped in vitriolic discourses and implementation stalemates, there are signs of inter-organization collaboration across sectors and levels of government in Niagara. Reaching compromise on resource allocation is still not entirely inclusive of environmental and social justice groups. However, the expressions of differences of opinion are more civil and the contestations are less pathological.

A recent example of this emergent trend is the region's decision four years ago to develop a Niagara-wide public transit system that will allow for more integrated inter-municipal bus services. The impetus behind this decision was a desire to address the patchwork of bus services that had frustrated the efforts of residents, especially those in the low-income bracket, from freely moving around for work and recreation purposes. More importantly, the region realized that a sense of collective identity in Niagara is undermined in the absence of a public transit system that can facilitate the free movement of people across a shared space. What initially started as an initiative between the Niagara region and the three largest cities – St Catharines, Niagara Falls and Welland – became a region-wide discussion. Despite some contestations over the technical details of the physical infrastructure and financial arrangements for such a major under-taking, much of the discussion was relatively civil. All the major municipalities eventually formally endorsed the plan for an integrated and modernized regional transit system which has now moved from a pilot project to a permanent fixture of the region (Niagara Falls Review, 2014). The inter-municipal transit system has taken on a life of its own over the past four years with new initiatives now underway by all municipalities and the Niagara region working jointly to solicit funds from the provincial and federal governments to create a train transit system connecting the region with the Greater Toronto and Greater Hamilton conurba-tions. Besides the economic and social benefits that come with an integrated public transit system, this policy issue has become one of the most compelling indicators of the region's capacity to overcome its endemic political polarization. Such a momentum could potentially evolve into a path-dependent wave that could spill over into other policy areas.

The imperatives of the new economic challenges in the region, and the NEDD's capacity to learn from the mistakes of its predecessors, have created a space for the emergence of concerted horizontal joint action and multilevel gov-ernance. Given the failure of its predecessor, the NEDD is keen to foster stra-tegic ties with all relevant actors within its sphere of operation. The agency thus seeks to synthesize top-down and bottom-up approaches to policy making and implementation in Canada's multi-tiered jurisdictions. NEDD's engagement with all these actors reflects a context of policy governance mechanisms that emphasizes the building of strategic alliances among a wide range of public and non-governmental actors in pursuing the goal of economic adaptability and resilience.

The Niagara case study illustrates how ongoing turbulence in the global economy and the attendant industrial restructuring across urban centres are impacting on the fundamental structures of governance in city-regions. A critical factor in the processes and outcome of Niagara's strategic pursuit of reinventing the region's ailing economy consists of creating governance structures that can address the simmering tensions among economic, social and environmental actors in the region. This was made possible by the configuration of institutions and processes to facilitate concerted planning and implementation across net-works of agencies and jurisdictions. Since the disbanding of the defunct NEDC and the creation of the NEDD, there is clearer evidence of attempts to synthesize top-down and bottom-up approaches to policy making and implementation in the multi-tiered jurisdiction in which the region is nested. The NEDD's relative success in carrying out its mandate is a function not merely of its expertise and resources but also of its adaptation to the imperatives of its external environment. A principal component of this outreach is engagement with third-sector organizations whereby economic development in the region must be understood as transitioning from simply delivering and directing business development incentives and programs to facilitating, coordinating and empowering a range of actors.

The Finger Lakes region, New York

The city-region of Rochester has an economic sphere of influence spanning the territory of Finger Lakes in upstate New York. The region has been through a difficult transformation over the past two decades from an economy based on a small number of leading manufacturing firms to an increasingly successful and diverse knowledge-based economy. For much of the twentieth century, the region's economy was dominated by four large manufacturing-based companies. Over the past two decades, these companies have lost tens of thousands of jobs. For instance, back in 1982, Kodak, one of the leading companies, had 60,400 employees in the region. Today that number has been reduced to 7,000 (Finger Lakes Regional Economic Development Council, 2011). Thirty years ago, the majority of the region's top employers were large industrial-based companies. Today, five out of the top ten private sector employers in the Finger Lakes are institutions of higher education and healthcare, and the University of Rochester ranks as the state's sixth largest employer. While this transformation has been painful, the region has successfully reinvented itself into a more dynamic, diverse and stable economy based on multiple sectors that have tremendous potential for future growth. Since 1980, total employment in the Finger Lakes has increased by 21 percent during a period of relatively flat population growth.

Finger Lakes' transformation over the past few decades illustrates the strategic commitment of the region to a vision of economic renewal, and its continued nurturing of a culture that identifies and supports that vision, rallying key agencies and resources in pursuit of an agenda and mission borne out it. A key strategic vision of the region over the past decade has been to accelerate its transformation to a diverse, knowledge-based economy by building on strengths that include renewable natural resources, a talented and highly educated workforce, a historic commitment to innovation, leadership as the state's top agricultural region, international recognition as a center for optics and photonics and national leadership in per capita intellectual property and degrees in higher education (Greater Rochester Enterprise, 2015). This vision rests on a culture of collaboration between public and private institutions to optimize the region's performance in advanced manufacturing, the arts, tourism and basic and applied research in medicine, science, engineering and technology.

The Finger Lakes economy was recently named one of 35 national "Innovation Hubs" by *The Atlantic* (Greater Rochester Enterprise, 2014). Many of the companies in the fields of advanced manufacturing, optics, imaging, photonics, fuel cells and computer technology emerged from the research and development labs of Kodak, Xerox and Bausch + Lomb and were founded by executives, engineers and technicians who were trained at these firms. These sectors have been further strengthened by a close partnership with the region's universities and colleges, which have provided industry with a steady supply of innovative technologies and highly skilled workers. University-based research has also helped propel the growth of new sectors, including life sciences and alternative energy. Such cross-fertilization extends beyond technology-driven sectors. For example, the region's expanding agriculture industry – specifically the rising international reputation of Finger Lakes wines – has in turn propelled growth in tourism.

Underneath this glamorous picture of transformation, however, lurk some ugly socioeconomic realities. In particular, Greater Rochester faces significant challenges in urban poverty and poorly performing schools, especially struggling K–12 education (from kindergarten through to twelfth grade), and stagnation in workforce development. The last two challenges deserve particular attention because as the region itself acknowledges, the twenty-first century economy demands a high level of literacy and numeracy, even for modest jobs at the bottom of the income scale (Finger Lakes Regional Economic Development Council, 2014). The fast pace of technological change can also render certain job skills obsolete. Too many of the region's schools are plagued with high dropout rates. This creates a barrier to the job market and traps many individuals and families in poverty.

Central to the region's effort to address these challenges and increase the pace of its economic reinvention is the creation of a regional strategic plan consisting of the nine counties that make up the region (Government of New York, 2011). It is worth noting that the new strategic plan is not exclusive to the Finger Lakes region; it is part of a 2011 policy initiative by Governor Andrew Cuomo for all regions of the state of New York. Another noteworthy point is that the institutional context of United States' federalism presents a somewhat different picture from that observed in the Niagara city-region in Canada in one significant respect. The federal presence at the local level tends to be quite passive. While a number of funds from federal departments support various sectors of the economy from which the Greater Rochester region benefits, these departments tend to be largely absent from the policy subsystems of local urban geographies. State-level agencies, however, are quite engaged in local economic restructuring, with the most principal player in New York being the Empire State Development Corporation (ESDC) (Government of New York, 2015).

At the regional, county and municipal level are a whole constellation of actors such as the Finger Lakes Regional Planning Council, the Greater Rochester Enterprise (GRE), the City of Rochester Economic Development Department (EDD) and the Industrial Development Agencies of the nine counties within the Finger Lakes region. The main non-state organizational actors within Rochester's economic development policy subsystem consists of the University of

Rochester and the other 17 post-secondary institutions in the Finger Lakes region. The University of Rochester is the principal player among these post-secondary institutions, with key knowledge generation and dissemination activities by its affiliates such as the University of Rochester Medical Center. Other influential non-state actors within the region's economic development policy system are the Rochester Business Alliance, Digital Rochester, High Tech of Rochester, the Rochester Regional Photonics Cluster and the Rochester Institute of Technology.

Even though these actors share a common aspiration for the region's economic reinvention, there are divergent and competing interests among the nine counties, the post-secondary institutions, business interests and the various agencies. However, to manage these differences from degenerating into crippling polarity, the GRE is the main regional economic development organization that acts as the primary conduit for supporting business attraction and expansion, entrepreneurship and innovation in the whole Finger Lakes region. The GRE is interesting because it is a form of hybrid organization created and funded by a pool of private and public sector organizations in the region. It is a form of public–private partnership supported by more than 120 local businesses, government and non-profit organizations. All the main partners from all levels of government and non-state actors within the region's economic development policy subsystems acknowledge and legitimize the GRE as the main policy conduit for pursuing the Rochester city-region's economic restructuring ambitions. However, this apparent consensus masks a deeper systematic exclusion of other voices such as anti-poverty and environmental groups. The predominant discourse of regional economic reinvention is framed in terms of supporting businesses. Initiatives aimed at poverty alleviation and ecological preservation are relatively marginal, carried out on the sidelines of mainstream policy debates. These groups have not been able to coalesce into a strong enough force to change the tenor of policy discourses. Thus, the absence of ideational intransigence is not indicative of deeper socioeconomic fissures and tensions in the region. The counter-narrative of regional reinvention are largely criticisms from the margin of the policy landscape that are viewed as nuisance rather than a threat to the infrastructure of governance.

Another factor in the nature of the policy discourse is that marginalized environmental and social justice groups to some extent acquiesce in the dominant narrative of economic reinvention in the region. The crisis of precipitous industrial decline back in the 1980s with massive job losses is so etched in the collective psyche of local actors that there has been a demonstrated willingness to accept the policy priority of supporting business. However, this acquiescence and cooperation has come at the expense of a balanced framing of regional reinvention.

Nevertheless, the case of the GRE illustrates how environmental factors such as a shared collective trauma can provide a backdrop of consensus strong enough to overcome polarizing tensions. The GRE has ridden on the wave of this local consensus in its engagement with non-state actors as critical sources of ideas and resources in the region's economic restructuring. More importantly, the GRE's operation reflects evolving governance arrangements in which various tiers of government facilitate intergovernmental and inter-sectoral cooperation through recurring platforms that reinforce the dominant narrative of local economic reinvention. It is the predominance of this narrative and its successful marginalization of ecological and other social justice concerns that have enhanced the relative success of concerted action in the region.

Discussion and conclusion

From the analysis of the two case studies, one can infer that there is evidence of manifest and latent divergent political, ideational, material and social schisms among key actors in both regions. A key lesson that emerges from the two cases is that polarization at the local level is often played out as conflicts among individuals and groups about the socioeconomic destiny of cities and how to allocate resources to combat problems such as economic stagnation, income inequality and poverty. The nature of the resulting contestation among actors within city-regions may have ideological underpinnings, but their immediate driving force is the material interests of actors. Both the Niagara and Rochester regions have seen such tensions and divides among actors. Left to themselves, these schisms can potentially derail the institutions of governance and entrap the regions in a vicious cycle of industrial decline and economic stagnation. The Niagara region witnessed such a stalemate for a brief period as it attempted to implement its 2005 Growth Strategy. However, the contestations seldom result in long-lasting pathological schisms largely because key coalitions emerge that either co-opt or marginalize other voices.

Another lesson to draw from the analysis of the two cases is that they illustrate the importance of bridge organizations or institutional intermediaries addressing existing and potential polarizing tensions among the various sectors and between tiers of jurisdiction. These bridge organizations serve as regional "champions" in establishing networks of knowledge exchange and building a collective regional consciousness. The GRE in Finger Lakes and the NEDD in Niagara serve as the bride organizations for their respective regions. The NEDD in particular learnt the lessons of its predecessor and was determined to adapt its mandate and strategy to reconcile (or bury) potentially crippling differences.

The third lesson is that there is strong evidence of a deliberative and strategic approach that includes various levels of government in managing crisis and change in both cases. The realities of global market forces impose severe constraints on the best efforts of city-regions. This means that cities cannot go it alone, and often requires the active presence of higher levels of government. Cities in federal systems such as Canada and the United States are nested within layers of jurisdictions and their strategies and prospects cannot be separated from these larger institutional and market contexts. A critical ingredient of adaptive and resilient city-regions is their willingness to open up and share their policy space with the active participation of other agencies. Surrendering some degree of jurisdictional autonomy in their strategic visioning, planning and implementation makes it possible for such city-regions to mobilize their key assets from various sectors and levels of government.

In terms of theoretical significance, the case studies illustrate the integrated conceptual framework's key proposition that the political legitimacy and coordinating capacity of public agencies are indispensable ingredients of concerted policy action in polarized policy environments. The policy environments in Rochester and Niagara are both cooperative and conflictual but not pathologically crippling. The key agencies responsible for regional economic development had to navigate through a constellation of actors. Indeed, some of their strategies for managing polarizing tensions, especially in the case of the Rochester region, involve excluding certain inconvenient voices that do not fit the dominant narrative. How long such exclusionary consensus will last is impossible to tell. However, there was recognition by key agencies that a significant aspect of effective governance is to maintain system stability by giving due attention to polarizing tensions in managing change.

Insights from the implementation literature help us understand the polarizing tensions between frontline agencies like the NEDD and GRE that operate at the strategic interface of state–society relations. This literature points to the need for governance in federal systems such as Canada and the United States that requires agencies to build core competences in managing intergovernmental jurisdictional rivalries in pursuit of concerted action. The complexity of managing change has necessitated the institutionalization of joint policy initiatives consisting of resources, organizations and agents drawn from various levels of government.

In addition, insights from organization theory helped us appreciate that the success of regional economic restructuring is a function not merely of any particular organization's expertise and resources but also of its ability to work with a range of orientations and actors (including community and private sector organizations), often as partners rather than subordinates. The new public governance literature further illuminated our understanding of this characteristic of governance. For instance, the Niagara and Finger Lakes regions embody in various ways the emergent phenomenon of third-sector engagement in co-production whereby policy implementation can be understood as transitioning from simply delivering and directing to facilitating, coordinating and empowering. Strategically minded regions have embraced the wisdom of creating self-sustaining networks through which public agencies engage in sharing power and administrative responsibility with non-state policy actors.

In conclusion, the multi-actor implementation framework provides a lens for understanding governance as encompassing diverse expressions of interorganizational cooperation among public agencies on the one hand, and between public agencies and organized non-state actors on the other. These interorganizational cooperative efforts can be seen as strategic networks for de-escalating polarization, pursuing concerted action and managing change.

Bibliography

Adams, F. Gerard. (2006). *East Asia, Globalization, and the New Economy*. London: Routledge.

Agranoff, Robert. (2007). *Managing within Networks: Adding Value to Public Administration*. Washington, DC: Georgetown University Press.

Agranoff, Robert and Michael McGuire. (1998). "Multi-network Management: Collaboration and the Hollow State in Local Economic Policy." *Journal of Public Administration Research and Theory* 8(1): 67–91.

Agranoff, Robert and Michael McGuire. (2003). *Collaborative Public Management: New Strategies for Local Governments*. Washington, DC: Georgetown University Press.

Andrews, Rhys, George Boyne, Jennifer Law and Richard M. Walker. (2011). *Strategic Management and Public Service Performance*. Basingstoke, UK: Palgrave Macmillan.

Atkinson, R.D. and D.K. Correa. (2007). *The 2007 State New Economy Index: Benchmarking Economic Transformation in the States*. Washington, DC: The Information Technology and Innovation Foundation (ITIF).

Baldassarri, Delia and Andrew Gelman. (2008). "Partisans without Constraint: Political Polarization and Trends in American Public Opinion." *American Journal of Sociology* 114(2): 408–446.

Bhagwati, J.N. (2004). *In Defence of Globalization*. New York: Oxford University Press.

Blakely, E.J. (2001). "Competitive Advantage for the 21st Century City: Can a Place-Based Approach to Economic Development Survive in a Cyberspace Age?" *Journal of American Planning Association* 67(2): 133–141.

Blakely, E.J. and N.G. Leigh. (2010). *Planning Local Economic Development: Theory and Practice*. Fourth edn. Los Angeles, London, New Delhi, Singapore and Washington, DC: Sage Publications.

Broome, André. (2007). "Seeing Like the IMF: Institutional Change in Frontier Economies." PhD dissertation, Australian National University.

Bryson, John M. (2011). *Strategic Planning for Public and Nonprofit Organizations: A Guide to Strengthening and Sustaining Organizational Achievement*. San Francisco, CA: Jossey-Bass Publishers.

Bunting, Trudi E., Pierre Filion and Ryan Christopher Walker. (2010). *Canadian Cities in Transition: New Directions in the Twenty-First Century*. Don Mills, Ontario: Oxford University Press.

Cepiku, Denita, David Jesuit and Ian Roberge (2013). *Making Multi-Level Public Management Work: Stories of Success and Failure from Europe and North America*. Boca Raton, FL: CRC Press.

Clark, G.L., M.P. Feldman and M.S Gertler. (2000). *The Oxford Handbook of Economic Geography*. Oxford: Oxford University Press.

Conference Board of Canada. (2013). "Mid-Sized Cities Outlook: Economic History of Canada's Mid-Sized Cities: 2013." Available at www.conferenceboard.ca/e-library/abstract.aspx?did=5487 (accessed March 3, 2017).

Conference Board of Canada. (2014). "Mid-Sized Cities Outlook 2014." Ottawa: Conference Board of Canada. Available at www.conferenceboard.ca/topics/economics/midsize-city.aspx (accessed March 3, 2017).

Conteh, Charles. (2013). *Policy Governance in Multi-Level Systems: Economic Development and Policy Implementation in Canada*. Montreal and Kingston, Canada: McGill-Queen's University Press.

Denhardt, Robert B. (2004). *Theories of Public Organization*. Belmont, CA: Thomson.

Denhardt, Janet V. and Robert B. Denhardt. (2003). *The New Public Service: Serving, Not Steering.* Armonk, NY: M.E. Sharpe.

Dewulf, Geert, Anneloes Blanken and Mirjam Bult-Spiering. (2011). *Strategic Issues in Public–Private Partnerships.* Chichester, UK: Wiley.

DiMaggio, Paul, John Evans and Bethany Bryson. (1996). "Have American's Social Attitudes Become More Polarized?" *American Journal of Sociology* 102(3): 690–755.

Finger Lakes Regional Economic Development Council. (2011). "Strategic Plan: Accelerating our Transformation." Available at https://regionalcouncils.ny.gov/themes/nyopenrc/rc-files/fingerlakes/FLREDCStrategicPlan.pdf (accessed March 29, 2017).

Finger Lakes Regional Economic Development Council. (2014). "Progress Report & Recommended Priority Projects." Available at https://regionalcouncils.ny.gov/themes/nyopenrc/rc-files/fingerlakes/FLREDC-2014PR.pdf (accessed March 29, 2017).

Fiorina, Morris P. and Samuel J. Abrams. (2008). "Political Polarization in the American Public." *Annual Review of Political Science* 11(1): 563–588. doi:10.1146/annurev.polisci.11.

Florida, Richard L. (2008). *Who's Your City?: How the Creative Economy is Making Where to Live the Most Important Decision of Your Life.* New York: Basic Books.

Fredrickson, H. George. (2007). "Whatever Happened to Public Administration? Governance, Governance, Everywhere." In Ewan Ferlie, Laurence E Lynn, Jr. and Christopher Pollitt (eds.), *The Oxford Handbook of Public Management.* Toronto: Oxford University Press.

Government of New York. (2011). "Finger Lakes Regional Economic Development Council." Available at www.facebook.com/pages/Finger-Lakes-Regional-Economic-Development-Council/397992706928732 (accessed March 3, 2017).

Government of New York. (2014). "Empire State Development." Available at www.esd.ny.gov (accessed March 3, 2017).

Government of New York. (2015). "Empire State Development Corporation: About Us." Available at https://esd.ny.gov/about-us (accessed March 29, 2017). Government of Ontario. (2006). "Growth Plan for the Greater Golden Horseshoe, 2006." Available at www.placestogrow.ca/index.php?option=com_content&task=view&id=9&Itemid=14 (accessed March 3, 2017).

Graham, Katherine. (2010). "No Joke! Local Government and Intergovernmental Relations in Canada." In Emmanuel Brunet-Jailly and John F. Martin (eds.), *Local Government in a Global World: Australia and Canada in Comparative Perspective.* Toronto: University of Toronto Press, pp. 213–237.

Greater Rochester Enterprise. (2014) "Innovation & Technology." Available at www.rochesterbiz.com/DoingBusinessHere/BusinessInformation/InnovationTechnology.aspx (accessed January 31, 2016).

Greater Rochester Enterprise (2015). "Doing Business Here." Available at www.rochesterbiz.com/DoingBusinessHere/BusinessInformation/BusinessIncentives.aspx (accessed March 3, 2017).

Greenspan, Alan. (2007). *The Age of Turbulence: Adventures in a New World.* New York: Penguin Press.

Hill, Michael J. and Paul L. Hupe. (2002). *Implementing Public Policy: Governance in Theory and Practice.* Thousand Oaks, CA: Sage.

Hill, Michael J. and Paul L. Hupe. (2003). "The Multi-Layer Problem in Implementation Research." *Public Management Review* 5: 471–490.

Hjern, Benny and Christopher Hull. (1987). *Helping Small Firms Grow: An Implementation Approach.* New York: Croom Helm in association with Methuen.

Joyce, Paul. (2000). *Strategy in the Public Sector: A Guide to Effective Change Management.* Chichester, UK: John Wiley.

Jreisat, J.E. (2002). *Comparative Public Administration and Policy.* Oxford: Westview.

Keast, Robyn, Myrna P. Mandell, Kerry Brown and Geoffrey Woolcock. (2004). "Network Structures: Working Differently and Changing Expectations." *Public Administration Review* 64(3): 363–371.

Kernaghan, Kenneth, D.B. Marson and Sanford Borins. (2000). *The New Public Organization.* Toronto: Institute of Public Administration of Canada.

Kettl, Donald F. (2000). "Public Administration at the Millennium: The State of the Field." *Journal of Public Administration Research and Theory* 10(1): 7–34.

Kooiman, J. (2000). "Societal Governance: Levels, Models and Orders of Social-political Interaction." In J. Pierre (ed.), *Debating Governance.* New York: Oxford University Press.

Kooiman, J. (2003). *Governing as Governance.* Thousand Oaks, CA: Sage.

Kresl, Peter and Balwant Singh. (2012). "Urban Competitiveness and US Metropolitan Centres." *Urban Studies* 49(2): 239–254.

Krugman, Paul R. (1990). *Increasing Returns and Economic Geography.* Cambridge, MA: National Bureau of Economic Research.

Krugman, Paul R. (1994). *Urban Concentration: The Role of Increasing Returns and Transport Costs.* Washington, DC: World Bank.

Krugman, Paul R. (2012). *End This Depression Now!* New York: W.W. Norton & Co.

Kurz, Heinz-Dieter. (2011). *Innovation, Knowledge and Growth: Adam Smith, Schumpeter and the Moderns.* New York: Routledge.

Lewis, Jenny, Mark Considine and Damon Alexander. (2011). *Networks, Innovation and Public Policy: Politicians, Bureaucrats and the Pathways to Change Inside Government.* Basingstoke, UK: Palgrave Macmillan.

Lindquist, Evert. (2006). "Organizing for Policy Implementation: The Emergence and Role of Implementation Units in Policy Design and Oversight." *Journal of Comparative Policy Analysis: Research and Practice* 8(4): 311–324.

Loorbach, Derk A. (2007). *Transition Management: New Mode of Governance for Sustainable Development.* Utrecht: International Books.

Mann, Thomas E. and Norman J. Ornstein. (2012). *It's Even Worse Than It Looks: How the American Constitutional System Collided with the New Politics of Extremism.* New York: Basic Books.

McCarty, Nolan, Keith T. Poole and Howard Rosenthal. (2006). *Polarized America: The Dance of Ideology and Unequal Riches.* Cambridge, MA: MIT Press.

Minnaar, F. (2010). *Strategic and Performance Management in the Public Sector.* Pretoria: Van Schaik.

Mintzberg, Henry. (2013). *Rise and Fall of Strategic Planning.* New York: Free Press.

Niagara Chamber of Commerce. (2013). "Blueprint for Economic Growth and Prosperity: Launching a Report Card for Niagara." Available at www.businesslinkniagara.com/publications/files/blueprintfinal.pdf (accessed March 3, 2017).

Niagara Community Observatory. (2015). "Niagara's Changing Economic Structure." Policy Brief #24. Available at https://brocku.ca/webfm_send/38197 (accessed March 29, 2017).

Niagara Falls Review (2014, September 24). " 'Historic' Moment for Regional Transit." Available at www.niagarafallsreview.ca/2014/09/24/historic-moment-for-regional-transit (accessed March 3, 2017).

Niagara Knowledge Exchange. (2013). "Economic Growth Strategy 2013–2015: Report to the Public." Available at www.niagaraknowledgeexchange.com/resources-publications/economic-growth-strategy-2013-2015-report-to-the-public (accessed March 29, 2017).

Niagara Region. (2009). "Niagara's Economic Growth Strategy 2009–2012." Available at www.pelham.ca/en/services/resources/Economic-Development/Research-Data-Centre/Niagara-Economic-Growth-Strategy-2009---2012.pdf (accessed March 3, 2017).

Niagara Workforce Planning Board. (2010). "The Changing Economic Structure of Niagara." Niagara Community Observatory, Policy Brief #5. Available at https://brocku.ca/webfm_send/13790 (accessed March 29, 2017).

OECD. (2009). "Investing for Growth: Building Innovation Regions." Meeting of the Territorial Development Policy Committee. Available at www.oecd.org/regional/ministerial/42531915.pdf (accessed March 3, 2017).

O'Toole, Laurence J. Jr. (2000). "Research on Policy Implementation: Assessment and Prospects." *Journal of Public Administration Research and Theory* 10(2): 263.

O'Toole, Laurence Jr. (2007). "Inter-organizational Relations in Implementation." In B. Guy Peters, and Jon Pierre (eds.), *Handbook of Public Administration*. London; Thousand Oaks, CA: Sage Publications

Pal, L.A. 2006. *Beyond Policy Analysis: Public Issue Management in Turbulent Times.* Scarborough, Ontario: ITP Nelson.

Peters, B. Guy and Jon Pierre. (2000). *Handbook of Public Administration*. London: Sage Publications.

Peters, B. Guy. (2001). *The Future of Governing: Four Emerging Models*. Lawrence, KS: University Press of Kansas.

Pierre, Jon. (2000). *Debating Governance*. Oxford and New York: Oxford University Press.

Pierre, Jon, and B. Guy Peters. (2005). *Governing Complex Societies: Trajectories and Scenarios*. New York: Palgrave Macmillan.

Poister, Theodore, David Pitts and Lauren Hamilton Edwards. (2010). "Strategic Management Research in the Public Sector: A Review, Synthesis, and Future Directions." *American Review of Public Administration* 40(5): 522–545.

Porter, Michael E. (1990). *The Competitive Advantage of Nations.* New York: Free Press.

Porter, Michael E. (2001). "Regions and the New Economics of Competition." In A.J Scott (ed.), *Global City-Regions: Trends, Theory, Policy*. Oxford: Oxford University Press, pp. 139–157.

Pressman, Jeffrey and Aaron Wildavsky. (1973). *Implementation: How Great Expectations in Washington Are Dashed in Oakland; or, Why It's amazing that Federal Programs Work at All, This Being a Saga of the Economic Development Administration as Told by Two Sympathetic Observers Who Seek to Build Morals on a Foundation of Ruined Hopes.* Berkeley, CA: University of California Press.

Rhodes, Rod A.W. (2000). "Governance and Public Administration." In Jon Pierre (ed.), *Debating Governance*. Oxford and New York: Oxford University Press.

Rothstein, Bo. (2007). "Political Legitimacy for Public Administration." In Guy Peters and Jon Pierre (eds.), *Handbook of Public Administration*. Thousand Oaks, CA: Sage Publications.

Roy, Jeffrey. (2006). *Business and Government in Canada.* Ottawa: University of Ottawa Press.

Schedler, Kuno, Isabella Proeller and John Philipp Siegel. (2011). *Strategic Management in the Public Sector*. London: Routledge.

Schofield, J. (2004). "A Model of Learned Implementation." *Public Administration* 82(2): 283–308.

Scott, Allen J. (2001). *Global City-Regions: Trends, Theory, Policy.* Cambridge, UK: Oxford University Press.

Scott, A.J., and Storper, M. (2003). "Regions, Globalization, Development." *Regional Studies* 37(6–7): 579–593.

Scott, A.J. and Storper, M. (2015). "The Nature of Cities: The Scope and Limits of Urban Theory.*" International Journal of Urban and Regional Research* 39: 1–15.

Simeon, Richard. (2006). *Federal–Provincial Diplomacy: The Making of Recent Policy in Canada.* Toronto: University of Toronto Press.

Sinclair, T.A.P. (2001). "Implementation Theory and Practice: Uncovering Policy and Administration Linkages in the 1990s." *International Journal of Public Administration* 24: 77–94.

Statistics Canada. (2006). "Census of Population." Available at www12.statcan.gc.ca/census-recensement/2006/index-eng.cfm (accessed March 3, 2017).

Statistics Canada. (2011). "National Household Survey." Available at www12.statcan.gc.ca/nhs-enm/2011/dp-pd/prof/index.cfm?Lang=E (accessed March 3, 2017).

Steiner, M. (ed.). (1998). *Clusters and Regional Specialisation.* London: Pion.

Steiss, Alan Walter. (2003). *Strategic Management for Public and Nonprofit Organizations.* New York: Marcel Dekker.

Stiglitz, Joseph. (2002). *Globalization and its Discontents.* London: Allen Lane/Penguin.

Stiglitz, Joseph. (2006). *Stability with Growth: Macroeconomics, Liberalization and Development.* Oxford: Oxford University Press.

Storper, M. (2013). *Keys to the City: How Economics, Institutions, Social Interactions, and Politics Shape Development.* Princeton, NJ: Princeton University Press.

Teisman, Geert and Erik-Hans Klijn. (2008). "Complexity Theory and Public Management." *Public Management Review* 10(3): 287–297.

Teisman, Geert, Arwin Buuren and Lasse Gerrits. (2009). "An Introduction to Understanding and Managing Complex Process Systems." In Geert Teisman, Arwin Buuren and Lasse Gerrits (eds.), *Managing Complex Governance Systems.* London: Routledge.

The Economist. (2010, October 7). "How to Grow" (Special Report: The World Economy). Available at www.economist.com/node/17173886 (accessed March 3, 2017).

Thompson, James D. (1967). *Organizations in Action: Social Science Bases of Administrative Theory.* New York: McGraw-Hill.

Tompkins, Jonathan. (2005). *Organization Theory and Public Management.* Belmont, CA: Thomson Wadsworth.

Treib, O., H. Bahr and G. Falkner. (2007). "Modes of Governance: Towards a Conceptual Clarification." *Journal of European Public Policy* 14(1): 1–20.

Waits, M.J. (2000). "The Added Value of the Industry Cluster Approach to Economic Analysis, Strategy Development, and Service Delivery." *Economic Development Quarterly* 14(1): 35–50.

Wamsley, Gary and Mayer Zald. (1973). *The Political Economy of Public Organizations: A Critique and Approach to the Study of Public Administration.* Lexington, MA: Lexington Books.

Wiarda, Howard. (2007). "Globalization in Its Universal and Regional Dimensions." In Howard Wiarda (ed.), *Globalization: Universal Trends, Regional Implications.* Boston, MA: Northeastern University Press.

Williams, Glyn. (2010). *The Knowledge Economy, Language and Culture.* Buffalo, NY: Multilingual Matters.

Wolfe, David A. (2010). "From Entanglement to Alignment: A Review of International Practice in Regional Economic Development." Toronto: Mowat Centre for Policy Innovation, School of Public Policy & Governance, University of Toronto.

World Economic Forum. (2013). "The Global Competitiveness Report 2013–2014." Available at http://reports.weforum.org/the-global-competitiveness-report-2013-2014 (accessed March 3, 2017).

Young, Robert. (2012). "Introduction." In Martin Horak (ed.), *Sites of Governance: Multilevel Governance and Policy Making in Canada's Big Cities.* Montreal and Kingston, Canada: McGill-Queen's University Press, pp. 3–25.

Young-Hyman, Trevor. (2008). "The Potential for Effective Regional Development Agencies in Turkey: A Comparative Analysis." *Regional & Federal Studies* 18(4): 375–402.

2 Lines in the sand

How Americans' polarization results in unwillingness to accept compromise policy outcomes

Michael R. Wolf, J. Cherie Strachan and Daniel M. Shea

Introduction: the nature of political compromise

Americans often frame compromise as an unqualified good. The American Political Science Association's Taskforce report, "Negotiating Agreement in Politics," for example, posits that popular desire for policy innovation and reform is often stifled by polarization among elected officials (Mansbridge and Martin 2013). This raises a question for scholars: To what extent does uncompromising elite political behavior reflect or conflict with the public's preferences towards compromise? We gauge the public's commitment to compromise with multiple political, cultural, and contextual measures from a national survey. We first asked respondents what political compromise means to them in a voice-captured open-ended question. Views on political compromise tend to cluster around compromise being a shared, positive, cultural norm, though a substantial number of Republicans reject political compromise as negative and do so with a negative tone.

We also look at factors that might expand or restrict the potential for compromise. Partisanship, strength of party identification, and differing worldviews affect attitudes toward compromise, as do preferences on specific issues. Meanwhile, exposure to disagreement in political discussion makes Republicans less likely to reject compromise completely.

Our findings suggest that lack of political compromise does not stem entirely from political leaders' intransigence. A substantial number of Americans do not want political compromise, with factors such as party identification, partisan strength, authoritarian worldview, and controversial issues eroding such inclinations. Democrats and Independents do desire more political compromise than Republicans, but even they are less inclined to tolerate compromise on specific issues. Exposure to disagreement through political discussion increases acceptance of compromise on hot-button issues. Yet these findings must be contextualized. First, exposure to disagreement makes voters less likely to reject compromise; it does not move them to embrace it. Second, exposure to disagreement has a greater effect on Republicans. Since Republicans often question the value of compromise, the ability to shift their attitudes is important. However, Democrats, who initially are far more likely to prefer politicians who compromise, become less supportive of it when exposed to political disagreement. Despite the impact of disagreement exposure on Republicans, few of the influences included in this analysis lead voters to embrace compromise on specific issues.

Literature review

Compromise vs. standing firm

Political compromise is essential in a diverse democracy. Positive views of compromise hold that deliberative negotiation can re-frame problems such that compromise solutions lead to satisfaction for all sides – the so-called "win–win" solution (Guttman and Thompson 2012; Mansbridge and Martin 2013). In this version, compromise yields a new position that all parties ultimately believe is better. Yet it seems unlikely that this ideal outcome results from every effort to seek common ground, or that most members of the public will regularly associate political compromise with these types of benefits. A more likely outcome is compromise resulting in moderation of the most extreme positions, producing a middle-ground solution. The most attractive aspect of this version of political compromise may be that each side is expected to make equal sacrifices to their ideal agenda. However, game theorists have long noted how subjective views lead individuals to defect from compromise even when it would provide a superior payoff, particularly when the payoffs are zero-sum. It is likely that Americans see some issues as more zero-sum than others, making some compromises neither win-win nor middle-ground.

Consequently, compromise may mean many different things depending on one's perspective, the nature of the issues, and the broader political context. Research has evaluated decreasing compromise among American politicians, though less focus or consensus exists on views toward political compromise among the broader electorate. Our findings present the public's direct perception of political compromise, as well as assessing specific political, cultural, and contextual factors that the extant literature suggests should affect the electorate's willingness to compromise: party polarization, distinct worldviews, different issue types, and disagreement in political discussion.

Partisan polarization

The realignment of southern conservative Democrats into the Republican Party and northeastern liberal Republicans into the Democratic Party over recent decades has resulted in clear public ideological divides (Black and Black 2002; Reiter and Stonecash 2011). Party scholars largely agree that elected leaders are increasingly divided, but disagree on whether the divisions exist among the general public. Fiorina and Abrams (2009) claim that the public is only superficially divided and that it disapproves of the elite's polarized positions, while Abramowitz (2010) counters that most partisans embrace the stark ideological positions of their party. Additionally, negative partisanship, or a second gut-level rejection of the other party among the public, may smother compromise substantively and procedurally (Wolf et al. 2012; Abramowitz and Webster 2015). This likely translates into difficulty in wanting to compromise with the other side. Indeed, in 2014 the Pew Center found that overall Americans wanted President Obama and Republican leaders to meet in the middle – 50/50 – on important issues facing the country, but only a third of consistently ideological partisans felt 50/50 was ideal and instead felt compromise should end up significantly favoring their party's leadership on such issues (Pew Research Center 2014). If partisans are becoming more ideologically divided, the propensity to want to compromise will be strained.

The Pew Center has also found that Democrats prefer politicians to compromise more than Republicans and that this divide has grown recently (Pew Research Center for the People & the Press 2007). We explore below how our findings fit this trend as well as offering potential explanations. Beyond other potential explanations such as New Deal Democrats being a coalition party, political cultural elements of the parties' bases, or changing competitive fortunes for the parties, one reason for differential appetite for compromise may hinge on the worldviews of those making up each party.

Separate worldviews in American politics

One core portion of the polarization literature argues that divisions are grounded in particularly divisive cultural issues that people want championed by politicians and that leave little room for compromise. Prominent issues such as gay rights, terrorism, immigration, and security have separated voters with two distinct worldviews. According to Hetherington and Weiler (2009), in one camp are authoritarians, who prefer social order and perceive America and its way of life as under threat by social change. Non-authoritarians, meanwhile, prioritize personal autonomy and civil rights, along with a level playing field for out-groups and minorities. The worldview divide has led to increasing party polarization as the crossover between Republicans and authoritarians and Democrats and non-authoritarians has been driven by these cultural issue divides (Hetherington and Weiler 2009). This is not to say that there are no authoritarians on the left or non-authoritarians on the right; in fact, these worldviews collided in the 2008 Democratic presidential primary (ibid.). The divide typically tends to polarize the parties ideologically (ibid.).

The reason why there are authoritarians on the left and non-authoritarians on the right despite the ideological divide is because the division affects voters' views of the proper political process too. Barker and Carman (2012) found that a similar traditionalist versus progressive divide led to differences as to how closely elected officials should follow (progressives) or work to counter (traditionalists) public opinion. Such core differences about the proper workings of representative democracy are likely to raise criticism of how each party attempts to achieve their ideologically divisive issue agenda by adherents of the opposing party. Further, Hetherington and Weiler (2009: 33–50) find that each worldview also has significant cognitive differences from the other side, which could likely affect how much a person would want to engage in deliberation and compromise. Non-authoritarians have an "accuracy motivation" that leads them to embrace deliberation and reject stark positions. This preference sets them apart from authoritarians, who favor clarity, avoid confusion, and have less tolerance of ambiguity, which is often a consequence in the process of compromising (Hetherington and Weiler 2009: 34–46). So the cultural divide not only potentially decreases compromise by adding another ideological divide, but also leads to disagreements on the proper process of politics with a willingness to compromise potentially being a key part.

Disagreement in political discussion

Political disagreement is not easy and cultural norms often suggest that people should avoid talking about politics in mixed company. How much people actually pursue discussion with people with whom they disagree about politics is a source of debate. Some argue that disagreement is frequent (Huckfeldt, Johnson, and Sprague 2004; Huckfeldt and Morehouse Mendez 2008). Others counter that disagreement is uncommon and that the frequency of political discussion is inversely related to political disagreement (Mutz 2006: 25–26). Avoiding divisive topics in interpersonal conversation is common, if not polite, but it could also help people to dodge compromise because their views remain unchallenged.

Political disagreement is important because it is a key aspect of deliberation, which leads to division but could also help the electorate grind toward greater consensus. Research on the flow of political information shows that exposure to conflicting views brings ambivalence, which leads people to hold conflicted political views (Zaller 1992). Compromise suggests that some level of ambivalence would be needed to see the other side of things or one's views would remain steadfast. The evidence from real-world political discussion demonstrates that disagreement can lead to better candidate evaluation, increased understanding of opposing political viewpoints (Mutz 2002a; Huckfeldt, Morehouse Mendez, and Osborn 2004), enhanced political tolerance (Mutz 2002b), and other positive democratic outcomes (Barabas 2004). These findings do not directly touch on compromise, but it is logical to assume that a person would be more willing to compromise when they become more ambivalent on an issue if tolerance and understanding the worth of the other side of an argument have been shown to increase as a result of engaging in political conversational disputes.

Hot-button issues

Consideration must also be given to different types of issues under debate. Some issues can fundamentally alter the political debate and partisan attachments based on how cognitively intricate or "gut-level" they are (Carmines and Stimson 1989). People have burned draft cards, flags, or bras in protests much more than spreadsheets or Internal Revenue Service code. Indeed, cultural issues have been powerful enough to pry loose, long-standing partisanship and deeply divide the American public (Hilygus and Shields 2010). Despite the American culture wars, scholars note that the rise of cultural issue divisions has not led to economic issues becoming less salient (Ansolabehere et al. 2006; Brewer and Stonecash 2007). Yet the culture divide literature does suggest that the growth of such issues helped to usher in this age of less compromise and motivate Americans who may have been less politically attentive. The nature of some issues may leave less 50/50 or win-win opportunity, as the culture war literature argues. Issue salience also has been shown to reduce a willingness to compromise (Pew Research Center for the People & the Press 2007). As a result, a voter's preference toward political compromise could very likely shift depending on the nature of the issue and the salience of that issue to the voter.

Propositions, data and measures

Four core propositions drive our study. First, our study allows respondents to describe political compromise in their own words. Perceptions of the usefulness and benefits of compromise are not uniformly embraced by politicians and may not be by the public. Further, the public could view compromise through procedural, issue-based, or multiple dimensions when provided with the opportunity to define it with their own voice. Second, the party polarization literature suggests that party identifiers should be less willing to compromise, though they differ on whether the public is polarized (Abramowitz 2010) or moderately more sorted ideologically (Fiorina et al. 2005; Levendusky 2009). In either case, we suspect partisanship and strength of party identification will suppress citizens' appetite for compromise. A third and likely related factor is the presence of either a non-authoritarian or authoritarian worldview. If citizens hold a non-authoritarian worldview, they should prefer compromise, while authoritarians should be more likely to reject compromise in defense of maintaining the social status quo.

The final propositions are more contextual and deal with exposure to political disagreement and with intransigence differing across different issues. Exposure to disagreement in political discussion should lead to a greater propensity for compromise and the nature of some issues provides different incentives for compromise. These propositions should hold both for voters' preference for political compromise in general and for their willingness to compromise on specific issues. Data comes from a survey commissioned by the Goldfarb Center for Public Affairs and Civic Engagement at Colby College that was fielded by SurveyUSA and included over 1,500 adults nationwide from November 13, 2012 to November 19, 2012.[1]

Dependent variables

Three dependent variables operationalize political compromise. First, the dataset included an open-ended response where respondents were asked to explain what political compromise means to them. Specifically, the question asked: "Some

Americans are more open to compromise on certain issues, but not on others. From your point of view, what does the idea of political compromise mean to you?"[2] Respondents were cued to think about compromise by two questions directly prior to the open-ended question. The first cue was: "Which do you think is more important in a politician: the ability to compromise to get things done, or a willingness to stand firm in support of principles?" The second was: "Given the outcome of the 2012 election, how likely do you think it is that elected officials in Washington will work together across party lines to find solutions to difficult issues?" The goal of the open-ended question was to provide inductive insight into Americans' understanding of political compromise.

The second dependent variable, measured by the first cue above, centers on a broader view of compromise and particularly whether politicians should employ it. While citizens may want compromise from politicians *generally*, they perhaps reject it for specific, contested political issues. So, issue-based compromise contingency measures were tapped by asking: "On the issue of ___, how likely are you to compromise with people who disagree with you?" We cited five separate issues: budget deficit, healthcare, immigration, abortion, and social policy such as gay marriage. Willingness to compromise will likely vary across these issues, but overall could demonstrate that people are less committed to compromise on specific issues than they are more generally.

Independent variables

The main independent variables deal with party identification, worldviews and exposure to political disagreement. The first contextual variable is the level of disagreement one experiences in political discussion. Respondents provided up to three potential political discussion partners and were asked how frequently they agree in these conversations.[3] Respondents were asked:

> From time to time, people discuss government, elections, and politics with other people. Think about the one person you talk with most about elections and politics … is that person your: spouse or partner, relative other than your spouse or partner, a friend, a co-worker, a neighbor, someone from your church, a member of a social group, or someone else?

Then the respondent was asked: "When you discuss politics and elections with this person, do you agree often, sometimes, rarely, or never?" These questions were repeated for a second and third political discussion partner. We then added the values from the first, second, and third political discussion partners with the value of zero given to respondents who did not have either a first, second, or third discussion partner respectively. Higher scores indicated greater disagreement, with the overall additive index ranging from 0–12. This index is drawn from the political science literature on individual exposure to disagreement. It is not intended to reflect the intensity of disagreement with individual conversation partners, but rather the overall amount of disagreement in a respondent's

political discussion partnerships.[4] To balance the distribution, we created a disagreement variable from the quintiles of this additive variable.

The second variable involves the respondent's political worldview. We use
the standard four-question battery to differentiate authoritarians from non-
authoritarians based on views of desirable childrearing goals. This involves
identifying preferable attributes of children: independence vs. respect for elders,
curious vs. good manners, self-reliance vs. obedience, and considerate vs. well
behaved. We use Hetherington and Weiler's (2009) same coding scheme to
produce the additive worldview index, but double the values so that respondents
are given a score of zero when the non-authoritarian option is chosen, one when
they say "both" attributes are positive, and two when they choose the authoritarian attribute. This produces an index from zero to eight, and we balance the
index's distribution in our worldview/authoritarianism by quartiles.

All other independent variables follow conventional measures for party
identification, ideology, attentiveness, religiosity, marriage status, gender, and
racial/ethnic group.

Findings

Our analysis unfolds in three stages. First, we content analyze respondents'
explanations of what political compromise means to them. Second, we assess
how partisan beliefs affect citizens' preferences for politicians who stand firm or
who compromise. Similarly, do voters' worldviews make them more or less
likely to want political compromise, and does disagreement in political discussion increase preferences for compromise? The third section explores how
partisanship, worldview, and political disagreement affect voters' embrace of
compromise on specific issues.

Open-ended responses to what political compromise means

Our content analysis of what "compromise means to you" resulted in six categories according to the underlying function of political compromise expressed.
These included:

1   a process that politicians can/should use to identify and do the right thing
    for the American people (example: "just talk to one another to figure out
    what the best policies are for the people");
2   a process that politicians can/should use to identify functional solutions to
    public problems (example: "be willing to listen to each other to find
    common ground for action on the problems we face");
3   a vaguer description of compromise as a process without a nod directly to
    the functional outcomes or "right thing" that can be produced;
4   a negotiating tactic that politicians use to gain a strategic advantage
    (example: "giving up something unimportant now in order to gain some-
    thing more important later");

5   an undesirable practice resulting in unsatisfactory/unacceptable outcomes; and
6   miscellaneous, not germane responses (which were excluded from the analysis).

Comments were also coded for positive, neutral, negative or hostile affect based on the respondent's tone of voice, with negative/hostile combined to achieve sufficient category size.[5] A factor analysis was run post-hoc on these coded categories and all of the categories are independent except for the "process without a nod directly to the functional outcomes or 'right thing'" and "a process that politicians can/should use to identify and do the right thing for the American people." These categories remain separate because they were objectively stated differently even though their underlying factor is shared. That all the other categories show factor independence demonstrates the strength of the coding into these distinct categories. For both the substantive categories and for affect, intercoder reliability far exceeded standard expectations and followed recommended content analysis protocol.[6]

Table 2.1 presents these voice captures by party and tone. The most prominent pattern is that voters overwhelmingly view compromise as a process to

Table 2.1 Respondents' open-ended evaluation of political compromise and tone of voice by party

	From your point of view, what does the idea of political compromise mean to you?					
	Rejects compromise (%)	*Negotiating tactic (%)*	*Process (%)*	*Functional process (%)*	*Process to do right thing (%)*	*N*
Democrat	3	3	13	32	50	244
Independent	21	2	4	36	37	53
Republican	20	7	10	29	36	213
Respondent's tone of voice						
Positive tone						
Democrat	0	0	4	7	89	134
Independent	0	0	0	4	96	20
Republican	0	1	2	6	91	83
Neutral tone						
Democrat	0	7	25	67	2	102
Independent	0	4	10	86	0	22
Republican	1	14	19	67	0	83
Negative tone						
Democrat	90	0	10	0	0	8
Independent	100	0	0	0	0	11
Republican	87	4	8	1	0	47

Note
Data are weighted. Coded from voice-captured open-ended responses.

produce either the most appropriate or functional political outcomes. Over seven in ten respondents described political compromise in one of these two ways.

The second trend is that Democrats view compromise differently than Republicans and Independents. Twenty-seven percent of Republicans and 23 percent of Independents either reject compromise or view it as a negotiating tactic, compared to only 6 percent of Democrats. In their own words, over a quarter of Republicans and nearly one-quarter of Independents (though their numbers are small) reject the idea of or view political compromise as only a tactic, not a positive substantive or procedural outcome. These differences are reflected in respondents' tones. Based on the number of partisans in each tone of voice category, many more Republicans (at 22 percent) and Independents (at 20 percent, though small overall) than Democrats (3 percent) had a negative/hostile affect toward political compromise. Though clearly a minority, a significant number of Republicans reject compromise or view it with suspicion and do so with sharp tones.

Still, political compromise was for all groups overwhelmingly described as the obvious way to identify and do the right thing for the American people, or to identify feasible solutions to problems and largely expressed as such in tone. Most people downplay the difficulty and highlight the "functional" aspects of political compromise in their open-ended responses.

The reasons why people express positive views of compromise could be multifaceted. They may see their work/home life functioning due to compromise. Subjective political views may also lead people to see their own preferences as superior and assume that "compromise" means persuading a yet-to-form majority toward his or her views. Finally, a willingness to compromise may be a socialized American "cultural default," so there could be a social desirability for compromise – especially given that the study followed the intense 2012 election, and as de Tocqueville (1969: 135) noted about such post-electoral periods: "... the ardor is dissipated, everything calms down, and the river which momentarily overflowed its banks falls back to its bed." Nevertheless, although many respondents felt compelled to support compromise they still raised secondary concerns. Indeed, a number of respondents added exceptions to their initial support, variously noting that people should not compromise on core principles, tenets of the Christian faith, or protection of individual/human rights. These respondents still felt obliged to express support for political compromise before making it clear that certain items were "off the table."

Preferences for politicians to stand firm or compromise to get things done

The findings from Table 2.2 support the claim that party and strength of party identification significantly influence preferences for politicians who compromise or stand firm. Table 2.2 shows clear differences stemming from partisanship (Republicans favor standing firm on principle and Democrats favor compromise) as well as well as party strength (stronger Republicans and Democrats favor

Table 2.2 Preference for politicians to stand firm or compromise by party ID strength 2012, and Pew findings by party on preference for leaders who compromise 1987–2012

	Which is more important in a politician?		
	Stand firm in support of principles (%)	Ability to compromise to get things done (%)	N
Strong Democrat	25	75	334
Weak Democrat	25	75	256
Independent Leans Democratic	18	82	128
Independent	37	63	133
Independent Leans Republican	45	55	128
Weak Republican	48	52	199
Strong Republican	60	40	236

Note
Data are weighted. Democrats and Republicans include Independents who lean to their party.

Pew Research Center Question 40h: I like political leaders who are willing to make compromises in order to get the job done

	Democrat agree (%)	Democrat disagree (%)	Independent agree (%)	Independent disagree (%)	Republican agree (%)	Republican disagree (%)
1987	77	16	70	20	66	27
1988	75	21	71	23	71	23
1990	74	21	77	18	67	29
1997	87	10	76	23	72	25
1999	83	14	80	17	70	26
2002	83	14	81	16	71	25
2003	81	17	78	18	72	24
2007	87	9	82	13	70	27
2009	89	9	79	16	66	29
2012	90	8	83	15	68	28

Note
Source Pew Research Center American Values Survey Question Database: www.people-press.org/values-questions/q40h/like-politicians-who-make-compromises-to-get-the-job-done/#party.

standing firm relative to less committed partisans), even if the absolute level of Republican compromisers falls far behind Democrats. As noted above, this finding is not a contextual effect of the 2012 election alone nor completely time-bound to the party polarized era, though this gap has surely increased as the polarization or sorting of partisans has grown. Decades of Pew Research Center studies (2007) presented in Table 2.2 show a higher percentage of Democrats liking politicians who compromise than Republicans, and this does not include the percentage of partisans who like politicians who "stick to positions, even if unpopular" where Republicans held a 55 percent to 37 percent advantage over Democrats in 2013.

Contextual influences on compromise: disagreement in political discussion and worldview

The previous sections provided a detailed picture of public views on political compromise, but were limited to partisan influences on compromise. Hence, we also include analyses of voters' worldviews and disagreement in their political discussion network. Worldview may predispose someone toward positive or negative views of compromise. Meanwhile, more disagreement in political discussion may enhance willingness to consider others' positions.

As anticipated, partisans – particularly stronger partisans – tend to discuss politics with like-minded conversation partners. In general partisans have double or triple the percentage of discussion with those they agree with most frequently, compared to Independents or weaker partisans. Strong partisans are less open to compromise and also less open to discussion that could challenge their partisan beliefs. Further, exposure to disagreement leads to greater attitudinal ambivalence, supporting the scholarly consensus, as indicated by later vote choice in the 2012 presidential election. Thus, our data fits broader attitudinal patters from discussion described in the literature.

A surprising finding in Table 2.3 suggests that increased disagreement may *not* uniformly lead to compromise. Independents' and Republicans' willingness

Table 2.3 Political disagreement and political worldview and preference for politicians to compromise by party

	% who think the ability to compromise to get things done is more important in a politician than the ability to stand firm in support of principles					
	Democrats (%)	N	*Independents (%)*	N	*Republicans (%)*	N
Level of agreement in political discussion						
Highest agreement	84	98	43	9	42	124
2nd Quintile	79	103	31	11	42	91
3rd Quintile	81	147	68	24	47	101
4th Quintile	74	161	69	29	55	106
Highest disagreement	64	77	68	31	51	62
Worldview						
Most nonauthoritarian	84	207	62	35	57	124
2nd Quartile	77	218	63	43	54	91
3rd Quartile	74	93	65	19	41	101
Most authoritarian	69	200	63	36	41	106

Note
Data are weighted. The questions used to measure authoritarianism were: "Although there are a number of qualities that people feel children should have, every person thinks that some qualities are more important than others. Even if you do not have children, I am going to read you pairs of desirable qualities about childrearing. Please tell me which one you think is more important for a child to have. Here's the first pair: Independence or respect for elders? Next pair: curiosity or good manners? Next: obedience or self-reliance? Last: being considerate or being well-behaved?"

to compromise increases with exposure to political disagreement. Yet Democrats tend to prefer compromise *less* as their disagreement increases. Perhaps Democrats who have disagreed with others may now feel that since they deliberated, disagreed, and their party won the presidency fair-and-square, their preference should be brought into policy from the election's mandate. Democrats still prefer compromise much more than Republicans.

How does worldview affect one's preference for politicians to compromise or to stand firm on principle? Republicans and Democrats differ on their world-views, as Hetherington and Weiler (2009) predict. Double the number of strong Democrats identified as non-authoritarians compared to strong Republicans.[7] Some 45 percent of strong Republicans were in the most authoritarian grouping (though 38 percent of strong Democrats were as well). Sharp worldview differences follow hypothesized patterns on compromise (non-authoritarians more than authoritarians) or standing firm (authoritarians more than non-authoritarians), though a slight majority of authoritarians do prefer compromise.

Table 2.3 presents the main findings on views of compromise, with the percentage of those who want politicians to compromise to get things done by both party identification and worldview. Expected patterns emerge. First, Democrats prefer politicians who compromise more than Republicans and Independents. Second, all partisans with greater authoritarian worldviews prefer politicians to stand firm on principle. When these patterns are combined one particular finding stands out: a majority of Republicans preferring compromise shifts to a majority preferring standing firm on principle as they move from the most non-authoritarian to the most authoritarian worldview. Just like disagreement, world-view affects partisans' preference for compromise in important ways.

Influence of partisanship, worldview, and disagreement on compromise on particular issues

Party identification, worldview, and political discussion disagreement all affect citizens' view of compromise. How much does each affect a willingness to compromise on specific issues? Our open-ended results suggested that except for a deviant minority, Americans generally embrace compromise but also frequently volunteered that they were inclined to avoid compromising on particular issues.

How much does the general appetite for compromise persist for particular issues? Table 2.4 shows how much a respondent's broad preference for politicians to compromise or to stand firm holds up with their own likelihood of compromising with others with whom they disagree on particular issues. Four out of ten people who want flexible politicians are very or somewhat unlikely to compromise with someone with whom they disagree about healthcare. Over half of those who claim to prefer flexible politicians report that they are very or somewhat unlikely to compromise on abortion or social issues such as gay marriage when they disagree with someone. The initial conclusion we draw from self-reported willingness to compromise on particular issues is that compromise is embraced far less in practice. Respondents overwhelming said in both open- and

Table 2.4 Preference for politicians to compromise or stand firm on principle and the likelihood a respondent will compromise with people they disagree with on issues, post-election 2012

	On the issue of ____, how likely are you to compromise with people who disagree with you?					
	Very unlikely (%)	*Somewhat unlikely (%)*	*Neither likely nor unlikely (%)*	*Somewhat likely (%)*	*Very likely (%)*	*N*
Deficit						
Stand firm	25	29	20	21	5	524
Compromise	8	17	21	43	11	887
Healthcare						
Stand firm	38	24	15	19	4	524
Compromise	15	24	20	32	10	911
Immigration						
Stand firm	31	24	21	18	6	524
Compromise	15	21	23	30	11	904
Abortion						
Stand firm	56	17	16	9	2	518
Compromise	35	22	20	14	8	899
Social Policy						
Stand firm	53	15	17	12	4	525
Compromise	33	20	20	17	9	910

Note
Data are weighted.

closed-ended responses that they want politicians to compromise, but they themselves do not want to compromise on the main issues of the day.

Table 2.5 presents the likelihood of respondents' willingness to compromise on each issue by party identification. For the most part, few respondents think it is somewhat or very likely that they will compromise on issues when they disagree with someone. On only one occasion is a majority of any partisan group somewhat or very likely to compromise with opponents on an issue (Democrats on budget deficit). Second, Democrats, Independents, and Republicans embrace compromise far less as the issues move from budgetary to social/cultural. Third, the partisan divide that emerged on preferences for politicians who compromise vs. stand firm exists here as well. On no occasion does a third, much less one-half, of Republicans say they are somewhat or very likely to compromise on an issue when they disagree with someone. They tend to be very or somewhat unlikely to compromise on all of these issues.

As citizens reject compromise on particular issues, even when they claim to prefer politicians who compromise, contextual influences that cultivate flexibility on issue positions become important. In particular, does exposure to disagreement make compromise more likely and does an authoritarian worldview

Table 2.5 Party identification and the likelihood of compromising with people who disagree on the deficit, healthcare, immigration, abortion, and social policy

On the issue of _____, how likely are you to compromise with people who disagree with you?

	Very unlikely (%)	Somewhat unlikely (%)	Neither likely nor unlikely (%)	Somewhat likely (%)	Very likely (%)	N
Deficit						
Democrat	7	16	21	44	12	719
Independent	14	27	26	26	7	130
Republican	24	27	19	26	4	569
Healthcare						
Democrat	16	25	17	31	11	732
Independent	22	15	28	29	6	132
Republican	34	25	17	20	4	577
Immigration						
Democrat	12	19	25	32	12	729
Independent	23	20	26	19	12	136
Republican	31	25	19	21	5	570
Abortion						
Democrat	39	21	18	14	8	720
Independent	34	17	30	15	4	130
Republican	50	21	16	10	3	572
Social Policy						
Democrat	35	22	19	15	9	731
Independent	35	15	23	18	9	136
Republican	50	15	16	14	5	577

Note
Data are weighted. The question on social policy reads: "Next, on social policy issues such as same-sex marriage, how likely would you be to compromise with people who disagree with you?"

decrease the likelihood of compromise? As anticipated, Table 2.6 illustrates that an authoritarian worldview decreases the likelihood of compromising on issues. Yet even among non-authoritarians, the likelihood of compromising on specific issues is rare. As one moves from budgetary, to healthcare, to immigration to social issues, it becomes less likely that people will compromise with their opponents. The distinction between non-authoritarian and authoritarian worldviews on *rejecting* compromise is not as pronounced as is the divide among Democrats and Republicans, but this worldview divide may be muted by the fact that it often manifests itself through party identification.

As posited above, party identification and separate worldviews shape compromise generally and on specific issues. Will disagreement in political discussion lead to greater likelihood of compromise on these specific issues? As Table 2.7 indicates, disagreement in political discussion does temper an uncompromising mindset. Again, expected patterns emerge. First, social/cultural issues elicit

Table 2.6 Worldview and the likelihood of compromising with people who disagree on the deficit, healthcare, immigration, abortion, and social policy

	On the issue of _____, how likely are you to compromise with people who disagree with you?					
	Very unlikely (%)	*Somewhat unlikely (%)*	*Neither likely nor unlikely (%)*	*Somewhat likely (%)*	*Very likely (%)*	*N*
Deficit						
Most nonauthoritarian	12	20	19	43	6	385
2nd Quartile	14	19	23	33	12	427
3rd Quartile	13	27	24	28	9	207
Most authoritarian	19	23	20	32	8	456
Healthcare						
Most nonauthoritarian	23	28	16	27	7	386
2nd Quartile	22	23	20	26	9	441
3rd Quartile	20	24	22	23	11	210
Most authoritarian	29	22	16	29	5	462
Immigration						
Most nonauthoritarian	16	21	23	32	8	383
2nd Quartile	18	21	25	25	12	442
3rd Quartile	25	17	23	25	9	209
Most authoritarian	27	25	20	22	7	459
Abortion						
Most nonauthoritarian	41	27	20	10	3	386
2nd Quartile	41	21	20	12	7	431
3rd Quartile	39	20	17	15	10	208
Most authoritarian	50	16	18	13	4	455
Social Policy						
Most nonauthoritarian	39	22	20	14	5	386
2nd Quartile	34	18	21	19	8	445
3rd Quartile	40	22	17	13	8	202
Most authoritarian	50	14	16	13	7	464

Note
Data are weighted. The question on social policy reads: "Next, on social policy issues such as same-sex marriage, how likely would you be to compromise with people who disagree with you?"

less willingness to compromise than more "nuts-and-bolts" budgets or healthcare policies. Yet even having the highest levels of disagreement in political discussion never leads to a majority of voters being somewhat or very likely to compromise on any particular issue. Rather, the effect of political discussion disagreement is to curb rejection of compromise. Disagreement does not make people more likely to compromise; it just makes it *less apt that people will be very unlikely* to compromise.

Yet partisan patterns complicate these effects. The more Democrats disagreed in political discussion, the less likely they were to prefer compromise, whereas the opposite is true for Republicans who became slightly more likely to want

Table 2.7 Levels of disagreement in political discussion and the likelihood of compromising with people who disagree on the deficit, healthcare, immigration, abortion, and social policy

| | On the issue of ___, how likely are you to compromise with people who disagree with you? | | | | | |
	Very unlikely (%)	Somewhat unlikely (%)	Neither likely nor unlikely (%)	Somewhat likely (%)	Very likely (%)	N
Deficit						
Highest agreement	27	22	14	25	11	241
2nd Quintile	15	25	17	37	6	208
3rd Quintile	14	21	21	36	8	281
4th Quintile	11	19	26	34	10	303
Highest disagreement	14	23	19	34	11	193
Healthcare						
Highest agreement	42	21	8	20	9	244
2nd Quintile	27	29	13	26	5	209
3rd Quintile	25	25	18	27	6	286
4th Quintile	16	28	21	27	9	311
Highest disagreement	19	21	22	30	8	192
Immigration						
Highest agreement	29	21	16	23	11	241
2nd Quintile	19	18	30	29	4	213
3rd Quintile	22	22	25	23	8	286
4th Quintile	20	23	23	25	10	312
Highest disagreement	21	24	20	25	10	192
Abortion						
Highest agreement	54	13	14	9	11	242
2nd Quintile	50	21	15	12	3	206
3rd Quintile	44	21	20	10	5	286
4th Quintile	37	18	22	18	5	308
Highest disagreement	40	22	20	11	7	191
Social Policy						
Highest agreement	54	15	10	11	9	244
2nd Quintile	51	15	19	13	2	211
3rd Quintile	41	21	19	13	6	286
4th Quintile	30	19	23	16	12	313
Highest disagreement	40	19	17	18	7	191

Note
Data are weighted.

politicians to compromise as their exposure to disagreement increased. This finding may result in part from a ceiling effect, as Democrats largely prefer politicians to compromise, thus leaving little room for further increases. Republicans start at a low pro-compromise rate, leaving nowhere to go but up as disagreement increases.

The results demonstrate that when voters are given the chance to report their likelihood of compromising on specific issues, they become less likely to prefer compromise, even when they claim to prefer politicians who are willing to do so. Party identification, worldview, and disagreement in political discussion do shift this calculus, but the take away is that Democrats, non-authoritarians, and those who disagree most in political discussion all tend to be *less uncompromising* compared to Republicans, authoritarians, and those with homogenous discussion networks. These patterns suggest that there is no singular overwhelming demand for the hard work of compromise among the American public.

Higher order models on compromise

The findings above describe relationships among party identification, worldview, and political disagreement and a preference for compromise at the elite level as well as on specific issues. The next step is to control for each of these factors simultaneously along with other explanatory attitudinal variables to see whether and when each significantly affects preferences for compromise.

Table 2.8 presents six models. The first model is in the first column and estimates how partisan identification, worldview, and disagreement in political discussion affects compromise generally when controlling for other important political and demographic variables. Specifically, it uses these explanatory variables in a logit model because the dependent variable is dichotomous. Positive coefficients indicate that the greater the value of the independent variable, the more compromise is preferred. The second set of models are ordered logits on the likelihood of compromising on each policy issue. Positive coefficients indicate that greater values of the independent variable lead to a greater likelihood of compromising on specific issues with those with whom one disagrees. Statistical significance was determined relative to the standard errors.

Further, we include the marginal effects of each statistically significant relationship. This reflects the change in probability of wanting politicians to compromise rather than to stand firm when the value of the independent variable moves from its minimum to the maximum value. For the ordinal logit models, this "margin" or marginal effect reflects the shift in likelihood from being very unlikely to compromise with someone who disagrees with you (a value of one) to being very likely to compromise with someone who disagrees with you (a value of five) as the value of the independent variable moves from its minimum to maximum value. In effect, the "margin" or marginal effect captures the relative substantive power each independent variable holds on the likelihood of being more apt to prefer politicians to compromise or being willing to compromise oneself on a policy issue.

In the logit model on the preference for politicians who compromise versus to stand firm, party identification, ideology, and worldview are all statistically significant. The more Republican, the more authoritarian, and the more conservative one is, the less likely one is to prefer a politician who compromises, which fit expectations from the findings above. Disagreement in political discussion is not significant, but the negative coefficient shows that exposure to disagreement in discussion makes it less likely that one will prefer

Table 2.8 Logit on whether politicians should stand firm or compromise and ordered logit models on how likely it is for a respondent to compromise with someone they disagree with on various issues

| | Logit: stand firm vs. Compromise | | | Ordered logit: very unlikely, somewhat unlikely, neither unlikely nor likely, somewhat likely or very likely to compromise on issues | | | | | | | | | | | | | | |
| | Compromise | | | Budget deficit | | | Healthcare | | | Immigration | | | Abortion | | | Social policy | | |
	Coef	SE	margin	Coef	SE	margin	Coef	SE	margin	Coef	SE	margin	Coef	SE	margin	Coef	SE	margin
Follow Politics Closely	0.039	(0.114)		0.154	(0.093)		0.104	(0.093)		0.031	(0.090)		0.098	(0.094)		-0.023	(0.093)	
Party Identification	-0.174	(0.037)	-0.226	-0.184	(0.031)	0.140	-0.108	(0.030)	0.118	-0.158	(0.030)	0.159	-0.051	(0.031)	0.073	-0.027	(0.031)	
Ideology	0.534	(0.110)	0.225	0.342	(0.092)	-0.083	0.256	(0.089)	-0.091	0.203	(0.088)	-0.066	-0.005	(0.091)		0.098	(0.089)	
Religiosity	-0.036	(0.084)		-0.028	(0.068)		0.032	(0.067)		-0.138	(0.068)	0.045	0.100	(0.069)		0.228	(0.068)	-0.106
Married	0.108	(0.136)		0.154	(0.119)		0.045	(0.109)		0.213	(0.049)	-0.035	-0.065	(0.112)		0.070	(0.111)	
Gender	-0.040	(0.132)		-0.011	(0.107)		0.073	(0.106)		0.087	(0.105)		-0.410	(0.109)	0.090	-0.136	(0.108)	
Race	0.058	(0.068)		0.048	(0.055)		0.171	(0.054)	-0.086	0.057	(0.055)	-0.084	0.239	(0.056)	-0.166	0.277	(0.056)	-0.184
Worldview/ Authoritarian	-0.219	(0.057)	-0.136	-0.743	(0.046)		0.011	(0.046)		-0.137	(0.046)	0.067	-0.047	(0.047)		-0.097	(0.047)	0.067
Pol. Disc. Disagreement	-0.032	(0.050)		0.107	(0.041)	-0.005	0.185	(0.041)	-0.133	0.034	(0.040)	-0.023	0.075	(0.042)	-0.071	0.161	(0.042)	-0.149
Constant	0.82	(0.523)																
cutpoint 1				-1.559			0.143			-1.652			-0.252			0.676		
cutpoint 2				-0.269			1.321			-0.577			0.548			1.438		
cutpoint 3				0.631			2.057			0.407			1.525			2.324		
cutpoint 4				2.736			3.921			2.115			2.788			3.570		

Notes

Data are weighted. Coef = logit or ordered logit coefficient. SE = standard error associated with coefficient. Margin = marginal effect/change in predicted probability of compromise vs. not compromise based on the shift from the minimum value of the variable to the maximum value of the variable. Compromise: 0 = Prefer politician willing to stand firm on principle; 1 = Compromise to get things done. *Budget deficit, Healthcare, Immigration, Abortion, Social policy:* 1 = Very unlikely to compromise; 2 = Somewhat unlikely to compromise; 3 = Neither unlikely nor likely to compromise; 4 = Somewhat likely to compromise; 5 = Very likely to compromise. Party identification: 1 = Strong Dem; 2 = Weak Dem; 3 = Lean Dem; 4 = Independent; 5 = Lean Rep; 6 = Weak Rep; 7 = Strong Rep. Ideology: 1 = Conservative; 2 = Moderate/not sure; 3 = Liberal. follows politics closely: 1 = Very closely; 2 = Somewhat closely; 3 = Not very closely; 4 = Not at all. Religiosity: 1 = Regular; 2 = Occasional; 3 = Almost never attend religious services. Married: 0 = Unmarried (single, separated, divorced, unmarried couple); 1 = Married (married or widowed). Gender: 1 = Male; 2 = Female. Racial/ethnic group: 1 = White; 2 = Asian; 3 = Hispanic; 4 = Black.

compromise-oriented politicians. This non-significance and negative sign may result from the counter-intuitive finding above that even though Democrats want compromise more than Republicans, they are less likely to do so after exposure to disagreement.

Not surprisingly when studying the marginal effect of each statistically significant variable relative to the other variables, party identification and ideology do much of the heavy lifting in explaining the likelihood of wanting politicians to compromise as well as being willing to compromise with people with whom one disagrees on particular issues. Still, as the statistical significance and marginal effects demonstrate, worldview and disagreement often also affect the likelihood of compromising on particular issues as demonstrated in the ordered logit models. The negative coefficients and positive signs of probability can be confusing, though they reflect the complicated nature of modeling so many powerful variables together and having some of the categories lack many cases of having anyone wanting to compromise on specific issues. Consequently, the signs of the likelihood of willingness to compromise are less important than their relative size. Nevertheless, from our cross-tabulations above and these models, an authoritarian worldview significantly reduces the likelihood of compromise with opponents on the budget deficit, healthcare, and immigration. This in turn means that non-authoritarians are significantly more likely to compromise than authoritarians on these issues.

Disagreement in political discussion is statistically influential on one's willingness to compromise on every issue except for immigration. Interpreting this finding's complexity is important given the evidence from the cross-tabulations above. At first blush, the more one encounters disagreement in political discussion, the more likely it is that one will compromise not only on the deficit and healthcare, but even on such contentious issues as abortion and social policy such as gay marriage. As the descriptive findings suggest, however, it is more accurate to say that engaging different-minded conversation partners makes respondents somewhat less intransigent – which fits with established literature indicating disagreement leads to ambivalence rather than completely flipped positions. Nevertheless, the importance of this finding is substantial as it means that uncompromising views on contentious issues can be offset somewhat if citizens are willing to discuss contested political issues. This finding is particularly noteworthy given the power of the explanatory and control variables in these models.

Because the bivariate analyses showed such distinct partisan reactions to disagreement exposure, the patterns in these models may cancel out some real effects. To check, we ran the same set of models separately for Democrats and Republicans. Here the contextual effects of worldview and particularly of disagreement in political discussion become much clearer. Table 2.9 demonstrates that disagreement exposure reduces Democrats' preferences for politicians who compromise. Political discussion disagreement, however, has little effect on their likelihood of compromising on specific issues. Interestingly, the reverse pattern occurs for Republicans, as disagreement exposure does not significantly affect

Table 2.9 Whether politicians should stand firm or compromise and how likely it is for a respondent to compromise with someone they disagree with on various issues among Democrats and Republicans

	Compromise Coef	SE	margin	Budget deficit Coef	SE	margin	Healthcare Coef	SE	margin	Immigration Coef	SE	margin	Abortion Coef	SE	margin	Social policy Coef	SE	margin
Democrats																		
Follow Politics Closely	-0.005	(0.173)		-0.247	(0.132)	0.064	-0.134	(0.129)		-0.134	(0.127)		-0.159	(0.132)		-0.245	(0.129)	-0.841
Ideology	0.169	(0.162)		0.241	(0.127)	-0.036	-0.169	(0.122)		-0.040	(0.119)		-0.224	(0.125)		-0.256	(0.120)	0.113
Religiosity	-0.115	(0.128)		0.028	(0.095)		-0.003	(0.092)		0.073	(0.092)		-0.222	(0.094)	0.102	0.043	(0.093)	
Married	0.234	(0.208)		0.099	(0.155)		-0.071	(0.151)		0.270	(0.151)	-0.030	-0.028	(0.154)	0.103	0.063	(0.152)	
Gender	-0.319	(0.208)		-0.280	(0.154)	0.015	0.105	(0.148)		0.014	(0.150)		-0.262	(0.152)		-0.112	(0.150)	
Race	0.059	(0.089)		0.080	(0.067)		0.181	(0.068)	-0.069	0.149	(0.067)	0.046	0.199	(0.067)	0.057	0.193	(0.069)	
Worldview/Authoritarian	-0.322	(0.091)	-0.167	-0.060	(0.066)		-0.035	(0.067)		-0.112	(0.067)	0.037	0.125	(0.066)	-0.136	0.064	(0.066)	-0.127
Pol. Disc. Disagreement	-0.257	(0.083)	-0.172	-0.057	(0.061)		0.063	(0.059)		-0.094	(0.059)		0.037	(0.061)	-0.087	0.030	(0.060)	
Constant	2.950	(0.795)																
cutpoint 1				-2.814			-1.646			-2.204			-1.236			-0.971		
cutpoint 2				-1.485			-0.306			-1.012			-0.422			-0.119		
cutpoint 3				-0.518			0.314			0.073			0.483			0.772		
cutpoint 4				1.679			2.106			1.774			1.624			1.903		
Republicans																		
Follow Politics Closely	0.110	(0.179)		0.635	(0.151)	-0.234	0.300	(0.153)	-0.169	0.101	(0.147)		0.229	(0.161)		0.078	(0.163)	
Ideology	0.913	(0.181)	0.403	0.276	(0.149)	-0.091	0.747	(0.152)	-0.270	0.473	(0.153)	-0.174	0.310	(0.154)	-0.138	0.526	(0.158)	-0.224
Religiosity	0.133	(0.131)		-0.092	(0.113)		0.027	(0.110)		-0.432	(0.115)	0.103	0.457	(0.117)	-0.208	0.513	(0.118)	-0.224
Married	-0.119	(0.209)		0.122	(0.181)		-0.058	(0.184)		0.056	(0.181)		-0.151	(0.191)		0.081	(0.194)	
Gender	0.171	(0.200)		0.143	(0.168)		0.058	(0.172)		0.251	(0.169)		-0.550	(0.184)	0.120	-0.207	(0.182)	
Race	-0.150	(0.145)		-2.220	(0.131)	0.129	0.028	(0.123)	0.129	-0.429	(0.135)	0.285	-0.127	(0.145)	0.083	-0.009	(0.137)	
Worldview/Authoritarian	-0.241	(0.085)	-0.165	-0.104	(0.072)		0.057	(0.073)		-0.221	(0.072)		-0.322	(0.077)		-0.330	(0.077)	0.216
Pol. Disc. Disagreement	0.053	(0.076)		0.344	(0.066)	-0.236	0.350	(0.066)	-0.290	0.220	(0.065)	-0.176	0.106	(0.068)	0.219	0.281	(0.069)	-0.247
Constant	-1.250	(0.618)																
cutpoint 1				0.644			2.050			-0.809			-0.055			1.369		
cutpoint 2				1.980			3.323			0.296			0.886			2.128		
cutpoint 3				2.838			4.127			1.179			1.959			3.078		
cutpoint 4				5.015			6.308			3.112			3.452			4.620		

broader preferences for compromise, but does shift their specific issue positions in the direction of compromise.

Again, the signs of these marginal effects are less important than their relative size given the fact that we know from the cross-tabulations that there are few cases among Republicans where people are somewhat or very likely to want to compromise. Still, the relative influence of political discussion disagreement is statistically significant and affects Republicans in a relatively large way on every issue but abortion – the change in probability sometimes even rivals ideology in its influence on the likelihood of compromise. Again, for the sake of accuracy, the results of the cross-tabulations need to be brought into these more abstract models to correctly describe the results. When Republicans engage with different-minded conversation partners, *they become less likely to completely reject compromise on these specific political issues.*

The real effects of political disagreement were masked by pooling partisan respondents together, as the cultural and contextual effects of worldview and disagreement in political discussion affect Republicans' preferences for compromise – or being uncompromising – far more than Democrats. Republicans' frequent authoritarian worldview makes them more apt to reject compromise but, unlike Democrats, exposure to political disagreement softens their uncompromising positions on a wide array of current political issues. Contextualizing compromise is important.

Discussion

Our research suggests that even though embracing political compromise appears to be a widely shared cultural norm according to citizens in their own words, many do not want their elected officials to compromise, and they are not very willing to compromise on specific issues themselves. Further, a substantial minority, who often use negative/hostile tones to describe political compromise, either reject it entirely or view it as a negotiating tactic. Citizens value the ability to achieve "win-win" solutions through compromise, yet few are willing to give ground for shared pain. On specific issues, compromise may seem like a zero-sum game, especially as issues move from economic to cultural issues.

This pattern holds especially for strong party identifiers and people with an authoritarian worldview, even among Democrats who are much more inclined than Republicans to favor cooperation. This partisan pattern on compromise versus standing firm does not emerge only in our time-bound research, but across three decades of Pew Research Center data as noted above, which suggests that although attitudes toward compromise might shift according to election outcomes, Republican preferences for politicians to stand firm is not a short-term 2012 electoral effect. Exposure to political disagreement improves citizens' willingness to compromise. Yet this pattern only occurred for Republicans, and they simply became *less likely to reject compromise completely.* Democrats, who start with higher initial preferences for political compromise, become less enamored by negotiated outcomes as disagreement exposure increases.

Our findings do not suggest that compromise needs to be viewed as a political end in itself. American political history is littered with horrendous political compromises that robbed people of rights and look terrible in our collective rearview mirror. Many of our political heroes achieved this status because they did not "sell out." Nor are eras of aggressive, uncompromising politics inherently bad. Often these were realigning moments that addressed unresolved issues and brought forth more stable and peaceful political epochs.

Nevertheless, many political observers see current gridlock as a consequence of insufficient efforts to compromise. Our findings show the public itself evaluates political compromise positively in their own words, but this does not easily translate directly into real-world preferences. These results will upset those frustrated at the lack of compromise in the American system. Other than the waning salience of social issues over time, we see few changes on the horizon that will encourage politicians or, notably, much of the electorate to embrace political compromise. This trend could be countered by purposefully creating circumstances that facilitate contested political conversations. The problem, of course, is whether voters will overcome natural disincentives to seek out such interactions – and whether marginal improvements in Republicans' (but not Democrats') attitudes toward compromise would be enough to make a difference in the stark patterns uncovered here.

Notes

1 SurveyUSA Methodology: 1,742 adults from the 50 United States and the District of Columbia were interviewed by SurveyUSA Tuesday November 13, 2012 through Monday November 19, 2012. Of the adults, 1,534 self-reported that they were registered to vote and were asked the questions reported here. Sixty-five percent of likely voters, reachable on a home telephone, were interviewed using recorded-voice telephone calls to landline phones. Sample was provided by Survey Sampling International. The youngest-male method of respondent selection was used on calls to landlines. Thirty-five percent of likely voters, unreachable on a home telephone, were shown an HTML questionnaire on their smart-phone or other electronic device. Sample provided by United Sample. Responses were minimally weighted to US Census targets for gender, age, race, and region. Where necessary, answer choices were rotated to prevent order bias, recency, and latency effects. SurveyUSA assigns each question within the instrument a theoretical margin of sampling error, and while such error is useful in theory and is commonly cited in the presentation of research results, sampling error is only one of many types of error that may influence the outcome of an opinion research study.

2 Instructions were:

> I'm going to ask you a question now that will require you to speak up and talk to me in your own voice. When you are done answering the question, be sure to stay on the line, don't hang up, because we're just getting started and we have a few more questions that we still want to get your feedback on. At the beep, speak for as long as you'd like, then press the pound key, and we will come back on the line.

The question has to do with compromise.

3 Political discussion partners are not identified with the broader name-generator battery that asks about people who they talk with about "important matters." This is impossible in an automated survey so we used the approach of other scholars who directly ask about the frequency of political discussion and disagreement.

4 Huckfeldt, Johnson, and Sprague (2004), Huckfeldt, Mendez, and Osborn (2004) and Mutz (2002a and 2002b) listed in the bibliography use the same question battery. The difference here stems from this being an automated survey. Nonetheless, the battery follows discussion network question conventions.

5 The six substantive categories were identified through qualitative content analysis of a randomly selected subset of the open-ended comments. Two coders worked together in a reiterative process in order to identify mutually exclusive categories that captured the fully array of respondents' comments, while minimizing the number of responses falling into an "other" or "miscellaneous" category. When coding instructions were difficult to follow, the coders revisited the instructions and added additional clarification and categories. This reiterative process ensures that the categories reflect the full array of substantive commentary provided in respondents' own words and prevents researchers from forcing answers into preconceived categories. After identifying these six categories and developing clear coding instructions, coders were able to apply them to the remaining responses with high levels of agreement.

6 After coding 50 randomly selected responses independently, the two coders reached high levels of inter-coder reliability for the most frequent combinations of function and affect codes: a process to do the right thing with positive or neutral affect, and a process to achieve functionality with positive or neutral affect. The coders achieved 100 percent agreement for all of the responses identified as a process to do the right thing with positive or neutral affect. In addition, they achieved 98 percent agreement for all of the responses identified as a process to achieve functionality with positive or neutral affect. As a result, the coders divided coding of the remaining responses, but set aside all those that did not fit into one of these four categories. The responses coded as either a tactic or as miscellaneous were classified by discussing the responses together until mutual agreement was reached. A similar approach was used to code responses that identified a generic process but provided no underpinning explanation of that process's function (example: "it is negotiating"), as well as responses that provided affect, but no further definition of political compromise (example: "it is really important").

7 For the specific results for these findings as well as details of the descriptive findings about disagreement discussed above please contact Michael Wolf: wolfm@ipfw.edu.

Bibliography

Abramowitz, Alan. 2010. *The Disappearing Center*. New Haven, CT: Yale University Press.

Abramowitz, Alan and Steven Webster. 2015. "All Politics is National: The Rise of Negative Partisanship and the Nationalization of U.S. House and Senate Elections in the 21st Century." Paper presented at the Annual Meeting of the Midwest Political Science Association, Chicago, Illinois, April 16–19, 2015.

Ansolabehere, Stephen, Jonathan Rodden, and James Snyder. 2006. "Purple America." *Journal of Economic Perspectives* 20(2): 97–118.

Barabas, Jason. 2004. "How Deliberation Affects Policy Opinions." *American Political Science Review* 98: 687–701.

Barker, David and Christopher Carmen. 2012. *Representing Red and Blue: How Culture Wars Change the Way Citizens Speak and Politicians Listen*. New York: Oxford University Press.

Black, Earl and Merle Black. 2002. *The Rise of the Southern Republicans*. Cambridge, MA: Belknap Harvard.

Brewer, Mark and Jeffrey Stonecash. 2007. *Split: Class and Cultural Divides in American Politics*. Washington, DC: CQ Press.

Carmines, Edward and James Stimson. 1989. *Issue Evolution: Race and the Transformation of American Politics.* Princeton, NJ: Princeton University Press.

de Tocqueville, Alexis. 1969. *Democracy in America.* Ed. J.P. Mayer. Trans. George Lawrence. New York: HarperPerennial.

Fiorina, Morris and Samuel Abrams. 2009. *Disconnect: The Breakdown of Representation in American Politics.* Norman, OK: University of Oklahoma Press.

Fiorina, Morris, Samuel Abrams, and Jeremy Pope. 2005. *Culture War? The Myth of a Polarized America.* New York: Pearson Longman.

Guttmann, Amy and Dennis Thompson. 2012. *The Spirit of Compromise: Why Governing Demands it and Campaigning Undermines It.* Princeton, NJ: Princeton University Press.

Hetherington, Marc and Jonathan Weiler. 2009. *Authoritarianism and Polarization in American Politics.* New York: Cambridge University Press.

Hilygus, Sunshine and Todd Shields. 2010. "Racial and Moral Issues in the Evolution of the 'Sothern Strategy,'" in *Controversies in Voting Behavior,* 5th Edn., Richard Niemi, Herbert Weisberg, and David Kimball (eds.), Washington, DC: CQ Press.

Huckfeldt, Robert and Jeanette Morehouse Mendez. 2008. "Moths, Flames, and Political Engagement: Managing Disagreement within Communication Networks." *Journal of Politics* 70(1): 83–96.

Huckfeldt, Robert, Paul Johnson, and John Sprague. 2004. *Political Disagreement: The Survival of Diverse Opinions within Communication Networks.* New York: Cambridge University Press.

Huckfeldt, Robert, Jeannette Morehouse Mendez, and Tracy Osborn. 2004. "Disagreement, Ambivalence, and Engagement: The Political Consequences of Heterogenous Networks." *Political Psychology* 25(2): 65–95.

Levendusky, Matthew. 2009. *The Partisan Sort.* Chicago, IL: University of Chicago Press.

Mansbridge, Jayne and C. J. Martin. 2013. "Negotiating Agreement in Politics." American Political Science Association, Washington, DC.

Mutz, Diana. 2002a. "Cross-Cutting Social Networks: Testing Democratic Theory in Practice." *American Political Science Review* 96(1): 111–126.

Mutz, Diana. 2002b. "The Consequences of Cross-Cutting Networks for Political Participation." *American Journal of Political Science* 46(4): 838–855.

Mutz, Diana C. 2006. *Hearing the Other Side: Deliberative versus Participatory Democracy.* New York: Cambridge University Press.

Pew Research Center for the People & the Press. 2007. *Broad Support for Political Compromise in Washington.* Washington, DC: Pew Research Center for the People & the Press.

Pew Research Center. 2012. "American Values Survey Question Database." *American Values Survey.*

Pew Research Center. 2013, January 17. "Obama in Strong Position at Start of Second Term: Support for Compromise Rises, Except Among Republicans."

Pew Research Center. 2014, June 12. "Political Polarization in the American Public."

Reiter, Howard L. and Jeffrey M. Stonecash. 2011. *Counter Realignment: Political Change in the Northeastern United States.* New York: Cambridge University Press.

Wolf, Michael R., J. Cherie Strachan, and Daniel M. Shea. 2012. "Forget the Good of the Game: Political Incivility and Lack of Compromise as a Second Layer of Party Polarization." *American Behavioral Scientist* 56(12): 1677–1695.

Zaller, John. 1992. *The Nature and Origins of Mass Opinion.* Cambridge: Cambridge University Press.

3 Can unequal distributions of wealth influence vote choice?

A comparative study of Germany, Sweden and the United States

*Lindsay Flynn and Piotr R. Paradowski**

It is widely accepted that income influences voting behavior. Does wealth? Is the effect similar across countries? Studies of wealth and voting behavior have not existed until recently, in part because of the absence of data on wealth holdings. The findings in this chapter indicate that wealth is related to voting behavior in some countries but not in others. The chapter models the effects of wealth on one form of voting behavior, vote choice, in three archetypal countries – the United States, Germany, and Sweden, each representing a distinct political and social welfare regime. If vote choice is predicated on wealth holdings above and beyond the effect of income, the growth in wealth inequality experienced since the 1970s serves to further polarize electoral outcomes. As other chapters in this volume point out, this polarization impedes decision making and implementation at both governmental and policy levels.

Citizenship grants a key political resource – the right to vote – regardless of economic resources. Yet this political resource is inseparable from economic resources. Those with similar economic resources tend to vote in similar ways (Brooks and Brady, 1999; Rehm, 2011). To date, economic resources have been operationalized almost exclusively through income as a measure, and links tested with data mostly from the United States. Yet in the United States and in Europe too, wealth is more unequally distributed than income (Davies and Shorrocks, 2000; Piketty and Saez, 2014). This chapter argues that, conceptually, a voter's position in the wealth distribution should affect voting behavior independently from the effect of income. Using probit regressions, it shows that wealth correlates with vote choice in a base model of the United States, Germany, and Sweden. But it only has an effect above and beyond the effect of income in the United States. In Germany, income and employment patterns correlate most strongly. In Sweden, economic resources do not correlate with voting behavior when the model includes other potential determinants. Since the effect of wealth is not consistent across the case countries, the chapter provides an additional analysis assessing the salience of economic issues during three election cycles. Citizens in Sweden are more likely to identify the importance of social policies as compared to Germany and especially the United States, where economic issues dominate.

The country-specific findings in this chapter lead to different conclusions with respect to political polarization. Growing levels of inequality may serve to

*Authors contributed equally to this work.

further polarize politics in cases where economic resources correlate with vote choice. This is especially true when wealth influences vote choice beyond the effect of income. Those with more resources can shape policy though monetary contributions to candidates directly and to organizations that hold lobbying power. While each eligible voter only has one vote, the consolidated block of votes at the upper end of the distribution hold more power. Put simply, a stronger relationship between economic resources and vote choice enables elected officials to adopt narrower political and policy positions. Those at the top of the distribution will benefit most from this polarization because of their economic position. Thus, in countries like the United States, where both wealth and income influence vote choice, growing inequality is poised to have the greatest effect on polarization, whereas in countries like Sweden, where neither independently influence voice choice, growing inequality is poised to have a smaller effect. However, it is unclear whether a tipping point exists, where inequality reaches a point at which it is more or less likely to lead to greater polarization.

This chapter proceeds as follows. First, it outlines the link between wealth, vote choice, and political polarization. Next, it describes wealth distribution in each of the three countries and justifies why some key conceptual and empirical differences between income and wealth warrant the analysis of these two economic resources separately. It then presents an empirical analysis that assesses the role of wealth as a determinant of vote choice in three case countries chosen to represent a range of political and social histories. It concludes with a discussion of these empirical findings in relation to political polarization. Because no studies to date link wealth, vote choice, and political polarization, most of the territory covered is new. As such, the claims made in this chapter are intended to prompt further conceptual discussion and empirical analysis.

Wealth, vote choice, and political polarization

The term wealth is often used in a colloquial sense, but it is used here to reference a very specific concept: net worth. Net worth is comprised of the assets held by an individual, household, or firm, less the debts held by that entity. Wealth, like income, is a measure of economic well-being. Wealth can, for instance, generate income, and income saved at time t becomes wealth at time $t+1$. Wealth can also serve as a tool to smooth consumption during times of lower income, such as unemployment, continuing education, or retirement. But, unlike income, wealth is measured by considering both sides of a household balance sheet. Various types of debt (e.g., mortgages, vehicle loans, educational loans) are subtracted from assets (e.g., one's residence, savings accounts, stocks and bonds).

Studies on the role of wealth on voting behavior are largely nonexistent. To date, scholars have developed and tested the link between economic resources and voting with income rather than wealth. This is likely due to a lack of data on wealth holdings rather than an argument against the use of wealth as a measure. In this section, studies on income and voting behavior are used to develop the conceptual scaffolding linking wealth to voting behavior. It identifies three related mechanisms – partisanship, class, and policy preferences – that could link wealth to voting behavior, specifically to vote choice. In a second step, it discusses what this dynamic means for political polarization.

Partisanship has been identified as one of the strongest predictors of vote choice (Campbell, 1980). If only one fact is known about a person – the party with which they identify – that person's vote can be guessed correctly nine times out of ten (Flanigan et al., 2014). Income differences reveal clear trends in partisan voting in the United States. Those with higher incomes are more likely to vote for the Republican Party and those with lower incomes the Democratic Party (Brooks and Brady, 1999; Gelman et al., 2010). The effect of income is weaker, however, in Europe (Huber and Stanig, 2007). Huber and Stanig attribute this to the strong welfare state in Europe that makes it more difficult for parties on the left and right to polarize on economic issues to the extent that the two parties in the United States can. As an economic resource, wealth may shape voting behavior through its influence on partisanship, just as income has been found to. In this case, those with larger stores of wealth should be more likely to support parties on the right. Additionally, the effect may be more pronounced in the United States.

A related set of studies look beyond income to consider the existence of class-based voting more generally, the presence of which has been both confirmed (Lipset, 1959; Inglehart, 1971; Manza and Brooks, 1999; Evans, 2000) and questioned (Clark and Lipset, 2001; Franklin et al., 2009). In these studies, class is measured in different ways, ranging from a dichotomous conception of blue-collar and white-collar workers, to a division across income categories, to divisions across educational and occupational categories. Most research using more refined measures of class has found it to shape voting behavior. Wealth has not yet been included in such analyses. Yet the existence of different types of wealth, especially one of its most tangible measures – property – is arguably an important component of class-based voting. After all, class conflicts throughout history have been rooted in a struggle between the propertied classes and the unpropertied.

Policy preferences may serve as the key mechanism that links class-based and partisan voting behavior, on the one hand, to wealth levels, on the other. In particular, wealth may mediate voters' views of governmental responsibility and regulation in redistributing resources. Previous research links partisan voting behavior to views on federal taxation in the United States (Kiewiet, 1984; Steinmo, 1989; Pierson, 1994). Specific regulations exist for various types of assets – housing consumption is taxed differently than other types of consumption, and capital gains from real estate are taxed differently than capital gains from mutual funds. Those with wealth and without may have different policy preferences, as might those with varying types of assets. This dynamic should hold in Europe as well. One recent study links housing wealth to social policy preferences in the United States, the United Kingdom, and a broader group of 29 industrialized countries (Ansell, 2014). Those with increasing wealth through the appreciation of their home lower their support for spending on social security (in the United States), full employment (in the United Kingdom), and reducing income differences (the broader group of 29 countries). Ultimately, policy preferences culminate in one main form of political activity – the vote.

What do high levels of economic inequality mean for politics and, in particular, political polarization? Polarization refers to the siloing of parties or people into distinct camps, with little ideological overlap, and less willingness to compromise. The vast majority of research on polarization is focused on the United States and takes two forms: elite polarization and mass polarization. Much of the literature is focused on ideology and, as with the literature on economic voting, those studies that do focus on economic polarization highlight the impact of income rather than wealth. Evidence of party polarization began in the 1960s and 1970s as Southern Democrats aligned with the Republican Party (Black and Black, 2009). By the 2000 and 2004 elections, the term "polarization" began to appear prominently in political commentary, both to reflect a divergence between party candidates and to describe a supposed "culture war" between citizens. There is consistent evidence for party polarization (Layman et al., 2006), but mixed evidence that voters have increasingly divided along ideological lines (Fiorina et al., 2005; Fiorina and Abrams, 2008; Abramowitz, 2012).

An exaggeration of an ideological culture war among citizens, however, does not preclude economic inequality among citizens leading to a polarization of elites. Indeed, findings indicate that income inequality of citizens correlates strongly with elite polarization of elected officials. For instance, elite polarization (measured by voting behavior of Democrats and Republicans in the U.S. House of Representatives) and the share of income held by the ultra-rich (i.e., the top 1 percent) both declined through the 1930s, stabilized mid-century, and increased substantially from the late 1970s to the present (McCarty et al., 2006). While correlation does not mean causation, the long historic relationship between income inequality and elite polarization is noteworthy.

Could increases in wealth inequality also be driving this relationship? Greater wealth inequality is expected to exacerbate political polarization in two ways. First, larger disparities among the haves and the have-nots will lead to the polarization of voters. A polarized electorate is more likely to breed polarized party politics, and one may even reinforce the other. Second, more extreme concentrations of wealth will lead to pandering. At the top, those commanding more resources can more effectively lobby for their interests. At the bottom, proponents of social justice and equity will be armed with more extreme visualizations of inequality. At both extremes, this will prompt elected officials to toe the party line, and take more extreme positions to reflect narrow constituencies. The next section outlines contemporary wealth distributions. It does so in relation to income distributions since income has been studied disproportionately in the literature. The section advances the argument that studies must be supplemented with measures of wealth in addition to income.

Economic resources: wealth versus income

Should wealth be included in analyses of voting behavior, or can income serve
as the sole indicator of economic well-being? This section argues that, while
related, wealth and income should not serve as substitutes for two reasons. First,
the relationship between wealth and income varies depending on which part of
the distribution is considered. Second, the dispersion of wealth and income
varies substantially. Trends in the relationship between wealth and income exist
in the middle of the distribution, the tails of the distribution, and the extreme
portions of each tail. Generally, the accumulation of one facilitates accumulation
of the other. But the tails of the distribution exhibit variation. For instance, fewer
than half of households fall in the top (or bottom) quintile of both income and
wealth distributions (Jäntti et al., 2012). In other words, the richest households
are not always the wealthiest, and those who are income-poor are not always
wealth-poor. However, at the very top and bottom of the distribution income and
wealth remain tightly linked (Kennickell, 2009). Put simply, for the share of
households that have both or neither, inequalities are felt more intensely than
might be expected if one considered only income, or only wealth. For the share
of households that have more of one relative to the other, models and estimates
will include unaccounted for noise, unless both wealth and income are included.

Wealth is distributed more unequally than income – upwards of twice as unequally in some cases – primarily because financial assets are more unequally distributed (Jäntti et al., 2012; Murtin and d'Ercole, 2015). For many people, most
of the wealth they hold is contained within their home. Because most home
owners also hold a mortgage, their asset is offset by a liability. For those with
housing wealth, then, the amount of equity in the home matters. For those with
other forms of wealth, debts are offset by a number of assets in the financial
sector, such as stocks and bonds, leading to, in relative and absolute terms,
greater levels of wealth. Figure 3.1 highlights the difference in income and
wealth levels across a group of 18 OECD countries. In a scenario of household
equality, the bottom 20 percent of households would hold 20 percent of the share
of income (or wealth). In actuality, the bottom 20 percent holds less than 10
percent of income and has negative net wealth. Conversely, the top 20 percent
enjoys a far larger share relative to size, commanding nearly 40 percent of
income and almost 70 percent of wealth. That leaves the middle 60 percent of
households with about half of the income and a third of the wealth. Wealth is
distributed particularly unequally in four countries – Austria, Germany, the
Netherlands, and the United States – where 60 percent or more of household
wealth is held by the top 10 percent (OECD, 2015).

Furthermore, the concentration of income and wealth in the hands of the few
has increased over time: since 1970, the share of income held by the top 10
percent has increased 17 percent in Europe and 43 percent in the United States.
The share of wealth has increased 6 percent and 11 percent, respectively (author's
calculations, from Piketty, 2014). Aggregate data from the OECD and Piketty
(2014) indicate that wealth disparities exist in all types of countries – liberal

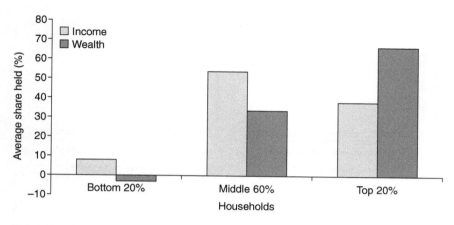

Figure 3.1 Share of income and wealth held by households, cross-country average.
Source: OECD, 2015.

Notes
Cross-country average for 18 OECD countries (2010 or latest available year): Australia, Austria, Belgium, Canada, Germany, Spain, Finland, France, Great Britain, Greece, Italy, South Korea, Luxembourg, the Netherlands, Norway, Portugal, the Slovak Republic, and the United States.

countries such as the United States, corporatist countries such as Germany, and even quasi-social democratic countries such as the Netherlands. What do the data show for the three case countries considered in this chapter? Figure 3.2 contrasts wealth and income distributions in the United States, Germany, and Sweden.

In Figure 3.2, countries are ordered by increasing differences between wealth and income – in the United States the distributions are most similar, and in Sweden the least. Both wealth and income distributions are very narrow in the United States, with a long right tail. This corresponds to a society in which the rich and the ultra-rich hold substantially more wealth and income than the middle class. One way to measure the effect of the tail on the distribution is to compare the mean to the median, since the mean is more sensitive to extreme values. Larger ratios indicate greater dispersion. In the United States, average wealth is 4.5 times that of median wealth and average income is 1.4 times that of median income. In other words, those with high wealth distort the distribution much more than those with high incomes. The case is similar but less pronounced in Germany. Wealth inequalities are high (a wealth mean to median ratio of 3.5) and income is distributed more equally (a ratio of 1.2).

In Sweden, income is more equally distributed than in the United States or Germany. The ratio of the mean to the median is only 1.1, meaning that the income of the rich does not substantially pull up the average. Sweden is known for a welfare system that pulls in the tails of the income distribution, imposing greater equality through taxes and transfers. This does not extend to wealth. The right tail of the distribution is not as long as in the United States or Germany

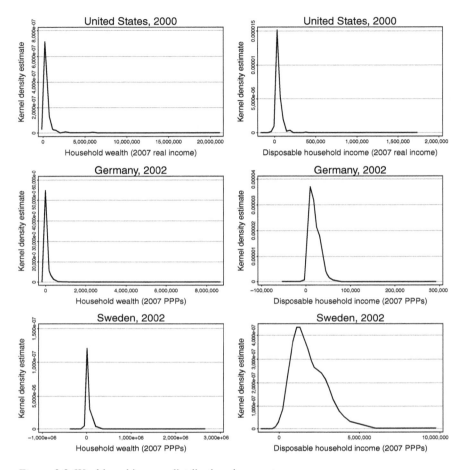

Figure 3.2 Wealth and income distributions by country.

Source: Luxembourg Wealth Study Database (LIS Cross-National Data Center, www.lisdatacenter.org).

(with a mean to median ratio of 2.7), but the differences between wealth and income are much more pronounced in Sweden than in the other two countries.

Another way to compare country-level wealth profiles is through the plotting of a Lorenz Curve. Figure 3.3 contrasts the Lorenz curves of Sweden and the United States. The Lorenz Curve shows how wealth is cumulatively held across a society. The line at 45° is the line of perfect equality. The poorest 20 percent hold 20 percent of wealth, the poorest 40 percent hold 40 percent of wealth, etc. The curved line represents the actual cumulative wealth holdings in each country. Curves further from the 45° line represent societies where wealth is more unequally held. In both countries, most of the wealth is held by a minority

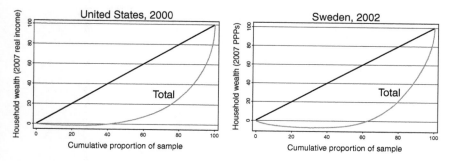

Figure 3.3 Lorenz curves in the United States and Sweden.
Source: Luxembourg Wealth Study.

of households. In the United States, the poorest 22 percent of households have more liabilities than assets. In Sweden, the bottom 30 percent do. In fact, it takes the wealth of the next 30 percent of households to average out to zero, which is why the portion of the Lorenz Curve representing the poorest 60 percent of households is comparatively more concave in Sweden. On the one hand, this can be interpreted as a somewhat equal distribution of wealth among the majority of Swedish households. But, put another way, 92 percent of the wealth held by those with positive net worth is captured by 40 percent of households. The latter describes a very unequal distribution, especially for a society known for economic equality. The wealth at the very top, however, remains more unequally distributed in the United States. Those in the top 5 percent have 15 times the wealth of the median household, calculated as a share of median wealth. In Sweden, the figure is 9 percent – not as unequal, but not evenly distributed either.

The figures above paint a picture of the overall wealth distributions in a country, but say nothing about the composition of wealth in each country. Table 3.1 provides an overview of wealth portfolios by country. It lists the median value of assets and debts in 2007 real dollars for those households that hold each asset or debt. The numbers reflect the nominal medians of wealth components multiplied by a measure of the relative prices, namely Purchasing Power Parity (PPP) and adjusted for the level of Consumer Price Index (CPI) and exchange rates. In particular, the values for 1995, 2001, and 2005 were brought to 2007 real dollars by multiplying the wealth figures by the appropriate CPI. CPI, PPP, and exchange rates were used to convert wealth components in Sweden and Germany to 2007 real dollars. The percentage of households holding each asset or debt is listed in parentheses.

Wealth inequality exists in all three countries. The United States stands out as the most unequal when considering income and wealth jointly. Sweden stands out as having a very unequal wealth distribution compared to income. The patterns in Germany align more closely with the United States, though they are less extreme.

Table 3.1 Wealth portfolios by country; median holdings in real 2007 dollars

	United States				Germany	Sweden
	1995	2001	2004	2007	2001	2001
Financial assets						
Deposit accounts	3,515 (91%)	5,731 (93%)	4,975 (92%)	5,100 (93%)	20,933 (78%)	76,402 (64%)
Risky assets	8,179 (51%)	17,543 (52%)	13,179 (49%)	13,000 (48%)	–	65,557 (71%)
Non-financial assets						
Principle residence	120,317 (73%)	143,860 (71%)	175,725 (73%)	200,000 (75%)	205,098 (48%)	890,171 (59%)
Investment real estate	67,594 (33%)	93,586 (29%)	104,336 (32%)	130,000 (34%)	133,488 (16%)	410,922 (17%)
Total debt						
Housing debt	70,974 (50%)	55,403 (50%)	81,163 (53%)	99,604 (53%)	43,746 (26%)	261,612 (73%)
Non-housing debt	7,706 (60%)	11,105 (66%)	12,537 (69%)	16,837 (69%)	6,041 (15%)	–
Net worth mean	152,428	248,192	275,093	295,917	182,009	699,255
median	35,149	50,421	52,140	60,300	72,742	250,732

Source: Luxembourg Wealth Study.

Notes
Median holdings calculated only for those with holdings in that category. Values in parentheses indicate the percentage of households included (i.e., the percentage holding that asset or debt).

Methods and case selection

Polling data on voting behavior has long existed. Wealth data is harder to collect. Recent efforts by the LIS Cross-National Data Center provide researchers with much-needed access to wealth data. Despite strong theoretical reasons to expect links between voting and wealth, no surveys collect data on both. Election data are drawn from the American National Election Studies (ANES) for the United States and the Comparative Study of Electoral Systems (CSES) for Sweden and Germany. Wealth data are drawn from the Luxembourg Wealth Study (LWS), one of the few databases available with comparable wealth data for multiple years and multiple countries. LWS was the first comparative wealth database established for public use.

Statistical matching procedures were employed to combine electoral and wealth data into one database. The data were statistically matched on labor force status, income quintile, home ownership, and education level with age groups serving as a donation class. These matching variables were standardized to a common framework and the nearest neighbor distance hot deck technique was conducted via the StatMatch package in R. The wealth surveys have larger sample sizes than the election surveys, and statistical matches work more reliably when datasets are similarly sized (D'Orazio, 2013: 9). Therefore, a random sample (without replacements) was selected from each of the LWS datasets to match with the observations in the electoral databases. Such data fusion allows for the joint analysis of wealth and voting, which is in itself a significant contribution to our understanding of voting behavior, but it does not come without caveats. The conclusions regarding the very rich voters are likely to be biased due to the fact that wealth surveys usually oversample the wealthy while electoral surveys do not. This also holds even when survey sample weights are used in statistical matching.

The United States was chosen as the primary case study for both theoretical and empirical reasons. Much of the literature on vote choice revolves around the United States. It is also known as a liberal country where citizens' economic well-being is most directly tied to their behavior in the market. Since this chapter argues for the integration of an additional concept into the voting behavior models, it is logical to situate the analysis in the United States. The primary test case is compared to two additional countries, which are chosen to represent different political and social regimes. Germany represents a European case with similarly high levels of wealth inequality, a history of a strong center-right parties, and a corporatist welfare state where citizens' economic well-being is tied to occupation. Sweden represents a European case of lower income inequality but high wealth inequality, a strong history of left party domination, and a social democratic welfare regime where citizens' well-being is less reliant on their behavior in the market. In the United States, data from the 1996, 2000, 2004, and 2008 presidential election cycles are used, and pooled together for the analysis. Data from the 2002 elections are used in Sweden and Germany. For each country, wealth data corresponds to the year before the election year, except in two cases where wealth data corresponds to the election year (the U.S. in 2004) or the year after the election (the U.S. in 2001).

In the United States, the presidential terms since Bill Clinton are seen as the most politically polarizing years in over a half-century. From Dwight Eisenhower's term in the 1950s through George H. W. Bush's term in the 1990s, gaps in Gallup-reported presidential approval ratings between Democrats and Republicans fluctuated from a low of 30 points during the Johnson administration in the 1960s to a high of 52 points under Reagan in the 1980s. Beginning with Bill Clinton's term, gaps between party supporters widened from 56 points (Clinton) to 61 points (George W. Bush) to 70 points under Barack Obama (Jones, 2015). Disparities in wealth accumulation were on an upward march by this time. What about partisan affiliation by wealth? As Figure 3.4 indicates, the self-identified partisans who belong to the wealth group that falls into the first three quintiles (the bottom 60 percent) are quite polarized in the 1996 and 2008 elections, but not so much in the 2000 and 2004 elections. The polarization between partisans who belong to the top 40 percent of the wealth group seems to be different. What is striking is that only about 45 percent of partisans in the top 20 percent of the wealth distribution affiliate with the Republican party in 2008. There are even fewer wealthy people who identify themselves with the Republican Party at the fourth quintile. The data presents no doubt that in the 2008 elections the Democratic Party attachment was on the rise among the rich. Yet, for the reasons mentioned above, the conclusions about those with a very high wealth share should be treated with caution.

In Germany, the 2002 election between incumbent Gerhard Schröder of the leftist Social Democrats (SPD) and Edmund Stoiber of the center-right Christian Democrats (CDU) was one of the closest in history. Stoiber conceded the election, but only after mistakenly declaring victory on the night of the election. Each party received 38.5 percent of the vote. Class as measured by occupation declined in importance as a cleavage among voters (Conradt et al., 2004), however the decade before the election saw an increase in wealth inequality after two decades of decreasing inequality (Hauser and Stein, 2003).

The story in Sweden is one of left-party domination for over a half-century. The Prime Minister of Sweden hailed from the Social Democratic Party (SAP) for 15 of 18 terms, almost continuously between the post-war period and 2002. In the 2002 election, parties on the right received only 29 percent of the vote, while parties on the left secured 53 percent. The politics of Sweden are overwhelmingly left leaning compared to Germany and the United States. Sweden is known for its generous and universal welfare state, and somewhat lower levels of income inequality. Wealth inequalities, however, are high. The case of Sweden serves as a particularly challenging test of the primary independent variables.

The dependent variable in the models is a dichotomous variable measuring the party for which the respondent voted. In the United States, the conservative party (Republicans) is coded 0, and the liberal party (Democrats) is coded 1. In Germany and Sweden, votes for parties on the left are coded 1 while parties in the center and on the right are coded 0. Parties were coded left, center, or right

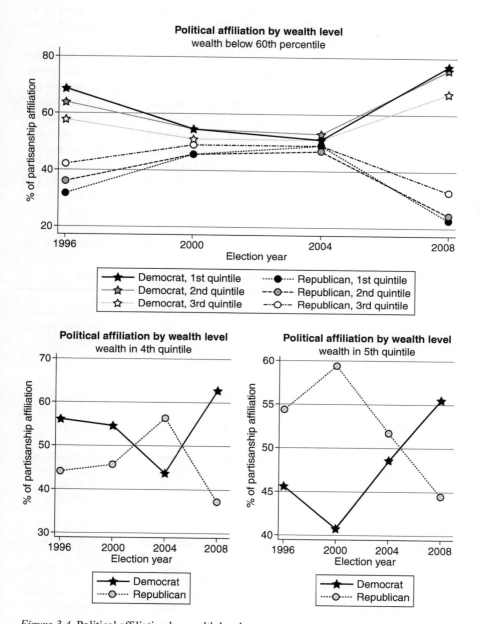

Figure 3.4 Political affiliation by wealth level.

Sources: Luxembourg Wealth Study and American National Election Studies data.

based on the Comparative Political Data Set developed by Armingeon et al. (2014). Only voters who voted for one of the major parties are included in the model. Table 3.2 lists vote shares for each party.

The primary independent variable of interest is a measure of wealth that captures the net worth of the household in which the person lives – the household assets less the household debts. Net worth is measured in quintiles to emphasize that absolute net worth is less important than the wealth position of an individual in respect to the society in which they live. It includes most of a household's financial and non-financial assets, including deposit accounts, bonds, stocks, mutual funds, principal residence and investment real estate, and all of the primary debt, including home-secured debt and non-housing debt like vehicle loans, educational loans, and other loans from financial institutions. The measure used here excludes business equity, pension assets, and life insurance because these types of assets are not always present in the wealth data and we believe it is better to use the most comparable net worth across countries that we analyze.[1] In part to account for this omission, age and retirement status are

Table 3.2 Vote choice

	Left	*Right*	*Center*
United States 1996 (Bill Clinton)	Democrats (49.2%)*	Republicans (40.7%)	Reform Party (8.4%)
United States 2000 (George Bush)	Democrats (48.4%) Green Party (2.7%)	Republicans (47.9%)*	
United States 2004 (George Bush)	Democrats (48.3%)	Republicans (50.7%)*	
United States 2008 (Barack Obama)	Democrats (52.9%)*	Republicans (45.5%)	
Germany 2002 (Gerhard Schröder)	Social Democratic Party (38.5%)* Alliance 90/Greens (8.6%) Party of Democratic Socialism (4.0%)	Free Democratic Party (7.4%)	Christian Democratic Union (29.5%) Christian Social Union (9.0%)
Sweden 2002 (Göran Persson)	Social Democrats (39.9%)* Left Party (8.4%) Green Party (4.6%)	Liberal People's Party (13.4%) Moderate Party (15.3%)	Christian Democrats (9.1%) Centre Party (6.2%)

Sources: Federal Election Commission; Office of the Federal Register; The Federal Returning Officer (Der Bundeswahlleiter); Statistics Sweden.

Notes
* Winning Party.
Only parties receiving at least 2% of the vote are listed. Inaugurated Head of Government listed in parentheses in column 1. In the 2000 election in the United States, Al Gore (the Democratic candidate) won the popular vote but George W. Bush (the Republican candidate) won the Electoral College and thus won the election.

included in the model, which serve as partial proxies to the likelihood of holding pension assets. A number of covariates are included in the model to incorporate the findings of previous research on vote choice. These include income, partisanship, gender, and age, as well as employment status, retirement status, and whether the individual owns a business. Separate probit regression models are run for each country. In the United States, data from all election years are pooled together, and a series of year dummies are included in the model. Models are interpreted using predicted probabilities.

Findings

Table 3.3 lists two models for each country. In Model 1, only wealth is included as an independent variable, and it is significant in all three countries. In Model 2, additional covariates are included that can generally be categorized in three groups: political, demographic, and economic. The political variables identify partisan affiliation, and are included in the model as a series of dummy variables. The comparison group holds no party affiliation. Partisanship is significant in each country, as expected, but especially in the United States. Two demographic factors often identified in the literature, age and gender, are also included. Gender is not associated with vote choice in any country, but age is associated with vote choice in both the United States and Sweden. Economic variables capture the tangible resources available to people, wealth and income, as well as employment circumstances, such as employment and retirement status. In the United States and Germany, economic variables explain variation in vote choice. For the United States, economic resources play a dominant role, whereas in Germany, employment variables are key. In Sweden, on the other hand, neither set of economic variables is significant in the full model.

Partisanship

Self-identified partisanship is a strong determinant of vote choice in the United States, but less so in Germany and Sweden. In the United States, those who affiliate with a party overwhelmingly vote for their party's nominee. In the 2000 election, the model predicts self-identified Democrats vote for the Democratic candidate with a 91 percent probability, but self-identified Republicans with only a 6 percent probability. Contrast this to Germany and Sweden, where the patterns are less stark. Self-identified left-leaning voters are more likely to cast a ballot for a candidate on the left, but only with a 62 percent probability in Germany and a 66 percent probability in Sweden. Moreover, self-identified right-leaning voters are also somewhat likely to vote for a left party, with a 52 percent probability in Germany and a 40 percent probability in Sweden.

The multi-party system in Germany and Sweden complicates questions of partisan identification. Over 60 percent of voters in the United States maintain a party affiliation. Over 60 percent of voters in Germany, and half of voters in Sweden, do not. The two-party system of the United States, while offering fewer

Table 3.3 Determinants of vote choice for left party; probit regression

	United States		Germany		Sweden	
	Model 1	Model 2	Model 1	Model 2	Model 1	Model 2
Wealth	-0.103*** (0.01)	-0.072*** (0.02)	-0.048** (0.40)	0.019 (0.03)	-0.54* (0.03)	-0.013 (0.03)
Income		-0.055*** (0.02)		-0.086*** (0.03)		-0.025 (0.03)
Partisanship (base category independent): Left		1.384*** (0.06)		0.146* (0.08)		0.407*** (0.10)
Partisanship (base category independent): Center				-0.196** (0.09)		-0.120 (0.18)
Partisanship (base category independent): Right		-1.447*** (0.06)		-0.088 (0.20)		-0.257* (0.14)
Business owner		0.134* (0.08)		-0.007 (0.16)		0.019 (0.15)
Age		-0.202*** (0.07)		-0.022 (0.06)		-0.146** (0.07)
Gender (female=1)		0.056 (0.05)		0.046 (0.07)		0.012 (0.09)
Employment status (employed=1)		-0.059 (0.07)		-0.241*** (0.09)		-0.067 (0.19)
Retirement status (retired=1)		-0.002 (0.10)		-0.331** (0.13)		0.054 (0.23)
Year (base category 1996): 2000		-0.305*** (0.07)				
Year (base category 1996): 2004		-0.355*** (0.07)				
Year (base category 1996): 2008		0.035 (0.07)				
Intercept	0.507*** (0.04)	1.019*** (0.18)	0.397*** (0.74)	0.602** (0.20)	0.213** (0.10)	0.462* (0.26)
N	4,355	4,355	1,627	1,609	904	904

Sources: Luxembourg Wealth Study; American National Election Studies; Comparative Study of Electoral Systems.

Notes

* $p<0.1$;
** $p<0.05$;
*** $p<0.01$;
robust standard errors in parentheses.

choices, captures more party supporters than in Germany or Sweden. Especially in the United States, all other variables in the model should be considered in the context of a strong partisan divide.

Economic voting: wealth, income and employment

Many scholars have found that those who are better off – as measured by income – are more likely to vote for right-leaning candidates. Does wealth also influence voting behavior? As argued above, wealth provides a more complete picture of economic well-being as a current and future income stream that needs to be protected, but also as a form of well-being that is not explicitly linked to wage employment. As such, wealth may have an effect on vote choice over and above any income effect. Because the voting literature has been developed in the American political and social context, the United States is the most important test case of the three countries. It is, indeed, the case where both wealth and income relate to vote choice. But wealth inequalities are growing across Europe, so it is worth assessing the possibility of an increased salience of economic voting. Evidence is found in the affirmative for Germany, but not for Sweden.

In the United States, both wealth and income are predictors of the vote. Those with higher levels of each are less likely to vote for the Democratic candidate. Not only is wealth a determinant of vote choice independent from income, but the magnitude of the relationship is larger. Table 3.4 offers a look at the

Table 3.4 Simulated probabilities, likelihood to vote for the Republican candidate, prime-aged employed men in the United States

	Wealth/income distribution		Change
	Low wealth/moderate income	High wealth/moderate income	Probability change
Self-identified Republican	0.856 (0.02)	0.911 (0.01)	0.055
Self-identified Democrat	0.039 (0.01)	0.071 (0.01)	0.032
Self-Identified Independent	0.354 (0.03)	0.464 (0.03)	0.110
	Low wealth/low income	High wealth/high income	Probability change
Self-identified Republican	0.829 (0.02)	0.927 (0.01)	0.098
Self-identified Democrat	0.031 (0.01)	0.087 (0.01)	0.056
Self-Identified Independent	0.314 (0.03)	0.508 (0.03)	0.194

Sources: Luxembourg Wealth Study; American National Election Studies; Comparative Study of Electoral Systems.

Notes
Low wealth/income corresponds to values falling in the 1st quintile, moderate wealth/income to values in the 3rd quintile, and high wealth/income to values in the 5th quintile. Probabilities are calculated for prime-aged (25–54) employed men. The probabilities for women are similar. One thousand simulations were performed using *Clarify* by Gary King.

magnitude through the use of predicted probabilities. Because partisanship is particularly important in the United States, the effect of wealth is assessed within partisan groupings. Two details are noteworthy. First, even holding income constant, wealth holdings have the power to nudge partisans on both sides of the aisle. While self-identified Republicans are likely to vote for the Republican candidate regardless of wealth level, each quintile of wealth is expected to increase the probability by over 1 percent. If income and wealth are both allowed to vary from low to high, the change among Republicans is ten points. Wealth levels provide one possible explanation for those atypical voters whose partisanship and vote choice do not align. Second, changes in wealth have the largest impact on those who do not self-identify with a political party. There is more than a ten-point difference in the likelihood that a voter with low wealth will vote for a Republican as compared to a voter with high wealth, holding income levels constant. When both income and wealth vary, there is nearly a 20-point difference. In other words, wealth and income can help explain voters who do not follow their identified partisan preferences, and those voters who are "up for grabs" in a given election.

Another way to assess the relationship between wealth and vote choice is to look across age groups. Older voters are more likely to vote for the Republican candidate and younger voters the Democratic candidate. This is accepted wisdom on the campaign trail, and conforms to the adage generally but falsely attributed to Churchill – if you are not a liberal when young you have no heart, but if you are not a conservative when old, no brain. Wealth holdings offer an alternative account. The young, especially those who are very early in their employment careers, have little to no savings. Median net worth is less than $5,000 (in 2007 real dollars) for those aged 25–34. Young home buyers have mortgages, but have not built equity in the home. Increasingly, they have high student loan debt. In other words, not only is their primary – and likely only – income stream from wages, but they are likely to have any assets offset by debt. The typical wealth profile of a young person can be juxtaposed with the typical wealth profile of an older person, particularly a retiree. Here, income streams are not primarily from wages, rather from pensions, equity built in a home (which can take many forms, from reverse mortgages, downsizing, or living rent free), and other sources of savings. Median net worth for those over the age of 65 is $130,000 (in 2007 real dollars). The median young person is almost completely reliant on current income streams. The median retiree has savings in one form or another, and is presumably drawing down on that wealth. Correspondingly, older voters are more likely to lend their vote to the Republican Party, known for policies that protect wealth, and young voters to the Democratic Party, known for policies supporting wage workers and those on the lower parts of the income distribution (though not necessarily only low income).

One additional economic variable – whether one owns an unincorporated business – is a significant predictor of vote choice. In the model, business owners are more likely to vote for a party on the left (with marginal significance), perhaps contrary to common wisdom. In the United States, there are 28 million small businesses accounting for over half of sales and jobs in the country (U.S. Small Business Administration, 2016). They range in size from less than five employees to up to 500, and are located in all sectors of the economy. In other words, small business owners are a diverse group. Among business owners, partisanship is still a strong predictor of vote choice. Self-identified Democrats remain unlikely to vote for the Republican candidate regardless of whether they are business owners. Predicted probabilities are 4 percent and 5 percent, respectively. The difference is greatest among Independents, who are predicted to vote for the Republican candidate with a probability of 41 percent if a business owner and 36 percent if not.

In sum, in the most important test case of economic voting, the United States, wealth is a significant predictor of vote choice. The effect persists independently of income. But while wealth holdings are unequally shared in Europe, increasingly so, wealth does not predict vote choice in either Germany or Sweden in anything beyond the base model. In Germany, holding other variables constant, income does predict vote choice. For instance, left-identified voters in the bottom income quintile are only predicted to vote for a left party candidate with a 55 percent probability, whereas similar voters in the top income quintile have a 68 percent probability of casting a ballot for the left. Wealth and income in Germany are more highly correlated than in the United States (a correlation of 0.45 compared to 0.36), but the model does not exhibit multicollinearity. Additionally, in Germany employment and retirement status influence the vote.

Germany is considered the quintessential corporatist welfare state. Benefits are linked to occupation and industry, stemming from Bismarck's policies in the 1880s that developed insurance schemes for old-age, sickness, and accidents that were financed and implemented jointly through a collaboration of employers and workers. Still today, a majority of workers (62 percent) are covered by collective agreements regarding pay and work conditions at either the industry or company level. The number is even larger when considering those companies who do not participate in collective bargaining, but nonetheless take account of the agreements when setting terms and conditions (Fulton, 2011). In the quantitative model, employment status and retirement status are significant predictors of the vote in Germany. Figure 3.5 illustrates the magnitude of the effect across the income distribution, holding all else constant.

Those who are not in the market, but not yet retired, are the least likely to vote for a party on the right – only a 25 percent probability for those in the bottom income quintile and a 36 percent probability for those in the top quintile. Those who are employed or retired are most likely to vote for a party on the right. For instance, the model predicts that those who are retired with income in the bottom quintile are about as likely (37 percent) to vote for a party on the right as those in the top quintile who are not employed (36 percent). Retirees in the top income quintile are predicted to vote for the right with a 50 percent probability.

In both Germany and the United States, economic factors are strong predictors of vote choice. Economic resources are important in the United States.

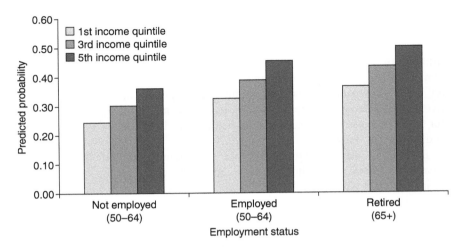

Figure 3.5 Simulated probabilities, likelihood to vote for a party on the right, by income quintile and employment status in Germany.

Sources: Luxembourg Wealth Study, American National Election Studies, and Comparative Study of Electoral Systems.

Employment factors are key in Germany. Neither type is significant in Sweden. If economic factors do not explain vote choice in Sweden, what might? Just as Germany is the archetypal corporatist welfare state, Sweden is the classic social democratic welfare state. Is vote choice instead moderated by non-economic factors?

Economic vs. non-economic factors: the case of Sweden

The variables included in the quantitate models were chosen to assess the impact of economic voting given increasing levels of wealth and income inequality. But perhaps Swedes base their vote decisions on social elements instead? An additional set of survey questions on the CSES provides some preliminary evidence of this possibility. The CSES survey identifies five of the most salient issues in each election year in Sweden and Germany, as well as the United States. The issues are identified through the expert judgment of CSES collaborators using open-ended and follow-up questions for each country, and are then aggregated to the country level. In other words, all respondents in a given country are coded with the same response. These variables cannot be included in the quantitative model since they do not vary by country, but it is possible to look across the three countries to consider differences in issue salience. Table 3.5 lists the most salient issues in each of three election cycles for each country. Issues range from economic and social, to domestic and international, to assessments of leadership and concerns about safety and security. Within each country, clear differences emerge in the types of issues that citizens identify as important.

Table 3.5 Most salient issue areas

	Election cycle 1 (1996–1998)	Election cycle 2 (2002–2004)	Election cycle 3 (2005–2008)
United States (1996, 2004, 2008)	Economic factors Taxes Health care Presence of "new" party candidates Finance	Terrorism, 9/11 War in Iraq Economy and unemployment Moral/cultural issues Health issues	State of the economy Wars (terror, Iraq, Afghanistan) Performance of incumbent Size of welfare state/ economic fairness/ inequality "Social" issues (abortion, religion, race, immigration)
Germany (1998, 2002, 2005)	Party performance Unemployment Leadership, "personalization" Media issues	Leadership of the Chancellor Economy and unemployment War on Iraq Social justice Flood in East Germany	Reform of social security (Hartz IV, unemployment benefits) Economy and unemployment Tax reform (goods and service tax) Snap elections Health system
Sweden (1998, 2002, 2006)	Worker's protection/ rights Support/opposition for EU Taxes Promises/trust of leadership Economic factors	Social welfare Health issues Education Childcare Taxes	Employment/ unemployment Social welfare/health issues Education Pensions/elderly care Taxes

Source: Comparative Study of Electoral Systems.

Note:
In Germany, the 2005 election was a snap election – called before expected.

Economic issues – either identified broadly as 'economic factors' or more specifically as taxes, unemployment, and finance – dominate discourse in the United States (except in 2004, the first post 9/11 national election). Social issues are based in moral debates, such as on abortion. In contrast, social issues in Sweden dominate, and are more directly linked to social policy – welfare, health, education, pensions, etc. – especially in the 2002 election (the election year used in the quantitative model). Notably, in a follow-up question about whether there would be a general consensus on the salience of issues, only Swedes stated that other Swedes would agree. Those in the United States said their fellow Americans would not agree with the issues they individually identified as important. Not only are the issues that Swedish respondents identified more social in nature, but they tend to think their views are similar to those held by the population as a whole.

The story in Germany is less clear. Views regarding the economy share the top spots with views on performance of the party and Chancellor. It is unclear whether performance is based on economic or social issues. If 2005 is an indication, where the top issue is the reform of unemployment benefits within the social security system, then it is a mix of both. In any case, all social issues are funded by taxes, and are fundamentally economic in nature. Distinctions between social and economic issues are undeniably fuzzy. However, this does not minimize the role that a difference in focus can have on political discourse. For instance, the data indicate Americans are focused on issues based on funding sources, like taxes, where Swedes are focused on the policy or policy outcome itself. A focus on funding sources may prompt a more individualistic political dialogue – should my tax dollars go to help the poor. A focus on social outcomes may be more likely to prompt collectively framed dialogues – should we address poverty and, if so, how. The issues that respondents in Sweden find politically salient are arguably more social in nature than in either Germany or the United States.

As in the United States, younger voters are more likely to vote for a party on the left in Sweden. Given the use of cross-sectional data, it is impossible to know whether this is an age effect (with voting behavior changing with age) or a cohort effect (where younger cohorts will continue to support the left as they age), but young people will experience wealth inequality in ways that older generations did not. Is it possible that the changing nature of wealth disparities will gain increased salience in the voting calculations of Swedes? After all, Sweden's long history of social democratic politics and solidaristic wage policy has not prevented inequalities in income and wealth from deepening. In fact, wealth inequalities are quite high, even compared to the United States, a country well-known for its unequal wealth distribution.

Discussion

The United States, Germany and Sweden represent three countries with diverse political and social histories. They are commonly used to represent three distinct regimes types, liberal, corporatist, and social democratic respectively. The role of economic voting is different in each. Individual level resources, wealth, and income, influence vote choice in the United States. Individuals in the United States are almost entirely reliant on market forces to secure their well-being; it is perhaps no wonder, then, that economic position and voting behavior are linked. However, studies typically use only income to assess the link. The findings in this chapter demonstrate that wealth should be included as well. In Germany, where social stratification occurs through occupation, income matters, and employment status does too. Wealth is significant only in the base model. In Germany, income and wealth are more highly correlated than in the United States, and income may serve as a proxy for wealth. No economic variables included in the model relate to vote choice in Sweden, where political discourse is framed by social issues and left-party dominance.

By choosing three very different countries to assess explanatory power, this chapter has attempted to define the scope of the relationship of wealth to vote choice. Next steps in the research agenda include extending the area of interest to include other aspects of voting behavior, using more detailed measures of wealth, and employing a most-similar research design to identify cases where wealth is most likely to hold explanatory power.

Is vote choice the variable with the closest link to wealth accumulation? While there is empirical support to link wealth to vote choice, partisanship operates very strongly in the models. In addition to the direct effect, wealth accumulation might influence partisanship. Rather than wealth at one point in time influencing vote choice in the next election, wealth accumulation in early adulthood may shape partisan preferences, which are typically relatively stable across time. These claims could be assessed with similar strategies and data sources as used in this chapter; however, panel data would be better suited to tracking behavior and preferences over time.

Wealth may also be linked to policy attitudes, as mentioned in the theory development section. Surveys collecting information on voting behavior often also collect information on policy preferences. Future research might consider the role of wealth in influencing policy preferences. One logical place to begin is to assess the link between wealth and knowledge of policies – with the hypothesis that those who have more at stake (i.e., are wealthier) will follow public policy more closely. Another possibility is that policy areas that are likely to affect wealth (e.g., taxation and macroeconomic policies) will be of interest to those with wealth, and the accumulation of wealth will be linked to views on tax treatment and fiscal policy.

In this chapter, overall net worth is used as the measure of wealth. There are many subcomponents which make up a person's wealth. These can be financial or non-financial in nature, and one's wealth is determined by both sides of the budget sheet. Furthermore, countries vary not just in the distribution of wealth, but in whether wealth is offset by debts and where assets are held. In looking at wealth subcomponents, multiple questions can be considered. For instance, will two people with a similar level of assets, but one with equity primarily in housing and the other with assets primarily in stocks and bonds act the same way? Are assets a better predictor of vote choice, or does debt drive behavior?

The models indicate that wealth and other economic variables operate differently in the United States, Germany, and Sweden. The inclusion of additional countries could help determine whether voting behavior is mediated by regime type, since each country is representative of a particular regime. In selecting countries, a most-similar design could be fruitfully employed, selecting countries with broadly similar political and economic dialogues. For instance, Australia, Canada, Ireland, New Zealand, and the United Kingdom are commonly categorized as having liberal welfare regimes where citizens secure well-being primarily through the market. The link between economic resources and voting should be stronger in these countries as compared to social democratic countries such as Denmark, Norway, and Sweden.

Heightened wealth and income inequalities lead voters to make decisions within an increasingly polarized arena. Likewise, heightened disagreements between parties and elites offer voters more polarized choices. This dual polarization can lead to less political compromise among elected officials and greater disparities in the voting behavior of citizens. Politicians' actions, in their campaigns and in their support of particular policies, are based in part on who they represent. In an increasingly polarized world, the haves and the have-nots command different levels of resources, and may contribute to an increasingly polarized political discourse. The political salience of wealth disparities is surely part of this story.

Note

1 We also ran our analysis of the United States with assets that were excluded here; the results do not change our conclusions. They are available upon request (email Piotr Paradowski, Luxembourg Income Study (LIS), at paradowski@lisdatacenter.org).

References

Abramowitz, A. (2012). "Forecasting in a Polarized Era: The Time for Change Model and the 2012 Presidential Election." *PS: Political Science & Politics,* 45(4): 618–619.

American National Election Studies. (2010). "Time Series Cumulative Data File (1948–2012)." Stanford University and the University of Michigan, release version: 20150514. Available at www.electionstudies.org/studypages/anes_timeseries_cdf/anes_timeseries_cdf.htm (accessed March 30, 2017).

Ansell, B. (2014). "The Political Economy of Ownership: Housing Markets and the Welfare State." *American Political Science Review*, 108(2): 383–402.

Armingeon, Klaus, Laura Knöpfel, David Weisstanner, and Sarah Engler. (2014). "Comparative Political Data Set III 1990–2012." Institute of Political Science, University of Berne.

Black, E. and M. Black. (2009). *The Rise of Southern Republicans*. Cambridge, MA: Harvard University Press.

Brooks, C. and D. Brady. (1999). "Income, Economic Voting, and Long-Term Political Change in the US, 1952–1996." *Social Forces*, 77(4): 1339–1374.

Campbell, A. (1980). *The American Voter*. Chicago, IL: University of Chicago Press.

Clark, T. N. and S. M. Lipset. (2001). *The Breakdown of Class Politics: A debate on Post-Industrial Stratification*. Washington, DC: Woodrow Wilson Center Press.

Comparative Study of Electoral Systems. (2015). CSES Module 1–3 Full Release.

Conradt, D. P., G. R. Kleinfeld, and C. Søe. (2004). *A Precarious Victory: Shroeder and the German Elections of 2002*. New York: Berghahn.

D'Ambrosio, C. and E. Wolff. (2001). "Is Wealth Becoming More Polarized in the United States?" Unpublished technical paper.

Davies, James B. and Anthony B. Shorrocks (2000). "The Distribution of Wealth." In *Handbook of Income Distribution*, edited by A. B. Atkinson and F. Bourguignon, Vol. 1, Ch. 11, pp. 605–675. Amsterdam; New York: Elsevier.

D'Orazio, Marcello (2013) "Statistical Matching and Imputation of Survey Data with Stat-Match." Available at http://citeseerx.ist.psu.edu/viewdoc/summary?doi=10.1.1.466.2015 (accessed March 30, 2017).

Esping-Andersen, G. (1990). *The Three Worlds of Welfare Capitalism*. Princeton, NJ: Princeton University Press.

Evans, G. (2000). "The Continued Significance of Class Voting." *Annual Review of Political Science*, 3(1): 401–417.

Federal Election Commission. Election Results. Available at www.fec.gov/pubrec/fe2000/cover.htm (accessed January 25, 2016).

The Federal Returning Officer (Der Bundeswahlleiter). (2002). Wahl zum 15. Deutschen Bundestag am 22. September 2002. Available at www.bundeswahlleiter.de/en/index.html (accessed March 30, 2017).

Fiorina, M. P. and S. J. Abrams. (2008). "Political Polarization in the American Public." *Annual Review of Political Science*, 11: 563–588.

Fiorina, M. P., S. J. Abrams, and J. C. Pope. (2005). *Culture war?* New York: Pearson Longman.

Flanigan, W. H., N. H. Zingale, E. A. Theiss-Morse, and M. W. Wagner. (2014). *Political behavior of the American electorate*, 13th edn. Los Angeles, CA: CQ Press.

Franklin, M. N., T. T. Mackie, and H. Valen. (2009). *Electoral Change: Responses to Evolving Social and Attitudinal Structures in Western countries*. Colchester, UK ECPR Press.

Fulton, L. (2011). Worker Representation in Europe. *Labour Research Department and ETUI.* Available at www.worker-participation.eu/National-Industrial-Relations/Across-Europe (accessed March 30, 2017).

Gelman, A., L. Kenworthy, and Y. Su. (2010). "Income Inequality and Partisan Voting in the United States." *Social Science Quarterly*, 91(5): 1203–1219.

Hauser, R. and H. Stein. (2003). "Inequality of the Distribution of Personal Wealth in Germany 1973–1998." Working Paper No. 398, The Levy Economics Institute.

Huber, J. D. and P. Stanig. (2007). "Why Do the Poor Support Right-Wing Parties? A Cross-National Analysis." Technical Report, Department of Political Science, Columbia University.

Inglehart, R. (1971). "The Silent Revolution in Europe: Intergenerational Change in Post-Industrial Societies." *American Political Science Review*, 65(4): 991–1017.

Jäntti, M., E. Sierminska, and P. Van Kerm. (2012). "Modelling the Joint Distribution of Income and Wealth." Paper presented at the 32nd General Conference of The International Association for Research in Income and Wealth, Boston, U.S.

Jones, J. M. (2015, February 6). "Obama Approval Ratings Still Historically Polarized." Available at www.gallup.com/poll/181490/obama-approval-ratings-historically-polarized.aspx (accessed January 25, 2016).

Kennickell, A. B. (2009). "Ponds and Streams: Wealth and Income in the U.S., 1989 to 2007." Finance and Economics Discussion Series, Divisions of Research & Statistics and Monetary Affairs, Federal Reserve Board, Washington, DC.

Kiewiet, D. R. (1984). "Macroeconomics and Micropolitics: The Electoral Effects of Economic Issues." *Business Horizons*, 27(5): 85–86.

Layman, G. C., T. M. Carsey, and J. M. Horowitz. (2006). "Party Polarization in American Politics: Characteristics, Causes, and Consequences. *Annual Review of Political Science*, 9: 83–110.

Lipset, S. M. (1959). "Democracy and Working-Class Authoritarianism." *American Sociological Review*, 24(4): 482–501.

LIS Cross-National Data Center. "Luxembourg Wealth Study Database." Available at www.lisdatacenter.org (accessed February 9, 2016).

Manza, J. and C. Brooks. (1999). *Social Cleavages and Political Change: Voter Alignments and US Party Coalitions*. Oxford: Oxford University Press.

McCarty, N., K. T. Poole, and H. Rosenthal. (1997). *Income Redistribution and the Realignment of American Politics*. Washington, DC: AEI Press.

McCarty, N., K. T. Poole, and H. Rosenthal. (2006). *Polarized America: The Dance of Ideology and Unequal Riches*. Cambridge, MA: MIT Press.

Murtin, F. and M. M. d'Ercole. (2015). "Household Wealth Inequality across OECD Countries: New OECD Evidence." OECD Statistics Brief, No. 21.

OECD. (2015). *In It Together: Why Less Inequality Benefits All*. Paris: OECD Publishing.

Office of the Federal Register. Historical Election Results. Available at www.archives.gov/federal-register/electoral-college/historical.html (accessed January 25, 2016).

Pierson, P. (1994). *Dismantling the Welfare State?: Reagan, Thatcher, and the Politics of Retrenchment*. Cambridge and New York: Cambridge University Press.

Piketty, T. (2014). *Capital in the Twenty-First Century*. Cambridge, MA: Harvard University Press.

Piketty, T. and E. Saez. (2014) "Inequality in the Long Run." *Science*, 334 (6186): 838–843.

Rehm, Philipp (2011). "Risk Inequality and the Polarized American Electorate." *British Journal of Political Science,* 41: 363–387.

Statistics Sweden. Historical Statistics of Elections 1910–2014. Available at www.scb.se/en_/Finding-statistics/Statistics-by-subject-area/Democracy/General-elections/General-elections-results/Aktuell-Pong/12275/Historical-statistics-of-election-results/32065/ (accessed January 25, 2016).

Steinmo, S. (1989). "Political Institutions and Tax Policy in the United States, Sweden, and Britain." *World Politics*, 41(4): 500–535.

U.S. Small Business Administration. (2016). Small Business Trends. Available at www.sba.gov/content/small-business-trends-impact (accessed January 25, 2016).

Part II

An example of polarization

The climate change debate

4 Consensual environmental policy in the Anthropocene

Governing what humanity hath wrought

Walter F. Baber and Robert V. Bartlett

> The problem is that no ethical system has ever achieved consensus. Ethical systems are completely unlike mathematics or science. This is a source of concern.
>
> Daniel Dennett

The phrase "global governance" developed a remarkable popularity over a decade. Whereas an internet search in 2004 produced fewer than 3,500 references to global governance (Biermann and Pattberg 2012), by December 2014 the count had approached 36.5 million references. If quantity is any indicator, global governance is an idea whose time has come. What is far less universal is the idea that global governance (in contrast to mathematics or science) can reasonably aspire to achieve a meeting of the minds – in short, a governing consensus. The reluctance to talk in terms of a global governing consensus most usually derives from two assumptions: that governance requires government and that polarization of the "unfathomable human diversity" we see around us is an insurmountable obstacle to a single, global government (Orwin 2014). These assumptions imply that global governance can never have a consensual character.

Against this background of a culturally diverse and politically divided global society, humankind's search for the self-governance required to protect the environmental preconditions of its own existence might seem especially problematic. This might be a problem that is among those least likely to prove an exception to the received wisdom about polarization and global consensus. Indeed, the complexity of environmental problematique (when added to the complexity of human culture) may make governing interaction with the earth's natural systems the most daunting challenge humans will ever face. For these reasons, determining whether it is possible to develop an approach to "earth system governance" that is both consensual and effective will turn upon the central questions, methods, and processes of global research on governance, rather than upon breakthroughs in the natural sciences. In particular, earth system governance must confront five core analytical problems (ESGP 2009).

First, the ***architecture*** of earth system governance includes questions relating to the emergence, design, and effectiveness of governance systems as well as the overall integration of global, regional, national, and local governance.

Second, understanding effective earth system governance requires an understanding of the ***agents*** that drive earth system governance and the role that each must play. The particular research gap here is the influence and responsibilities of actors apart from national governments (such as businesses, social action networks, and non-profit organizations), the ways in which authority is granted to these agents, and how they exercise that authority.

Third, earth system governance must respond to the inherent uncertainties in human and natural systems. It must combine the stability necessary to ensure long-term governance solutions with the flexibility needed to react quickly to new findings and developments. In other words, humans must better understand and further develop the ***adaptiveness*** of earth systems and their governance.

Fourth, the greater the regulatory competence and authority that is conferred upon larger institutions and systems of governance – especially at the global level – the more we will be confronted with questions of how to ensure the ***accountability*** and legitimacy of that governance.

Fifth, earth system governance is (like any political activity) crucially about the distribution of material and nonmaterial values. It is, in essence, a conflict about ***access*** to goods and about their ***allocation***. It is about justice, fairness, and equity.

These challenges of governance are not, of course, challenges of a scientific or technical nature. The advent of the Anthropocene – grounded though it may be in the scientific progress that has invested humanity with responsibility for our own environment – seems not to have given us an equivalent ability to resolve the differences that we discover among ourselves. Although environmental governance must be broadly democratic if it is to be effective (Baber and Bartlett 2005), the course of our development seems not to have provided us with a clear path leading to principles that will command the assent of humanity in the way those of mathematics or science do.

A source of concern, indeed.

Observations and analysis

> Uniform ideas originating among entire peoples unknown to each other must have a common ground of truth.
>
> Giambattista Vico

In order to better understand the role of consensus in democratic environmental governance, we analyze here the concept of transparency. Transparency does not rely on uniformity among entire peoples unknown to each other to play its role in environmental governance. To say that the concept of transparency in governance involves some kind of consensus is not to suggest that this is uncontested ground – as the heated dispute over the 2010 WikiLeaks controversy amply demonstrates. Calls for greater transparency in governance have become a standard element in diverse areas ranging from the "design of 'robust' international monitoring, reporting, and verification systems for global climate mitigation" to "calls for transparency to combat opaque business practices implicated in the global financial crisis" (Gupta and Mason, 2014, 3). The concept of transparency in environmental governance has a long history. Its origins can be traced to the "right-to-know movements in the 1960s and 1970s, particularly in the United States and other advanced industrialized democracies" (Mol 2014, 39) and even earlier to the US Administrative Procedures Act of 1946. But the transparency bandwagon has travelled more widely – stopping in both rich countries and poor, democratic and authoritarian (Fiorini 2007). This broadly emerging consensus has been driven in part by trends toward democratization and marketization, but also by processes of transnational learning that have both led to a growing domestic receptivity to transparency-based governance (Florini and Jairaj 2014) and to public disclosure obligations imposed by the 1998 Convention on Access to Information, Public Participation in Decision-Making and Access to Justice in Environmental Matters (Mason 2014).

Before exploring its manifestations across a range of environmental governance issues, it is worth pausing briefly to consider the general outlines and core assumptions of this "transparency consensus." At neither the national nor international level do transparency's advocates claim that it is a panacea. Never can they be heard claiming that public disclosure, by either government or industry, will actually solve environmental problems. They do, however, have compelling arguments to make on transparency's behalf. As a starting point, it has been observed that access to information is an indispensable prerequisite for the development and deployment of environmental rights generally (Hayward 2005). Moreover, a normative argument can be made that people who are subject to risk as a consequence of environmental decisions taken by others have a fundamental *right to know* about their circumstances (Beierle 2004). Beyond this fundamental moral commitment, there are a number of procedural advantages commonly thought to result from transparency. For instance, strong transparency policies are likely to make public participation in decision-making processes more effective by fostering a process of public learning through disclosure (Auld and Gulbrandsen 2014). Moreover, transparency policies are potentially useful in holding environmental decision makers *accountable* – a particularly challenging problem in the global governance context, where accountability mechanisms are necessarily detached from electoral or representative accountability systems (Keohane 2006); this makes accountability of global environmental governance and transnational private governance all the more elusive (Biermann and Gupta 2011). These procedural advantages, when realized, could be expected to result in the empowerment of the recipients of disclosure – redressing in some measure the information gap between elite groups and average citizens. Transparency policies have as one of their important aims the adoption of public policies that reduce ecological damage, mitigate risk, and lead to overall environmental improvements (Fung et al. 2007). Finally, transparency policies are expected to be valuable in efforts to achieve policy coordination and integration (Buhrs 2009; Bartlett 1990). These fundamental values – effective public participation, the right to know, public accountability, citizen empowerment, and effective environmental protection – constitute the normative consensus underlying what has been described as "governance by disclosure" (Gupta and Mason 2014). The consensual nature of this normative perspective is amply demonstrated by the fact that not even the critics of this form of governance dispute its underlying normative objectives. Its critiques invariably focus on the disclosure policy models that are adopted and the implementation actions taken in their pursuit – as we can see in examining transparency through the lens provided by the five analytical problems of global governance described above.

The architecture of transparency

In the context of earth system governance, the concept of "architecture" draws our attention to widely shared and interlocking webs of institutionalized principles and practices in a given area of environmental policy. As with other phenomena for which the term "governance" is preferable to "government," our analysis here is directed to the interactions among formally constituted and fully public organizations and non-governmental organizations (NGOs) and more loosely identified elements of civil society. From early research on the formation and structure of international regimes (Krasner 1983; Young 1989, 1998) to more recent analysis of how different international norms and verification procedures, compliance management systems, and external factors influence regime effectiveness (Stokke 2012), these emergent networks of global political order have become prominent in thinking about international relations.

In applying the concept of architecture to the question of transparency, a useful example is "the form of governance by disclosure through prior informed consent" (Jansen and Dubois 2014, 107) represented in the Rotterdam Convention on the Prior Informed Consent Procedure for Certain Hazardous Chemicals and Pesticides in International Trade (hereinafter "the Convention"). The Convention is a multilateral treaty with 154 current signatories. Its general objective is to promote shared responsibilities in relation to the importation of hazardous chemicals. The Convention promotes open exchange of information by requiring exporters of hazardous chemicals to use proper labeling, include directions on safe handling, and to inform purchasers of any known restrictions or bans. Signatory nations can decide whether to allow or ban the importation of chemicals listed in Annex III of the Convention. Exporting countries are obliged to ensure that producers within their jurisdiction comply with the terms of the Convention.

This relatively simple disclosure architecture is the institutional expression of a fundamental *normative consensus* (Baber and Bartlett 2015) that nations have an inherent right to control the flow of hazardous chemicals into their territory. It is, however, an implicit rejection of the far stronger demand for an outright ban on the use of hazardous pesticides that might better serve the needs of developing nations which often lack both analytical and enforcement capacities (Jansen

2008). The policy model embodied by the specific provisions of the Convention reflects a "techno-statist" *political consensus* about an approach to governance that emphasizes networks of science specialists delivering pesticide risk information as a public good, which governments can then use to regulate their exposure to the uncertainties of a complex and technologically sophisticated global market. It rejects both the "neoliberal" alternative of leaving chemical end users and providers to negotiate their own arrangements in a *caveat emptor* environment and the "deliberative democratic" option of problematizing the tacit normative framings of markets and prescribing a participatory risk management system grounded in a democratized form of science and technology (Kraft et al. 2011; Tyfield 2012). Finally, the Convention institutionalizes a "meta-consensus" that the *social consensus* required for the implementation of its particular expression of governance by disclosure should be crafted below the level of international governance through the political processes of the various signatory states. The core aim of the Convention is to help states exert their sovereign power to regulate the flow of listed substances into their territories. The broader (and more challenging) issues of accountability, legitimacy, and democracy are of a distinctly secondary concern (Biermann and Gupta 2011; Mitchell 2011).

The architecture of the Convention is the result of several decades of experimentation, which has led to a "more-or-less functioning, though modest, governance-by-disclosure regime" (Jansen and Dubois 2014, 124). With respect to pesticides and other hazardous chemicals. Its prior informed consent system seems to produce the public good that its designers sought – more "information regarding regulatory decisions on banning and restricting the use of pesticides" as well as "scientific evidence of harm" resulting from their misuse (Jansen and Dubois 2014, 124). When it comes to the question of empowering substantively better and procedurally more democratic environmental decision making, the record is decidedly more mixed. Regime effectiveness at the level of implementation is limited by a deficit in the "analytical and decision-making abilities of some nations" (Jansen and Dubois 2014, 125). To the extent that these broader objectives require "shifts in unequal power relations" – either among nations or within them – little appears to have been accomplished (Jansen and Dubois 2014, 125). It may well be that this possible outcome was surrendered when a techno-statist norm was adopted instead of a deliberative democratic approach that would challenge the implicit commitments underlying the ideas of value-neutral science and national sovereignty (Baber and Bartlett 2015).

The agents of transparency

As a field of scholarly inquiry, earth system governance poses the challenge of identifying which groups and individuals (agents) actually produce governance outcomes – real-world changes in human behavior. It is, by now, a commonplace observation that processes of global environmental change challenge the capacity of nation-states to respond to and mitigate the impact of those changes. Of course, this capacity varies among various regional, national, and subnational governments (Baber and Bartlett 2009). The effectiveness with which governments are able to deploy their existing capacities depends to a significant degree upon the balance of cooperation and resistance that they encounter in their dealings with non-governmental actors.

One governance-by-disclosure approach designed to address these difficulties with governmental responses to environmental challenges is the creation of non-state certification programs. Non-state certification shares with other transparency policies the attractive quality of allowing the end users of goods and services to make their own market decisions, having been provided with the "public good" of information that would otherwise be difficult (or impossible) for them to acquire. The *normative consensus* embodied in this approach is the hope that certification will serve as a tool for NGOs, investors, governments, and consumers to identify and support (via their market selection of labeled products) high performing businesses. In this way, all of these groups and individuals can be agents in the creation of upward pressure on entire sectors of an economy that does not involve coercive regulation (Auld and Gulbrandsen 2014).

The *political consensus* supporting non-state certification as an approach to governance-by-disclosure exhibits an interesting form of bifurcation. One policy model is for participants in a production market to create a membership organization to design and implement a certification system (consisting of both certification standards and procedures). An example of this approach is the Forest Stewardship Council (FSC). The FSC is a result of the widely shared disappointment at the failure of the 1992 Earth Summit to achieve any significant progress on the topic of deforestation. Frustrated with the inability of international politics to produce results, various NGOs turned their attention to industry itself to provide more results-oriented "soft law" solutions (Welford and Starkey 2001). With membership to its environmental, social, and economic chambers open to both organizations and individuals, the FSC seeks to maintain a highly participatory and "transparent" approach to transparency (Kirton and Trebilcock 2004).

A second policy model falling under the general heading of non-state certification is represented by the Marine Stewardship Council (MSC). At its inception, the MSC was a joint undertaking of the World Wide Fund for Nature and Unilever (Fowler and Heap 2000). Now independent of its founding organizations, the MSC has developed a set of standards for sustainable fishing in consultation with approximately 300 organizations and individuals worldwide. But the MSC has not followed the FSC's model of membership organization in its search for political legitimacy. Instead, it relies on the consistency of its standards with the "Guidelines for the Eco-labelling of Fish and Fishery Products from Marine Wild Capture Fisheries" adopted by the UN Food and Agriculture Organization (FAO) in 2005 *and* upon an "assessment" program conducted by professional staff and overseen by the MSC Board of Directors which is open to the submission of information by interested parties. The MSC approach to transparency, therefore, appears more instrumental and science driven than that of the FSC (Auld and Gulbrandsen 2014).

This apparent "diversity" within the political consensus supporting non-state certification transparency can, perhaps, be explained (and even justified) by the fact that this particular instance of political divergence does not necessarily suggest any lack of *social consensus* at the level of policy implementation. This is possible because of the operating assumptions about how eco-labeling actually works in practice. Unlike product labels mandated by various national product safety standards, eco-labels provide the individual consumer with relatively little information. In the absence of a very significant (and costly) outreach and marketing effort, most consumers cannot reasonably be expected to critically assess either labeling standards or the organizations that develop and implement them. Research suggests that the operative influence of non-state certification is actually a function of public interest NGO targeting of major buyers, who respond by demanding certified products from firms in their supply chains (Gulbrandsen 2006). If this is correct, then the public preference for sustainable products is effectively mediated by NGOs, which are better suited to assess certification standards (and their authors) than are individual consumers. As a result, the provenance, organization, and governance of certifying organizations may matter far less than one would ordinarily assume. It may be that governance-by-disclosure can, in fact, tolerate something less than complete transparency. As long as transparency of procedures and outcomes is sufficient, policy models featuring either robust or relatively leaner patterns of stakeholder monitoring can be sustained (Auld and Gulbrandsen 2014, 289–290).

Transparency and adaptiveness

Adaptiveness, in the context of earth system governance, is something of a catch-all for a set of distinct but related concepts – including "vulnerability, resilience, adaptation, robustness, adaptive capacity, social learning," and so on (ESGP 2009, 45). Each of these concepts captures something important about changes made by social groups in response to, or anticipation of, changes in the natural environment. Adaptiveness includes at least three kinds of social-ecological responses to environmental change. These include "narrowing" the gap between current responses to change and imagined best responses, "tracking" changes in what counts as a best response (when that shifts as a result of environmental change), and "transforming" institutions when a best response requires a change from one governance regime to another (ESGP 2009). In effect, the concept of adaptiveness suggests a constant need for information about our policy target, how it is moving through the governance space we share, and when it might be approaching a boundary of that space as we understand it.

Insofar as governance-by-disclosure always involves the flow of information among actors in governance processes, any techniques falling under that heading might be assumed to involve adaptiveness as we have described it. One problem area of earth system governance is particularly appropriate as a focus for inquiry into the relationship between transparency and adaptiveness – the problem of risk governance. Focusing on this governance problem allows us to examine a policy arena in which narrowing, tracking, and transforming seem to take place simultaneously and (according to the varying accounts of particular "agents") point us in conflicting directions. This can be seen most clearly in the case of risk governance associated with the transboundary transfer of genetically modified organisms (GMOs).

The Cartegena Protocol on Biosafety (hereinafter "the Protocol") is an expression of one of the most widely subscribed to principles in earth system governance – the precautionary principle. In brief, this principle declares that where there are threats of serious or irreversible damage, lack of full scientific certainty shall not be used as a reason for postponing cost-effective measures to prevent environmental degradation. The Protocol, which currently has 168 signatories worldwide, applies the precautionary principle to international trade in GMOs. The form this application takes is a requirement for an "advance informed agreement" for the importation of GMOs. This requirement (an offspring of the longer established notion of prior informed consent) is a virtually uncontested corollary of the basic principle of national sovereignty as it applies to environmental governance (Gupta 2000). And, as with all informed agreement regimes, a broad *normative consensus* on the value of transparency is fundamental.

The Protocol also represents a *political consensus* of exactly the sort that one might expect from a prior informed consent arrangement. It promotes biosafety by establishing rules and procedures for the safe transfer, handling, and use of GMOs, with a specific focus on transboundary movements. It features one set of procedures for GMOs that are to be intentionally introduced into the environment (the advance informed agreement procedure) and another procedure for GMOs that are intended to be used directly as food or feed or for processing. Parties to the Protocol must ensure that GMOs are handled, packaged, and transported under conditions of safety. The shipment of GMOs involving transboundary movement must be accompanied by appropriate documentation specifying, among other things, the identity of GMOs and a contact point for further information. These procedures and requirements are designed to provide importing parties with the necessary information to make informed decisions about whether or not to accept GMO imports and for handling them in a safe manner. The importing party is required to make its decisions in accordance with scientifically sound risk assessments. The Protocol also sets out principles and methodologies on how to conduct a risk assessment. In case of insufficient relevant scientific information, the importing party may rely on the precautionary principle in making its decisions on importation. Where the Protocol reveals its essential nature, however, is in the character of the social consensus exhibited in its implementation.

The implementation of the Cartegena Protocol is an outstanding example of the aphorism that policy is procedure. The central issue of implementation is application of the Protocol's disclosure requirement to agricultural commodities – a task that is daunting in both scope and complexity. Four of the most heavily traded food commodities (soy beans, maize, canola, and cotton) have GMO varieties and GMO varieties of other commodities (wheat and rice) are under development (James 2012). Moreover, many politically critical countries wear more than one hat in the GMO arena – alternately playing the roles of GMO exporter and importer (Falck Zepeda 2006). Also, to make matters just a bit more difficult, the crucial axis of GMO politics pits economic powerhouses against one another – with the United States leading an export-oriented coalition and the European Union at the center of a somewhat more diverse import-oriented group of nations (Gupta 2014). Finally, the quality of the discourse in which this array of forces has engaged has not been significantly improved by the efforts of scientists. GMO proponents appear to have profited little from meta-data research which indicates that an increasing number of primary research studies fail to show any health risk associated with GMO use (Domingo and Bordonaba 2011; Snell et al. 2012). GMO opponents are generally unfazed when confronted with objections that absolute proof of a negative is impossible and demanding it is unreasonable.

This description of the universe of discourse within which Protocol implementation is taking place might seem to be the very antithesis of the idea of *social consensus*. But that impression ignores the underlying commonality of the views being advanced on the subject of GMO crops. Both the opponents and proponents of GMO technology are convinced that a sufficient quantity of science-based information will eventually acquit their views. Against that backdrop, a regime of minimal disclosure (labeling which declares that GMOs *may* be contained in a bulk shipment) together with a *caveat emptor* standard for decision-making may be the uniquely appropriate one for the circumstances. GMO import decisions differ from other risk-based decisions in that they are actually decisions about the risk of risk. Given the logic of a "no measurable risk" conclusion, from research that can never meet the standard of "no possible risk," decision makers are deprived of probabilistic reasoning. So, the transparency policy involved in an "advance informed agreement" system leaves disclosure recipients no better off than they were prior to disclosure because they have always known that commodity shipments might contain GMOs. Of course, the converse is true – disclosure of a risk of risk leaves GMO exporters no worse off because no genuinely new information has been exchanged.

Outcomes of this sort are often produced where a "least common denominator" agreement is regarded as better than no agreement at all. But where a problem like the risk of risk is at issue, an agreement that imposes little but initiates much may actually constitute a "best practice" rather than a poor compromise – and especially so from the perspective of institutional adaptiveness. Much of the effort to implement the Protocol has shifted from the disclosure mandate to the improvement and standardization of sampling, testing, and verification infrastructures. This, of course, runs the risk of privileging some forms of expertise over others (Gupta 2004). It also provides an opportunity to address what is probably the most telling criticism of the Protocol – precisely that it helps the least those countries that need help the most (Gupta 2014). As seen in other contexts, governance-by-disclosure can place unsupportable burdens on developing countries that lack both the analytical and institutional capacity to effectively interpret and utilize disclosed information.

In the case of GMOs, however, a mirror image of that inequity can be discerned. Many developing countries that could benefit from GMO technology will not take it up as long as they believe that there remain significant areas of concern about GMO safety and that they would not be able to export their food commodities to the European Union market (Key et al. 2008). In the light of these considerations, the Protocol should not be condemned for the apparently undemanding quality of its social consensus with respect to what it mandates. It should, rather, be appreciated for the adaptive potential it provides by addressing the inescapably political challenge of ensuring biosafety through the development of institutions and practices of sampling, testing, and verification that can be recognized to be reliable, accurate, and trustworthy means for discovering the true risks of GMO risk (Gupta 2010). If GMO policy is ever to go beyond narrowing the gap between the status quo and best practices, much less track the ongoing changes in what best practices really are, it is likely to be because the kind of basic empirical work that the Protocol sustains will eventually allow us to transform our perceptions of the boundaries of GMO discourse.

Transparency and accountability

The very concept of "governance" involves a central question of accountability. At its most basic level, environmental governance refers to the multifaceted and multilayered nature of "governing" the borderless and state-indiscriminate natural environment. How one does that in a way that holds agents accountable (in any traditional sense) is a persistent challenge – especially for those who argue that environmental governance must be fundamentally democratic in order to be effective. Accountability is rendered even more attenuated in the area of transparency policy because governance-by-disclosure so often depends in critical ways on non-state actors. An excellent example of this is provided by the Global Reporting Initiative (GRI).

Sustainability reporting is a recent concept that encourages businesses and institutions to report on their environmental performance (Herzig 2006). Given its entirely voluntary character, it is unsurprising that a high level of *normative consensus* exists in support of this form of transparency. Moreover, by its very definition, sustainability reporting is somewhat self-regarding. It is a way in which businesses assess their own environmental accomplishments and failings, reflect on this performance and subsequently transfer this information into the public domain. This broad conceptual enterprise has been described as "reflexive environmental law" by some academics. Reflexive environmental law is an approach in which industry is encouraged to "self-reflect" and "self-criticize" the environmental externalities that result as a product of their activity, and thus act on these negative social impacts in a way that dually safeguards growth and protects the environment (Orts 1995). Not unrelated to this reflexive quality of GRI's self-criticism process is the fact that other environmental actors who wish to use GRI disclosures for their own purposes are often frustrated by a certain degree of user-unfriendliness. That problem becomes clearer when we examine the policy model at work in the GRI.

GRI is entirely a private sector effort, the purpose of which is to harmonize reporting standards for all organizations, of whatever size and geographical origin, on a range of issues with the aim of elevating the status of environmental reporting to that of, for example, financial auditing (Willis 2003). Environmental transparency is one of the main areas of business within the scope of the GRI. The GRI encourages participants to report on their environmental performance using specific criteria. The standardized reporting guidelines concerning the environment are contained in the GRI Indicator Protocol Set. This indicator set includes criteria on energy, biodiversity, and emissions – with the 30 specific environmental indicators ranging from "materials used by weight" to "total environmental expenditures by type of investment." In theory at least, disclosure of this kind of data and its collection in an organized database does more than allow business to engage in self-criticism. It should also empower environmental actors outside the corporate sector by redressing the information imbalance from which they often suffer. The prospect of providing a more level playing field for the three-sided contest among businesses, governments, and civil society sustains a powerful *political consensus* in support of such voluntary disclosure regimes. The devil, as is so often the case, is to be found in the details of implementation.

Implementation of the GRI is, almost by definition, an expression of *social consensus*. In this instance, however, the consensus (though genuine enough) occurs in too small a "society" for it to serve all the purposes that it might. The effectiveness of GRI's social consensus is limited by a number of factors. First, the disclosure language of GRI fails to adequately specify what counts as transparency and what purposes it is meant to serve. A second weakness, not unrelated to the first, is that corporations can be in compliance with GRI's basic transparency requirement while having disclosed their information in forms that are not easily compared to one another. Finally, the information infrastructure surrounding GRI remains relatively weak. In contrast to other disclosure schemes, civil society actors have not gathered around GRI in sufficient numbers to translate its data into more valuable, accessible, comprehensible, comparable, and actionable forms (Dingwerth and Eichinger 2010).

Advocates of GRI are not unaware of these concerns, nor have they been entirely unresponsive. However, the most significant response to these limitations of GRI has been among other business organizations. In particular, GRI (as well as other disclosure systems) supports a thriving market in the management and delivery of that data. Some companies collect and aggregate data, rendering it in a comparable and consistent format to their clients. Other firms go further, offering interpretations of the data and investment recommendations based upon them (Dingwerth and Eichinger 2014). As a basic tool for large individual and institutional investors, a service of this kind may be invaluable. If this were as far as GRI went, it could plausibly argue that it is held accountable for its performance by precisely the same investment market that its disclosure regime seeks to influence. But neither GRI's own rhetoric nor our hopes for governance-by-disclosure will allow us to stop there. When we extend our analysis of disclosure systems of this character, two central challenges become apparent.

First, the introduction of a class of environmental actors who serve as intermediaries between information disclosers and end users creates a new level of complexity – and, with it, a new accountability challenge. The history of governance-by-disclosure may be judged to have been positive (on balance), but that is no guarantee that it will always be so. Information intermediaries play a role in the development of transparency-based governance that is somewhat similar to that of lawyers in the development of hard law regimes. Lawyers serve as a sort of translation matrix for those seeking to acquit the political values associated with the rule of law, helping members of divergent knowledge communities to communicate with each other (Habermas 1996). In that context, lawyers are subordinates in a clear principal/agent relationship. The contours of that relationship are well defined and the lawyer's relationship of accountability to his client is enforceable by law. Information intermediaries in governance-by-disclosure systems occupy a more ambiguous position. They will commonly have valuable contractual relationships between both disclosers of information and end users of their restatements of that information. As demanding as it may be to navigate that interstitial territory, success in doing so is no guarantee at all that the result will either serve the public interest or protect the environment. So, the first question we face in the era of transparency's lost innocence (Mol 2014) is: Who will watch the watchers?

Second, the advent of the information intermediary as a business concern poses another question worth pondering. Information disclosed by GRI has come to represent a tradable good that profit-seeking intermediaries seem to value (Dingwerth and Eichinger 2014). Yet not-for-profit intermediaries have seemed to shy away from this particular source of information. In the light of this asymmetry, one must ask whether transparency regimes of this sort contribute to the marketization of transparency (Gupta and Mason 2014). If not, we can reasonably wonder whether the ideal of governance-by-disclosure advocates to level the political playing field and empower the historically disadvantaged will prove viable in the long run, or whether transparency policies will eventually end up replicating the inequities that motivate the environmental justice movement.

Transparency, access, and allocation

A critique of transparency policy for risking the replication of socioeconomic inequities reminds us of something that contemporary discourses of governance can lead us to forget. Governance is inescapably political – and politics involves questions about who gets what, when, and how (Lasswell 1950). In the context of earth system governance, this key question has been conceptualized as the problem of *allocation and access*. This analytical problem is likely to be ever present in global environmental governance, because "the most vulnerable to earth system transformation will be those who live in the marginalized lands and coastal zones of the developing world" (ESGP 2009, 59). In exploring the politics of equity in earth system governance, and its relationship to transparency, it will be useful to concentrate on a governance-by-disclosure approach that is centrally concerned with access to and sharing of environmental goods.

The Convention on Biological Diversity (CBD) identifies transparency as a key element in the international governance of genetic resources. Central to the governance of genetic resources under the CBD is the concept of access and benefit sharing. Access and benefit sharing constitutes recognition by the CBD of the inherent right of nations to utilize their genetic resources under environmental laws of their own choosing. To acquit this right, genetic resource users are required to secure permission from the states that provide those resources within their territories. The CBD also established fair and equitable benefit sharing as the standard for evaluating schemes that compensate genetic resource providers for permission to exploit resources found within their borders (Orsini et al. 2014). For this equitable standard to be met, it is clearly necessary that both the conditions under which access to genetic resources is granted and the benefits accruing from their eventual use should be as transparent as possible. That necessity was answered by adoption under the CBD of the Nagoya Protocol on Access to Genetic Resources and the Fair and Equitable Sharing of Benefits Arising from their Utilization in 2010 (hereinafter "the Protocol").

In addition to affirming the right of nation-states to benefit equitably from the utilization of their genetic resources through transparent agreements, the Protocol also recognizes the role in access and benefit sharing of traditional knowledge related to genetic resources that is possessed by indigenous and local communities (ILCs). It is frequently the case that genetic resources utilization results, in the first instance, from the accumulated traditions, practices, and know-how of ILCs and that these communities often continue to rely on those resources in their day-to-day existence. The special interest of ILCs in the utilization of genetic resources is clearly distinguishable from the market-oriented interests of the national governments within whose territories those ILCs lie. So, in addition to achieving an equitable balance in the allocation of benefits from genetic resources utilization between providers and users, the *normative consensus* supporting the Protocol also provides a forum for the assertion of access rights to genetic resources on the part of those who were responsible originally for their development and stewardship (Suiseeya 2014). In effect, the Protocol extends the concept of transparency to include the "disclosure" of traditional forms of knowledge that the complex architecture of biodiversity governance (Oberthür and Pozarowska, 2013) all too often overlooks.

The transparency requirements of the Protocol must be implemented at two distinct levels – in the negotiation of utilization agreements on mutually agreed terms between users and providers and in the allocation of genetic resources benefits. The CBD explicitly extended the sovereign rights of states over the genetic base of life and coupled it with the commitment of contracting parties to facilitate access to genetic resources for environmentally sound uses and not to impose restrictions that run counter to the CBD's objectives. Moreover, the CBD obliged all contracting parties to take appropriate measures to share in a fair and equitable way the results of research and development and the benefits arising from the commercial and other utilization of genetic resources with the contracting party providing these resources. Sharing the benefits arising out of the utilization of genetic resources constitutes one of the three major objectives of the CBD (which also include conservation and sustainable use of biological diversity). The Protocol significantly expands and fleshes out this general framework on access and benefit sharing using a well-established governance-by-disclosure technique. Article 6.1 of the Protocol (on "Access to Genetic Resources") places the right of parties to require prior informed consent in the context of the exercise of sovereign rights over genetic resources. Furthermore, Articles 6.2 and 6.3 (f) of the Protocol obliges parties to ensure that prior informed consent or approval and involvement of ILCs be obtained for access to genetic resources where these communities have the established right to grant access to such resources (Buck and Hamilton 2011). This *political consensus* on prior informed consent as the appropriate transparency policy model for genetic resources access, and access and benefit sharing, is the core achievement of the Protocol.

The Protocol came into being against the backdrop of a general lack of transparency in negotiations over genetic resources access. Often, the terms of access agreements were denied to the public by a norm of industrial confidentiality (Orsini et al. 2014). Moreover, a general reluctance to disclose information was exacerbated by resistance to the very idea of selling public natural resources to private companies – an attitude often most pronounced among ILCs (Miller 2006). The resulting "biopiracy" characterization by developing countries, ILCs, and NGOs of almost any use of genetic resources that did not respect the principles of prior informed consent and mutually agreed terms was a dominant force for transparency by the time the Protocol came into force (Bled 2010). The Protocol's uptake of transparency as tool of governance was, therefore, "directly linked to the marketization of genetic resources on the one side and to concerns over biopiracy on the other" (Orsini et al. 2014, 163). This accounts for the "decentralized, contract-based marketization approach" upon which this governance system is based (Orsini et al. 2014, 166). With the requirement of mutually agreed terms as a precondition for the granting of prior informed consent, access agreements become dense contractual arrangements containing detailed terms and conditions that are imposed upon both provider and user (Pisupati 2007). This pre-existing *social consensus* regarding the commercialization of genetic resources both structured the Protocol and was, in turn, refined by it. But this social consensus may have unfortunate implications.

The liberal market logic of the system could be regarded as a major achievement in international biodiversity policy-making and, more broadly, in global environmental governance. Optimistically, its implementation may lead to collaboration and partnerships in research that could provide for fruitful multi-party dialogue, because most access activities are undertaken by researchers (often with non-commercial intent) and because their activities will primarily focus on the research and development part of the innovation chain. A collaborative approach to implementation could further be facilitated by a major emphasis on the exchange of best practices in the prior informed consent process between parties and stakeholders – eventually resulting in the development of research and industry standards on access and benefit sharing (Buck and Hamilton 2011). But there is a long-existing imbalance between transparency for access and transparency for benefit sharing. The Protocol enhances transparency of access conditions, but it does nothing to redress the comparative disadvantage with respect to access and benefit sharing (Orsini et al. 2014).

Access and benefit sharing negotiations at the CBD's 2010 biennial Conference of the Parties (COP 10), and experience with the issue since then, demonstrate the challenges and complexities of the pursuit of justice for ILCs. The lack of progress in this area demonstrates the limited nature, scope, and engagement in the justice discourse at Nagoya and suggests the existence of a justice meta-norm that is indifferent (or even hostile) to the pursuit of ILC justice. Not only was ILC justice pursued primarily by a handful of actors in a small subset of events, but their engagement centered on deliberating how to deliver a pre-established notion of justice rather than tackling the questions of what and whose justice is demanded. Although plural and multivalent understandings of justice were represented at COP 10, there was a convergence in the access and benefit sharing negotiations towards a pre-existing set of justice practices underpinned by market-liberal justice norms and ideas (Suiseeya 2014). This absence of contestation over meaning is troubling because achieving ILC justice ultimately demands shifts in the normative fabric and orientation of global environmental governance – shifts that are only possible through debates over the substance of justice, which the social consensus underlying the Nagoya Protocol appears to inhibit.

A way forward

> We must indeed all hang together, or, most assuredly, we shall all hang separately.
>
> Benjamin Franklin

Having examined the implications of transparency policies for five core problems of earth system governance, what conclusions are warranted? The most obvious, perhaps, is that the concept of consensus must be understood in a more complex and contingent way than it often is (Baber and Bartlett 2015). In the context of environmental governance, consensus is that level of agreement among all parties to the decision process that allows them to "hang together" as they move from one stage of that process to the next. Consensus in governance cannot, and never could, be usefully thought of as simple unanimity. The major elements of consensus – the normative, the political, and the social – all relate to different kinds of agreement, each with its own regulative standard. These elements vary in relative importance as participants in a shared decision process move between the poles of general and abstract discourse and the specific and concrete actions of everyday life. So consensus does not need to have a reach that is either wide or deep to merit our approbation as a source of democratic legitimacy.

A second conclusion is that the character of each distinct analytical problem of governance places its own demands and limitations on the transparency consensus. For instance, a prior informed consent approach can provide satisfactory *architectural* solutions for governance-by-disclosure (it can be stable, useful, and consensual) while failing to resolve (or even exacerbating) problems of *access* and *allocation*. Third, and finally, transparency policies can provide an institutional and procedural context for environmental *agency* that is widely supported in spite of the fact that it does little to advance environmental governance outcomes that actually improve the environment or governance in any substantial way.

To have, at this stage, produced a patchwork quilt of observations might seem to be a disappointing result. But that is only a problem if one insists that our accounts of governance phenomena have the character of nomothetical explanations grounded in general theory. A more appropriate set of expectations results if we accept the fact that governance (especially at the global level) can most appropriately be represented by models that both describe and explain. Commonly referred to by philosophers of science as pattern explanations (Kaplan 1964), these models explain both a theme and a relationship simultaneously by specifying their place in an empirical pattern. If further explanation of other phases or aspects of the same theme is desired, one traces out more relations between the theme and other things (Diesing 1971, 157–160). Having recognized that having a better understanding of earth system governance requires pattern explanation of this sort, the scattering of insights produced by looking at the relationship between the core analytical problems of polarization, governance, and a collection of variations on the theme of transparency should be far more satisfying. Like pieces in a complex puzzle, they represent touch points for further development of the explanatory pattern. The shapes that they have begun to reveal may as yet be impossible to fully specify. But their colors are sufficiently rich and harmonious to suggest that additional work on the puzzle is likely to be highly rewarding.

References

Auld, Graeme and Lars Gulbrandsen (2014). "Learning through Disclosure: The Evolving Importance of Transparency in the Practice of Nonstate Certification." In Aarti Gupta and Michael Mason (eds.) *Transparency in Global Environmental Governance: Critical Perspectives*. Cambridge, MA: MIT Press, pp. 271–296.

Baber, Walter and Robert Bartlett (2005). *Deliberative Environmental Politics: Democracy and Ecological Rationality*. Cambridge, MA: MIT Press.

Baber, Walter and Robert Bartlett (2009). *Global Democracy and Sustainable Jurisprudence Deliberative Environmental Law*. Cambridge, MA: MIT Press.

Baber, Walter and Robert Bartlett (2015). *Consensus and Global Environmental Governance: Deliberative Democracy in Nature's Regime*. Cambridge, MA: MIT Press.

Bartlett, Robert V. (1990). "Comprehensive Environmental Decision Making: Can It Work?" In Norman J. Vig and Michael E. Kraft (eds.) *Environmental Policy in the 1990s: Toward a New Agenda.* Washington, DC: CQ Press, pp. 235–254.

Beierle, Thomas (2004). "The Benefits and Costs of Disclosing Information about Risks: What Do We Know About Right to Know?" *Risk Analysis* 24 (2): 335–346.

Biermann, Frank and Aarti Gupta (2011). "Accountability and Legitimacy in Earth System Governance: A Research Framework." *Ecological Economics* 70 (11): 1856–1864.

Biermann, Frank and Philipp Pattberg (2012). "Global Environmental Governance Revisited." In Frank Biermann and Philipp Pattberg (eds.) *Global Environmental Governance Reconsidered.* Cambridge, MA: MIT Press, pp. 1–24.

Bled, Amandine (2010). "Technological Choices in International Environmental Negotiations: An Actor–Network Analysis." *Business and Society* 49 (4): 570–590.

Buck, Matthias and Clare Hamilton (2011). "The Nagoya Protocol on Access to Genetic Resources and the Fair and Equitable Sharing of Benefits Arising from their Utilization to the Convention on Biological Diversity." *Review of European Community and International Environmental Law* 20 (1): 47–61.

Bührs, Ton (2009). *Environmental Integration: Our Common Challenge.* Albany, NY: State University of New York Press.

Diesing, Paul (1971). *Patterns of Discovery in the Social Sciences.* New York: Aldine.

Dingwerth, Klaus and Margot Eichinger (2010). "Tamed Transparency: How Information Disclosure under the Global Reporting Initiative Fails to Empower." *Global Environmental Politics* 10 (3): 74–96.

Dingwerth, Klaus and Margot Eichinger (2014). "Tamed Transparency and the Global Reporting Initiative." In Aarti Gupta and Michael Mason (eds.) *Transparency in Global Environmental Governance: Critical Perspectives.* Cambridge, MA: MIT Press, pp. 225–247.

Domingo, José. L. and Jordi Giné Bordonaba (2011). "A Literature Review on the Safety Assessment of Genetically Modified Plants." *Environment International* 37 (4): 734–742.

ESGP (Earth System Governance Project) (2009). *Earth System Governance: People, Places, and the Planet.* International Human Dimensions Programme on Global Environmental Change, IHDP Report No. 20. Bonn: The Earth System Governance Project.

Falck Zepeda, José (2006). "Coexistence, Genetically Modified Biotechnologies and Biosafety: Implications for Developing Countries." *American Journal of Agricultural Economics* 88 (5): 1200–1208.

Florini, Ann (2007). *The Right to Know: Transparency for an Open World.* New York: Columbia University Press.

Florini, Ann and Bharath Jairaj (2014). "The National Context for Transparency-Based Global Environmental Governance." In Aarti Gupta and Michael Mason (eds.) *Transparency in Global Environmental Governance: Critical Perspectives.* Cambridge, MA: MIT Press, pp. 61–80.

Fowler, Penny and Simon Heap (2000). "Varieties of Participation in Complex Governance." *Public Administration Review* 66 (1): 66–75.

Fung, Archon, Mary Graham, and David Weil (2007). *Full Disclosure: The Perils and Promise of Transparency.* New York: Cambridge University Press.

Gulbrandsen, Lars (2006). "Creating Markets for Eco-Labelling: Are Consumers Insignificant?" *International Journal of Consumer Studies* 30 (5): 477–489.

Gupta, Aarti (2000). "Governing Trade in Genetically Modified Organisms: The Cartagena Protocol on Biosafety." *Environment* 42 (4): 23–33.

Gupta, Aarti (2004). "When Global is Local: Negotiating Safe Use of Biotechnology." In Shelia Jasanoff and Marybeth Long-Martello (eds.) *Earthly Politics: Local and Global in Environmental Governance*. Cambridge, MA: MIT Press, pp. 127–148.

Gupta, Aarti (2010). "Transparency to What End? Governing by Disclosure through the Biosafety Clearing-House." *Environment and Planning C: Government and Policy* 28 (2): 128–144.

Gupta, Aarti (2014). "Risk Governance through Transparency: Information Disclosure and the Global Trade in Transgenic Crops." In Aarti Gupta and Michael Mason (eds.) *Transparency in Global Environmental Governance: Critical Perspectives*. Cambridge, MA: MIT Press, pp. 133–156.

Gupta, Aarti and Michael Mason (2014). "A Transparency Turn in Global Environmental Governance." In Aarti Gupta and Michael Mason (eds.) *Transparency in Global Environmental Governance: Critical Perspectives*. Cambridge, MA: MIT Press, pp. 3–38.

Habermas, Jurgen (1996). *Between Facts and Norms: Contributions to a Discourse Theory of Law and Democracy*. Cambridge, MA: MIT Press.

Hayward, Tim (2005). *Constitutional Environmental Rights*. Oxford: Oxford University Press.

Herzig, Christian (2006). "Corporate Sustainability Reporting: An Overview." *Sustainability and Accounting* 21: 301–324.

James, Clive (2012). *Global Status of Commercialized Biotech/GM Crops 2012*. ISAAA Brief 44. Ithaca, NY: ISAAA (International Service for the Acquisition of Agri-biotech Applications).

Jansen, Kees (2008). "The Unspeakable Ban: The Translation of Global Pesticide Governance into Honduran National Regulation." *World Development* 36 (4): 575–589.

Jansen, Kees and Milou Dubois (2014). "Global Pesticide Governance by Disclosure: Prior Informed Consent and the Rotterdam Convention." In Aarti Gupta and Michael Mason (eds.) *Transparency in Global Environmental Governance: Critical Perspectives*. Cambridge, MA: MIT Press, pp. 107–131.

Kaplan, Abraham (1964). *The Conduct of Inquiry*. San Francisco, CA: Chandler.

Keohane, Robert (2006). "Accountability in World Politics." *Scandinavian Political Studies* 29 (2): 75–87.

Key, S., J. Ma, and P. Drake (2008). "Genetically Modified Plants and Human Health." *Journal of the Royal Society of Medicine* 101 (6): 290–298.

Kirton, John J. and Michael J. Trebilcock (2004). *Hard Choices, Soft Law: Voluntary Standards in Global Trade, Environment and Social Governance*. Burlington, VT: Ashgate.

Kraft, Michael E., Mark Stephan, and Troy D. Abel (2011). *Coming Clean: Information Disclosure and Environmental Performance*. Cambridge, MA: MIT Press.

Krasner, Stephen (1983). *International Regimes*. Ithaca, NY: Cornell University Press.

Lasswell, Harold (1950). *Politics: Who Gets What, When, How*. New York: Peter Smith.

Mason, Michael (2014). "So Far but No Further? Transparency and Disclosure in the Aahus Convention." In Aarti Gupta and Michael Mason (eds.) *Transparency in Global Environmental Governance: Critical Perspectives*. Cambridge, MA: MIT Press, pp. 83–106.

Miller, Michael (2006). "Biodiversity Policy Making in Costa Rica: Pursuing Indigenous and Peasant Rights." *Journal of Environment and Development* 15 (4): 359–381.

Mitchell, Ronald (2011). "Transparency for Governance: The Mechanisms and Effectiveness of Disclosure-based and Education-based Transparency Policies." *Ecological Economics* 70 (11): 132–143.

Mol, Arthur (2014). "The Lost Innocence of Transparency in Environmental Politics." In Aarti Gupta and Michael Mason (eds.) *Transparency in Global Environmental Governance: Critical Perspectives*. Cambridge, MA: MIT Press, pp. 39–59.

Oberthür, Sebastian and Justyna Pozarowska (2013). "Managing Institutional Complexity and Fragmentation: The Nagoya Protocol and the Global Governance of Genetic Resources." *Global Environmental Politics* 13 (3): 100–118.

Orsini, Amandine, Sebastian Oberthur, and Justyna Pozarowska (2014). "Transparency in the Governance of Access and Benefit Sharing from Genetic Resources." In Aarti Gupta and Michael Mason (eds.) *Transparency in Global Environmental Governance: Critical Perspectives*. Cambridge, MA: MIT Press, pp. 157–180.

Orts, Eric (1995). "A Reflexive Model of Environmental Regulation." *Business Ethics Quarterly* 5 (4): 779–794.

Orwin, Alexander (2014). "Can Humankind Deliberate on a Global Scale? Alfarabi and the Politics of the Inhabited World." *American Political Science Review* 108 (4): 830–839.

Pisupati, Balakrishna (2007). *UNU-IAS Pocket Guide – Access to Genetic Resources, Benefit Sharing and Bioprospecting*. Yokohama: United Nations University Institute of Advance Studies.

Snell, Chelsea, Aude Bernheim, Jean-Baptiste Bergé, Marcel Kuntz, Gérard Pascal, Alain Paris, and Agnès E. Ricroch (2012). "Assessment of the Health Impact of GM Plant Diets in Long-term and Multigenerational Animal Feeding: A Literature Review." *Food and Chemical Toxicology* 50 (3–4): 1134–1148.

Stokke, Olav (2012). *Disaggregating International Regimes: A New Approach to Evaluation and Comparison*. Cambridge, MA: MIT Press.

Suiseeya, Kimberly R. Marion (2014). "Negotiating the Nagoya Protocol: Indigenous Demands for Justice." *Global Environmental Politics* 14 (3): 102–124.

Tyfield, David (2012). "A Cultural and Political Economy of Research and Innovation in an Age of Crisis." *Miberva* 50 (2): 149–167.

Welford, Richard and Richard Starkey (2001). *The Earthscan Reader in Business and Sustainable Development*. London: Routledge.

Willis, Alan (2003). "The Role of the Global Reporting Initiative's Sustainability Reporting Guidelines in the Social Engineering of Investments." *Journal of Business Ethics* 43 (3): 233–237.

Young, Oran (1989). *International Cooperation: Building Regimes for Natural Resources and the Environment*. Ithaca, NY: Cornell University Press.

Young, Oran (1998). *Creating Regimes: Arctic Accords and International Governance*. Ithaca, NY: Cornell University Press.

5 Polarized climate debate?

Institutions and structure in subnational policymaking

Russell Williams and Susan Morrissey Wyse

> Effective mitigation will not be achieved if individual agents advance their own interests independently. Climate change has the characteristics of a collective action problem ... cooperation is therefore required to effectively mitigate GHG emissions.
>
> International Panel on Climate Change

> For the implementation of Kyoto, we need the collaboration of the provinces. We don't have the jurisdiction to do it.
>
> Jean Chretien (Former Prime Minister of Canada)

> We have no intentions of waiting for the authorization or the permission from anyone in order to act on reducing greenhouse gases.... Québec has set objectives in order to abide by Kyoto and we expect the federal government to do its part.
>
> Jean Charest (Former Premier of Québec)

Introduction: the road to Paris

Under the auspices of the United Nations Climate Change Conference (COP 21), held in Paris in the late fall of 2015, states were directed to table their own *Intended Nationally Determined Contribution* (INDC) for greenhouse gas (GHG) reduction targets. The goal was to achieve the deep cuts in carbon emissions scientists say are needed by 2030 if global temperature increases are to be kept to only 2 degrees Celsius. The goals of the Paris Summit were understandably ambitious, but they reflect two decades of global consensus building on both what needs to be done and the political process by which carbon emissions should be managed.

For Canada's Conservative government, in office in the lead up to the Paris Summit, the timing was problematic. Following the country's provocative withdrawal from the commitments made under the Kyoto Protocol, and a confusing welter of Canadian government proposals for "made in Canada" solutions to climate change (including an ambiguous commitment to meet whatever "standards the United States ultimately agrees to in international negotiations"), the Paris Summit forced the government to table some sort of national target, prior to the fall 2015 election. Given the Conservative's position on climate change, insiders argued that the government would like to "punt" and avoid any further serious engagement for the time being. Since a Canadian INDC effectively requires a deal with the provinces on just how Canada should "put a price on carbon" and a complex set of intergovernmental negotiations given the growing divergence of provincial policy on climate change – the subject of this chapter – Canada's announced INDC was unsurprising. The government simply announced that they would seek to reduce Canadian emissions to 30 percent below 2005 levels by 2030 (the "30/30" target). In the absence of a serious implementation strategy, the credibility of this commitment was problematic, but more to the point, it reflects a significantly "lighter" proposal than that tabled by either the EU or the US. The *World Resource Initiative* estimated that Canada's INDC commitment effectively watered down the earlier Copenhagen Accord commitments (that Canada was already failing to meet) and crucially amounted to little more than half the level of carbon emission reductions offered by the US: "Canada's level of mitigation would put it – the world's ninth largest emitter – noticeably behind its peers in terms of how fast it aims to decarbonize in the post-2020 period" (Damassa and Fransen 2015). On top of this, other national delegations were quick to question the credibility of Canada's commitment to that target given past experience.

For students of Canadian climate change policy, well aware of the polarization of policy debate on the issue, none of this was very surprising. The fact is that federalism has emerged as a major challenge to Canada's participation in UN climate change initiatives, and it provides institutional opportunities for partisan polarization over the issue. As this chapter will illustrate, provincial climate change policies and the attitudes behind them seem irreconcilable and, as such, an *effective* national strategy seems unlikely. Climate change policy, much like other key international policy domains (trade, finance and immigration policy), all theoretically the preserve of federal authorities, are increasingly "provincial" – effectively, this case illustrates deep changes in the nature of Canadian federalism broadly, but also the emergence of a new and necessarily "confederal" style of foreign policy on economic affairs. This dynamic is compounded in the climate policy sector by the huge differences in the structure of each province's economy – Canada includes some provincial "petro-states" and some provinces that had have emissions and policy regimes comparable to EU members. At Paris, representatives of Canada's federal government were in an awkward position, superficially responsible for Canada's international commitments, while everyone knew real action would need to be generated in the increasingly autonomous provincial capitals – essentially, there were some important empty chairs in Paris.

While it is almost too common in the study of Canadian politics to suggest federalism is in "flux," or in "transition," or to offer some new typology of federal–provincial relations (Bickerton 2010), the fact remains that globalization, the expansion of multilevel governance, increasingly intrusive trade agreements etc., all challenge the traditional logic and assumptions of the Canadian Division of Powers which allocate responsibilities between the different levels of government. As Janice Stein (2006, 47–50) argues, this is a reality we have to adapt to or we run the risk of failing to come to terms with key policy challenges. At the same time, while there has been an understandably growing interest in the role of the provinces in Canadian foreign policy generally (Dyment 2006; Kukucha 2008), much of the literature focuses only on the increased engagement of the provinces in policy fields still dominated by federal officials (e.g., international trade). Provinces are usually characterized as "participants" in internal deliberations over policies directly affecting their jurisdiction, rather than important drivers of foreign policy.

This chapter explores the case of Canadian climate change policy in order to illustrate what Stein would call the "reality" of the policy challenge facing Canadian governments. In the absence of an early intervention by the federal government in the Kyoto implementation process to impose either a "carbon tax" or a national "cap and trade" system, provinces have effectively become the prime movers of climate policy. Coupled with the fact that the provinces are moving in very different directions in regard to climate change, the reality is that no matter what federal leaders say about the issue the important action is at the provincial level – despite the fact that those provinces have no control over the nature of national GHG reduction commitments. In its most simple terms, no matter what Canadians think about climate change, there is a deep-seated opposition to a federally imposed "national" solution. Even provincial governments that want to meet international standards have fought against a national strategy, in defense of provincial autonomy. When it comes to climate policy, discourses of federalism and the rights of provinces are more important.

Federalism and climate change

Although climate change is frequently viewed in the framework of global politics, it is increasingly recognized that local and regional governments have a major role to play in developing strategies (Gore 2010). Indeed, many see climate change mitigation as a particularly "vexing" problem for federations where global collective action challenges are reproduced within the state and underlying structures in political economy and broad attitudinal differences make it more difficult to impose the costs necessary to tackle GHG emissions (Brown 2012). In Canada, where provinces have jurisdiction over their natural resources and there is a long history of regional antipathy to federal intervention in the distribution of economic benefits, it not only seems necessary for provinces to be heavily involved in any national climate mitigation strategy, but increasingly it is seen as a *constitutional* requirement. Many argue that the federal government lacks the power to unilaterally "put a price on carbon" in the manner required to achieve real reductions in Canada's emissions.[1] However, because climate change is a global policy problem, provinces and other subnational governments are not often considered to be important independent actors in climate policy debates (Rabe 2007, 424). Considering the lack of climate policies that have been put forward in Canada at the national level, it is important to assess provincial action in order to understand the benefits and limitations of subnational climate policies in the Canadian context (Williams 2013).

While the federal government has been reluctant to implement meaningful climate mitigation policies, the provinces have been experimenting with a wide range of strategies for reducing emissions even though reductions have not been mandated at the federal level and provinces are not legally bound to international obligations. Several Canadian provinces have experimented with carbon taxes, cap and trade systems and other market-based regulations. A closer examination of these policies and their political impacts is essential to understand the difficulties surrounding the Paris Summit and the broad trajectory of Canadian foreign policy on climate change. Provincial action is generally designed with particular regional interests in mind, and federalism has been seen as a major obstacle for a national climate strategy.

Generally, analysis of subnational politics over climate change have fallen into two camps. On the one hand, some argue that the preoccupation with international agreements has overlooked the progress made by subnational governments (Rabe 2007). In fact, subnational governments in North America have undertaken considerably more GHG reduction strategies than their national counterparts. Several Canadian provinces and US states have introduced carbon taxes or cap and trade systems. On the other hand, there is also a great deal of skepticism that subnational governments will take on the costs of *effective* climate policies when the benefits are likely to be highly diffused (Harrison 2013, 96). While subnational governments have acted on climate change, their actions are woefully inadequate in terms or real GHG reductions. Furthermore, if there is little incentive for subnational governments to act, why would these governments take on such politically risky policy innovations, particularly when intra-state "race-to-the-bottom" dynamics are likely worse than at the global level?

Across Canada, each provincial government has developed its own unique climate strategy, which tailors a plan consistent with local interests and contexts. According to Rabe (2007), subnational actors are the most capable of reducing emissions because they often have jurisdiction over resources (the oil and gas sector is Canada's largest single emitter of GHGs) and therefore have a greater institutional capacity to act. Thus far, the international regime has seemed ineffective in cutting global emissions, despite the common expectation that climate change will be best addressed at the international level. Rabe points out that a country's willingness to sign international climate agreements – the Kyoto Protocol, for example – has not actually resulted in a greater willingness or ability to enact national GHG reduction strategies (Rabe 2007, 423–424) as implementation of international targets has proven far more politically difficult. In the Canadian case, Rabe's argument reflects the reality that provinces retain control over their resources and the federal government's authority *appears* to be limited (Rabe 2007, 432).

Although the difficulties surrounding the implementation of the Kyoto Protocol illustrate the challenge of reaching a national consensus on climate change policy, as well as the importance of provincial involvement, other scholars argue that without guidance from the federal government, provinces will be unable to effectively reduce Canada's GHG emissions. Harrison, for example, expresses a "guarded enthusiasm" concerning the "scope and impact" of provincial and state action in North America (2013, 96). While Harrison acknowledges that subnational governments have experimented with climate policies more than their national counterparts, she also points to some significant limits of subnational action. For example, she argues that state and provincial action most often emerges where there are perceived benefits for the local environment or economy. In addition, these states and provinces are often the lowest emitting jurisdictions anyway, meaning the real world GHG reductions are quite limited. By contrast, the highest emitting jurisdictions not only avoid such policies, but instead use federalism and intergovernmental relations as an opportunity to obstruct the actions of other subnational jurisdictions as well as effective policies at the national level (Harrison 2013, 96). Indeed, federalism is often deployed in symbolic terms – a federal intrusion into what is claimed as a provincial matter is seen as more problematic then global warming itself.

The challenge in Canada is that the underlying political economy of carbon emissions exacerbates interprovincial conflicts over who should pay the costs of mitigation. Emissions vary widely from one province to the next – in large part based on the presence of a large oil and gas sector (see Table 5.1).

Harrison's main argument is that a disproportionally high share of Canada's emissions come from "oil and gas" provinces like Alberta and Saskatchewan, and this is "a challenge unlikely to be overcome by other provinces in the absence of federal leadership" (Harrison 2013, 107). A detailed examination of Harrison's concerns across the provinces tends to illustrate this because even with bold

Table 5.1 Provincial and territorial GHG and per capita emissions: 2005–2010

	GHG emissions (Mt CO_2e)		Per capita emissions (t/capita)	
	2005	2010	2005	2010
British Columbia	63	56	15.0	12.4
Alberta	232	236	69.8	63.4
Saskatchewan	71	73	71.1	69.8
Manitoba	21	20	17.9	16.3
Ontario	206	172	16.4	13.0
Québec	86	82	11.4	10.4
New Brunswick	22	18	29.8	24.5
Nova Scotia	24	20	25.3	21.7
Newfoundland	10	9	19.8	16.9
Prince Edward Island	2	2	16.2	13.8
Territories	2	2	21.9	18.8
Canada	740	692	22.9	20.3

Source: Environment Canada, "Canada's Emission Trends 2012," August 2012, Table 16: www.ec. gc.ca/Publications/253AE6E6-5E73-4AFC-81B7-9CF440D5D2C5%5C793-Canada's-Emissions-Trends-2012_e_01.pdf.

emission reduction plans from several provinces, Canada's overall emission reductions are nowhere near international commitments (Environment and Climate Change Canada 2014, ii). Alberta emits almost the same amount of GHGs as Canada's two largest provinces, Ontario and Québec, *combined* (Flanagan 2015, 4). If meaningful policies are not taken on by the highest emitting provinces, Canada's emission reductions will continue to be limited and regardless of who is in office in Ottawa, international climate summits will be uncomfortable.

It is important to recognize, however, that outside of this structural reality, Canadians want something done about climate change. Indeed, survey data from the Angus Reid Institute suggests a relatively uniform level of support for "putting a price on carbon" in Canada (see Table 5.2). When Canadians are asked about the desirability of taxing or imposing a cap and trade system on carbon emissions, they tend to overwhelmingly support these initiatives, regardless of what province they live in and the extent to which that province's economy is dependent on carbon emissions. The puzzle, of course, is why this does not translate into an effective national strategy.

The literature on Canadian climate change policy leaves us in an uncertain place. Federalism, in combination with the regional nature of the economy, seems to be a significant disincentive to the development of effective climate policies. However, there is innovation occurring at the provincial level and broad public support. Rabe is not wrong when he argues that subnational governments can have more institutional capacity for climate policy, but without international and/or national pressure on provinces the largest emitting regions are not using their capacity to actually effect change.

Putting a price on carbon – no, really ...

What can we say about the polarization of provincial climate change policies, subnational politics and the difficulty of managing Canada's involvement in global negotiations? Over the last decade, provincial policies and their impact have diverged, and this is having a "feedback" effect on the likelihood of future action on climate change.

Table 5.2 Public support for national cap and trade system to combat climate change (%)

	Support	Oppose
Canada	75	25
British Columbia	78	22
Alberta	71	29
Manitoba and Saskatchewan	77	23
Ontario	70	30
Québec	81	19
Alberta	81	19

Source: Angus Reid Institute, "Most Canadians Support Carbon Pricing; but Less Consensus on Effectiveness of Such Measures," May 2015: http://angusreid.org/carbon-pricing/.

Québec – an early, if incomplete innovator

Québec currently represents the only Canadian province to have both a carbon tax and cap and trade system. The province has made the deepest voluntary GHG emissions reduction – 20 percent below its 1990 levels by 2020 (Government of Québec 2012, 1). Quebec also has the lowest per capita emissions in Canada at 10.4t (Environment Canada 2012, 32). Québec has been perceived as a leader in provincial climate policies. However, as Harrison argues, "subnational climate leaders tend already to be the cleanest states and provinces, and even they have been strategic in the sectors they regulate and the instruments they employ" (Harrison 2013, 95). Québec's activities on climate change tend to illustrate these dynamics.

In 1995, Québec became the first Canadian province to put forward a *Climate Change Action Plan*. At the time, Québec already had among the lowest per capita emissions in Canada, largely due to hydroelectricity (Séguin 2009). For this reason, the government argued that Québec would only need to introduce voluntary instruments to tackle climate change, rather than more coercive market-based instruments – such as carbon taxes – which might hurt Québec's competitiveness (Houle 2011, 10). Québec was concerned with the potential impact any federal initiatives would have on the province's industries and, importantly, on provincial autonomy.

During the failed intergovernmental negotiations on how to implement the Kyoto Protocol, Québec was ironically both a firm supporter of the Protocol, but simultaneously opposed to federal proposals for a national strategy. The provincial government was concerned that the federal government, which favored a sector-by-sector approach within its national climate policies (treating industries differently), would put the interests of Canada's western oil and gas sector over those of Québec, such as the province's pulp and paper industry. Québec favored a provincial approach in which the other provinces would essentially have to play "catch up." Ultimately, during the Joint Meeting of Ministers (JMM) of Environment and Energy in 2002, Québec walked away from talks because other regions (as well as the federal government) preferred the sector-based approach (Macdonald 2013, 52). Québec had also expressed frustration that provinces were unable to develop their own separate GHG reduction targets – a symbol of lost provincial autonomy (Stilborn 2003, 7). For Québec, concern for provincial industries and autonomy were enough for the province to withdraw from the Kyoto implementation negotiations entirely (Pembina Institute 2000, 5).

The inability to reach consensus between provinces on a strategy for GHG emissions reductions left Canada collectively incapable of meeting its targets under Kyoto. However, when Canada walked away from its Kyoto obligations in 2011, Québec's provincial Liberal Party expressed considerable frustration and claimed that the environment was a "national identity issue" in Québec; the provincial government announced that it would unilaterally remain committed to Kyoto's GHG reduction targets (Handal 2012, para. 2). Indeed, the province has forged ahead with the development of a cap and trade system. Then premier Jean

Charest, his environment minister, Pierre Arcand and the opposition Parti Québecois (PQ) all attacked the federal government for withdrawing from Kyoto (Lalonde, 2011). Scott McKay, the PQ shadow minister for the environment, claimed that "the gap is widening between Québec and the rest of Canada on climate related issues" (Handal 2012, para. 1), and the party argued that Québec's environmentalism was connected to the province's unique identity within Canada. This cross-party support for strong environmental leadership has led to competition between parties as they attempt to "out-green" each other; election promises have included commitments to deepen Québec's GHG reduction targets further than Kyoto targets (from 20 percent to 25 percent below 1990 levels by 2020).

Consensus has reached further than national identity issues in Québec, as each party has also consistently advocated market-based instruments as an economic opportunity, where the province could benefit by linking directly with international cap and trade initiatives. Considering Québec's concerns with federal intrusion, as well as the political incentives to pursue alternative climate strategies, the Western Climate Initiative (WCI) ultimately provided a valuable framework for approaching a climate policy on its own terms. The WCI is a voluntary subnational intergovernmental organization whose central aim is to create a decentralized North American cap and trade system. At its peak, 11 partners had committed to the system: Arizona, California, Montana, Utah, New Mexico, Washington, Oregon, British Columbia, Manitoba, Ontario and Québec; a further 16 states held "observer status." However, by 2012 it appeared that the WCI would be reduced to one province and one state: Québec and California. While British Columbia, Manitoba and Ontario have remained members of the WCI, plans for developing a cap and trade system have stalled in all provinces with the exception of Ontario, which has recently committed to moving forward with the system. As Klinsky (2013, 150) notes, some members saw the WCI as a stopgap means of achieving a much larger, national climate change policy. However, as momentum at the national level has waned, support for the WCI also declined. For Québec, the WCI provided an important symbolic opportunity to stake a claim over its own climate policies and protect its individual interests in the light of what seemed like inevitable federal climate change regulation (Klinsky 2013, 150).

Under the auspices of the WCI, Québec became the first Canadian province to introduce both a carbon tax and a cap and trade system. The carbon tax, implemented in 2007, is an annual levy set at $4 per ton of CO_2. At such a low rate, Québec's carbon tax is not primarily designed to deter fossil fuel consumption. Rather, tax revenues (roughly $200 million per year) are intended to contribute to the provincial Green Fund. The tax also only applies to approximately 50 large industrial emitters. Fund revenues contribute to the 26 priorities in the *2013–2020 Climate Change Action Plan*, which include public transport, improved land-use planning, sustainable mobility and fuel efficiency.[2] It is notable that Québec's transportation sector currently accounts for the largest share of GHG emissions (43.5 percent), and emissions are growing (Government of Québec 2012, 22). The carbon tax would have to be significantly higher to impact consumers' transportation practices (Bernard and Duclos 2009, 7).

Québec's cap and trade system first came on-stream on January 1st, 2013 as part of the WCI. Within Québec's first compliance period (between 2013 and 2014), any "persons or municipalities" operating a facility whose annual GHGs were greater than or equal to 25 kilotons of CO_2 (or equivalent) were subject to the system; this applied to about 80 facilities from the industrial and power generation sectors. The second compliance period, which began on January 1st, 2015, brought all fossil fuels into the system, meaning that it now covers 85 percent of GHGs in Québec (Government of Québec 2013a, 1). All emitters in Québec must register with the Compliance Instrument Tracking System Service (CITSS), which is a market tracking system that was created to support the WCI's cap and trade system. While emitters now require emission allowances for each ton of CO_2 released into the atmosphere, most allowances will be provided free by the government; once an emitter exceeds its particular industry's emissions cap, additional units will need to be purchased. The minimum price for an emission unit in 2013 was $10.75, and it is scheduled to increase at a rate of 5 percent plus inflation every year until 2020 (Government of Québec 2013b, 2). In addition, in order to encourage continuing improvements in efficiency and innovation, annual caps on "free" emission units dropped between 1–2 percent each year, starting in 2015.

Due to the flexibility of the WCI system, some critics argue that jurisdictions will be able to weaken the effectiveness of the system. According to the David Suzuki Foundation's extensive analysis of Canadian climate policy, flexibility mechanisms such as offsets and early reduction credits reduce the integrity of the system by reducing the certainty that emission reductions are the same on paper as they are in reality (Marshal et al. 2011, 2). The Foundation recommends these be phased out over time. Another potential limitation of Québec's system is that the free permit allocation is based on the intensity of that particular sector's emissions, rather than an absolute cap on the quantity of emissions (Marshall et al. 2011, 4). With an intensity-based approach, industries that have significantly increased production, therefore contributing to an increase in overall GHG emissions, can continue to receive free permits from the government.

Despite the lack of a serious federal GHG mitigation strategy prior to the Paris Summit, Québec has introduced innovative environmental policies designed to achieve internal GHG reduction targets. The motives for Québec's policies are rooted in concern for the province's industries and political autonomy. In addition, unlike other Canadian provinces, a strong consensus exists among Québec's provincial parties: these initiatives are uncontroversial – so much so that the issue has been connected to the province's national identity. Nonetheless, consistent with Harrison's concerns, Québec's economic interests have greatly influenced policy. Quebec's emissions, already low, have been reduced by targeting a limited array of industries with a fairly "light touch" to date – for example, little has been done to address its politically more problematic transportation related emissions.

British Columbia: the "best case" scenario for GHG policy in Canada

Over the past decade, British Columbia has transformed into the provincial leader in Canadian climate policies. Boasting the highest carbon tax in the country (at $30 per carbon tonne), British Columbia has reduced its GHG emissions after more than a decade of emission increases (Environment and Climate Change Canada, 2014). Prior to 2007, Gordon Campbell's Liberal government in British Columbia showed little interest in taking climate change seriously. However, the 2007 Throne Speech declared that British Columbia would voluntarily aim to reduce its GHGs by at least 33 percent below current levels by 2020, therefore placing British Columbia's GHGs at 10 percent below 1990 levels by 2020.[3] In order to reach these targets, the province would be the first subnational jurisdiction in North America to implement a comprehensive carbon tax. The province also announced a carbon offset program which would require the public sector to become carbon neutral by 2010.

There are several key factors that contributed to the development of British Columbia's climate policies. During the federal–provincial negotiations on the implementation of Kyoto, the Liberal government had expressed grave concerns about the consequences of ratifying the Protocol, and Gordon Campbell is said to have spearheaded significant opposition (Macdonald 2001, 19). In an editorial letter in the *National Post* in 2002, he argued essentially that British Columbia had a good emissions profile (mainly due to hydroelectricity) and that a federal-led system would impose an unfair burden on a province that was not really the source of the problem – essentially action should be focused on provinces like Alberta and Saskatchewan. British Columbia's position was similar to that of Quebec – GHG emissions reductions were laudable, but the federal government should not impose a policy. However, Campbell's administration was also deeply at odds with the environmental movement on a range of issues – his government was not seen as "green" (Wright 2005). Indeed, the move from environmental laggard to environmental leader in just two years came as a shock to many. Andrew Weaver, a Green Party Member of the Legislative Assembly and University of Victoria climatologist who has worked on Intergovernmental Panel on Climate Change (IPCC) reports, claimed that "it came from nowhere," referring to the province's sudden push towards serious GHG mitigation strategies (Hunter 2008, para. 17). Campbell seems to have simply been a genuine convert to the urgency of climate policy. However, it is also notable that from 2006 to 2008, support for more serious action on climate was high in Canada, and in particular enjoyed a high level of support from British Columbia voters.

Importantly, because more aggressive climate action was coming from a "right-of-centre," pro-business party, there was limited opposition from the business community (Harrison 2013, 3). Debate did not polarize in the way it has in other jurisdictions. Also important was the decision to ensure that the carbon tax was revenue neutral (Harrison 2013, 11). Indeed, the deftness in the way the tax was designed, in combination with the extent to which the left-leaning New

Democratic Party's opposition was necessarily muted given their own environmental commitments, helped pave the way to a rapid consensus in support of the tax (Harrison 2012, 9).

The province's carbon tax is charged to the consumer at point of sale and applies to all emissions from burning fossil fuels within the province, which in 2012 accounted for 77 percent of British Columbia's total emissions. Non-energy agriculture uses such as landfills, fugitive emissions (which cannot be measured) and non-combustion industrial process emissions are not included in the carbon tax. In order to give consumers and businesses adequate time to adjust their carbon profiles, the tax was phased in over four years. It initially started at $10 per ton in 2008, and increased by $5 per year until reaching $30 per ton in 2012. Unlike Québec's carbon tax, which supports the provincial Green Fund, British Columbia's tax is revenue neutral, which means that every dollar must, by law, be returned to taxpayers through reductions in other taxes. "Revenue neutrality" was seen to be a key selling feature in generating support, an assurance that the carbon tax was not merely "a tax grab" by government (Harrison 2012, 6). Most tax cuts (62 percent) have come in the form of personal income taxes – reductions in income tax were designed to offset some of the burden for consumers negatively impacted by the carbon tax – with the rest coming in the form of corporate and small business tax rate reductions. Since its introduction, the carbon tax has not only met revenue neutrality, but has also been lower than the total of business and personal tax cuts and credits, making the carbon tax revenue negative (Barrett 2011).

The strategy for a "carbon neutral government," where public sector organizations within the province (including provincial ministries, public schools, universities, Crown Corporations and hospitals) are mandated to either reach carbon neutrality or purchase carbon offsets, was also important. Initially, carbon offsets were purchased through the government's newly established Pacific Carbon Trust (PCT) at a rate of $25 per tonne. The PCT was a crown corporation with a mandate to purchase quality British Columbia-based offsets, but concerns were expressed about the program by the British Columbia Auditor General. "Credible" offsets, according the provincial government, must be "measurable, permanent and additional to business-as-usual," but programs through the PCT were not always demonstrably additional to business-as-usual (meaning that the programs would have gone forward regardless of PCT funding). The Auditor General's report looked at two of the largest offset projects, *Darkwoods Forest Carbon Project* and Encana's *Under Balanced Drilling Project*, which accounted for 70 percent of the offsets in 2010. The report concluded that because both projects were not additional to business-as-usual their funding under the guise of carbon neutrality was a waste of taxpayer's money (Government of British Columbia 2013, 5).

While the carbon neutrality of the public sector remains a bit fuzzy, it has been seven years since British Columbia began to tax carbon in a serious fashion. The evidence suggests that the program is effective. A 2013 report by Sustainable Prosperity found that per capita fuel consumption had dropped by roughly 19 percent in comparison with the rest of Canada; and emissions dropped by 17.4 percent at the same time as they rose across Canada by 1.4 percent (Sustainable Prosperity 2012, 1). Overall, actual GHG emissions in the province have dropped by at least 10 percent since 2008 and, as the report points out, GHG reductions are trending in the same direction as European countries that implemented similar policies a decade earlier – British Columbia's carbon tax is currently higher than in most European countries (Sustainable Prosperity, 2012, 4). British Columbia's carbon tax has received praise from both Canadian and international sources. While there are critics, particularly in regard to the problem of cross border "leakage" as British Colombia may choose to buy more gas across the border in the US to avoid the tax, an OECD Environmental Paper (2012) claimed that the tax has been very effective and the Pembina Institute stated that "all available evidence indicates [the carbon tax] has been successful" (Pembina Institute 2013, 1).

British Columbia's move from environmental laggard to environmental leader on climate change policies is an important story of subnational climate policy development. Most studies seem to agree the province developed meaningful strategies that have effectively reduced its GHG emissions. With such progress at a time when emissions had been steadily increasing, the British Columbia case suggests that meaningful action can occur in provinces that are not already the lowest emitters – from a political economy perspective British Columbia is also dependent on a number of high emission industries. Where the British Columbia case is most important is in the context of subnational policy experimentation.

Alberta – an innovator ... of sorts

As Canada's largest emitter of GHGs, representing roughly 35 percent of overall emissions (David Suzuki Foundation 2012, 24), Alberta has expressed grave concerns over any national climate strategy. Of course, considering that the energy sector in Alberta is the single largest contributor to its provincial GDP, income, employment and government revenue (Meadows and Crossman 2010, 2), Alberta's opposition was predictable. Alberta was vocally skeptical of Canada's ratification of the Kyoto Protocol. Instead of agreeing with the Kyoto targets, which were seen as damaging to Alberta's economy, the government has consistently focused on developing its own "made in Alberta" approach.

In 2002 Alberta became the first Canadian province to pass climate change legislation and implement a market-based regulatory system. Indeed, even the right-of-centre Progressive Conservative government (which was spectacularly defeated by the left-of-centre New Democratic Party in 2015) had increasingly recognized that Alberta's interests would be better served if the province acted as an active negotiating partner instead of standing in isolated opposition to all policy development. Nonetheless, Alberta's innovations have been slow, ineffective and largely seek to insulate the oil and gas sector from paying for emissions.

During the intergovernmental discussions leading up to Kyoto, while federal environment minister, Sheila Copps, hoped for "a massive commitment beyond voluntary measures" to reduce emissions (Stilborn 2003, 3), then Alberta premier Ralph Klein called the Kyoto targets "the goofiest, most devastating thing" ever proposed by the federal government (Rabe 2007, 438). Once it was clear that the US would not be ratifying Kyoto, Alberta (along with several other Canadian provinces) expressed grave concerns that Canada's oil and gas sector would be at a considerable competitive disadvantage.

In May 2002, Alberta released a draft climate change plan in direct response to the potential ratification of the Kyoto Protocol. The draft plan warned that Canada would not be able to meet the Kyoto targets without a "... serious and detrimental impact on the national economy" (Government of Alberta 2002a, 8). Ironically mirroring Quebec's position, Alberta proposed that the provinces simply be left to determine their own policies as a "national plan." When the federal government pressed ahead and ratified the Kyoto targets, Alberta quickly released its first (and indeed the first of its kind in Canada) climate change action plan, *Albertans & Climate Change: Taking Action*. Most significant in the "made in Alberta" approach was the development of a market- based approach to carbon pricing – an Alberta-based offset trading system with intensity-based emissions limits and investments in carbon capture and storage research (Meadows and Crossman 2010, 22). Alberta argued that it had the most to lose from federal regulation, and decided that the most effective way to avoid such regulation was by acting first. The post-Kyoto perspective from Alberta has focused on convincing other provinces, as well as the federal government, not only of Kyoto's "failures" but also of Alberta's own success in climate policy (Stilborn 2002, 8).

Alberta's plan has eschewed meeting the Kyoto targets (6 percent below 1990 levels by 2012) and instead focused on reducing "emission intensity" (i.e., emissions per unit of production) arguing that this would be the only effective way of tackling GHG emissions "without jeopardizing economic growth" (Government of Alberta 2002b, 11). The problem with this approach is that while energy use may become more efficient (intensity-based emissions decrease), real GHG emissions could continue to rise dramatically (Chalifour 2008, 127). Under the plan, Alberta committed to a 20 Mt reduction below "business-as-usual" levels by 2010, a 50 Mt reduction below "business-as-usual" levels by 2020 and a 200 Mt reduction below "business-as-usual" levels by 2050. As the Pembina Institute (2009, 1) argued, in reality this would mean that Alberta's overall emissions would be 58 percent *above* 1990 levels in 2020, and 16 percent above 1990 levels in 2050. Essentially, Alberta's approach rendered all other Canadian provincial strategies irrelevant as the province's projected emission increases alone would far exceed Canada's international commitments (Pembina Institute 2009, 1).

In 2007, Alberta became the first Canadian province to implement a credit-based emissions trading system. The Specified Gas Emitters Regulation (SGER) applies to "major facilities" emitting more than 0.1 Mt per year. The facilities that fall under this regulatory framework account for roughly 50 percent of Alberta's GHG emissions (Government of Alberta 2009, 32). These facilities were required to reduce their emissions intensity to 12 percent below baseline, which was the average intensity for that facility between 2003 and 2005. If facilities were unable to meet emissions-intensity limits, they were required to pay $15 per carbon tonne into the *Climate Change Emissions and Management Fund*. Alternatively, emitters also had the option of purchasing offsets from other facilities in Alberta that do not fall under emissions-intensity regulation, but have nonetheless reduced their emissions intensity.

According to the Government of Alberta, SGER achieves roughly 7 Mt of emission-intensity reductions per year. In addition, $398 million has gone towards the *Climate Change Emissions and Management Fund*, $213 million of which is allocated to 51 "clean technology projects" (Government of Alberta 2014b, 5). However, it is widely believed that Alberta will not come close to meeting its 2020 targets. The David Suzuki Foundation (2012, 22) has reported that under the plan Alberta will likely only achieve one-third of its reduction target, and a recent Auditor General report found that the province's targets were simply not in line with its climate change strategy. The report actually found no evidence that the Department of Environment and Sustainable Resource Development had even monitored the performance of its strategy against the province's targets (Government of Alberta 2014b, 39).

The SGER had been scheduled for renewal on September 1st, 2014, but the regulation was instead extended until June 2015. Reports suggested that both the levy and emissions-intensity percentage would be doubled (Sustainable Prosperity 2012, 7). In fact, in 2013 several media reports suggested that the provincial government actually proposed a "40/40 plan," raising the 12 percent emissions intensity and the $15 carbon levy to 40 percent and $40, respectively. However, the Conservative government later claimed that this was only an "idea." As was widely documented, there was pushback from the oil and gas industry which argued that the 40/40 program, while putting a higher burden on their members, would not actually reduce emissions (Paris 2013, para. 16).

Indeed, the real purpose of many of Alberta's climate change initiatives had little to do with meeting serious emissions targets; instead, in the wake of Canada's withdrawal from Kyoto, many saw these proposals as merely ways to buy the credibility or "social license" necessary to get a variety of pipeline projects approved to meet the needs of expanded Alberta oil and gas production (Green 2013).

In the subsequent provincial election of 2015, Alberta's long-time Conservative government was defeated and replaced by a left-leaning New Democratic government which almost immediately began the process of rolling out a more aggressive set of carbon pricing mechanisms. Indeed, the launch of Alberta's own "British Columbia-style" carbon tax in January 2017 has been lauded as a major change in direction in the province, and could be seen as a key building block for any "confederal" style national strategy on climate change. While the situation is still very fluid, a few points are important in evaluating this "change in direction." While Alberta's carbon tax looks like British Columbia's in terms of how it impacts consumers (there will be tax hikes on gas at the pumps, for example), the tax does not apply to the production emissions of the oil and gas sector. Indeed, Alberta's entire strategy is predicated on the idea that oil and gas production and GHG emissions in the sector will continue to grow (Harrison 2016). While there will be a partially applied carbon tax, that tax is also seen as part of a "grand bargain" in which other provinces will then approve the building of new pipelines and oil and gas export infrastructure in support of Alberta's oil and gas sector. Essentially, Alberta's new plan, while certainly more serious than past plans, still does not address the core problem of its uniquely high (and increasing) emissions.

Considering Alberta's contribution to Canadian GHG emissions, and the contribution of fossil fuel production to the province's economy, the province likely presents the most challenging case in Canadian climate policy. Despite the recent praise that Alberta's current strategy has received it is difficult to avoid seeing the Alberta case as one of climate policy avoidance. Alberta's policies have always been heavily influenced by the desire to prevent Canada from adopting a real national GHG reduction strategy – one that might, for example, ratchet back the oil and gas development which has been a key driver of Canada's emission increases. Alberta concluded that its interests would be better represented if it acted on its own, rather than being a constant voice of opposition. Thus, the various "made in Alberta" systems are not clearly aimed at reducing emissions in a meaningful way. Even in a best-case scenario, where Alberta reaches the targets it has set (which is unlikely), the province's emissions would still increase dramatically at a time when the trend is supposed to be going in the opposite direction.

Where is Canada at on GHG mitigation?

This overview of three key provinces' carbon mitigation strategies (or lack thereof) highlights one key finding: in the absence of a serious national strategy, Canada has been failing to meet GHG reduction targets, including those agreed in international negotiations. Moreover, there is considerable divergence in both the kinds of policy instruments Canadian provinces are employing and in their effectiveness in reducing emissions. While provinces such as British Columbia and Quebec (and Ontario) are reducing emissions, others are actually increasing their emissions. What is also relevant, from the perspective of understanding the increasing complexity of Canadian foreign policy in this area, is that the divergence in policy instruments and GHG outcomes is mirrored by a peculiar kind of institutional polarization between provinces over the trajectory of climate policy. For example, at the level of public opinion, voters in those provinces that have done little in terms of climate change mitigation have become increasingly skeptical about the desirability of government protection of the environment. For instance, longitudinal data from the *Canadian Election Study* illustrate the extent to which fault lines have hardened over time: attitudes in Alberta and British Columbia concerning the trade-off between "jobs" and the "environment" have diverged (Williams and Morrissey Wyse 2015).

Essentially, while the Canadian public's support for putting a price on carbon is high in the abstract, public support for federal involvement in managing environmental problems has diverged since the 1990s, suggesting that at the level of public opinion, the notion of a national response to climate policy is harder to sell, given how importantly Canadians seem to value provincial autonomy. Indeed, the differences between the "petro-provinces" (Alberta, Saskatchewan and Newfoundland) and the other provinces can also be seen among policymakers in administrative survey data. While longitudinal data is not available, a snapshot provided by data collected in 2010 illustrates significant differences in the attitudes of senior public officials toward climate change and its importance as a policy issue (see Table 5.3).[4] Fundamentally, there is no "Canadian" discourse universe on climate change. In the absence of a federal policy, provinces have undertaken their own voluntary strategies; they are increasingly directly involved in international frameworks like the WCI, and both voters and public officials are increasingly happy with their divergent choices.

Indeed, one of the most notable facets of the emerging politics of climate policy is that ideological partisanship may be less important in this polarizing landscape than "provincialism." Essentially, where a government "lives" may be

Table 5.3 Differences in attitudes and activities regarding climate change among public administrators

	AB/SK/NL	ON/BC	p-value
How concerned are you personally about climate change?*	3.87	4.04	0.080
How concerned is your department or agency about climate change?*	3.51	3.82	0.004
Overall, how would you rate your department or agency's capacity to deal with adaptation to climate change?*	2.67	2.96	0.006
Within my organization there exists a general consensus regarding the need for adaptation to climate change*	3.05	3.34	0.012
Mitigation should be considered part of a larger adaptation strategy*	3.78	3.89	0.020
International agreements will affect domestic adaptation policies*	3.82	3.88	0.303
Within your department or agency, what is the demand for:* – climate change-related policy analysis – climate change-related scientific research	 3.58 2.56	 3.81 3.22	 0.041 0.000
Are you involved in any aspects of climate change in your work?**	0.52	0.70	0.000

Notes
* Responses to questions are on 1–5 scale, where 5 reflects greater level of agreement/demand/concern, and so on.
** Responses to question on 0–1 scale (yes/no) where 1 = yes.
AB = Alberta; SK = Saskatchewan; NL = Newfoundland; ON = Ontario; BC = British Columbia.

more important than its broad ideological commitments in explaining its orientation to climate action, and this is a fact all future climate initiatives in Canada will have to deal with.

Conclusion – Paris and beyond

What does this provincially based polarization on climate policy mean for Canada and the growing role of the provinces in international policy? Perhaps the best illustration is the federal–provincial "consultations" in preparation for the Paris Summit.

In the fall of 2014, during routine engagement between federal officials and provincial climate change officials, the federal government announced the need for additional data on the state of provincial carbon profiles and the likely impacts of provincial initiatives on future emissions – all of this was necessary in preparing Canada's Paris INDC commitments for the Paris Summit. At best, the purpose of this process was simply to put forward a plausible Canadian proposal based on what the provinces were already planning to do, however uneven and inadequate – at least this is how participants expected the process to unfold. No one was under any illusions that the Conservative Harper government would propose a more decisive national response. In March 2015, the minister of the environment, Leona Aglukkaq, conveyed to the media that there was an ongoing process of consultation with the provinces: "As this is a national contribution, the provinces and territories hold many levers for taking action on emissions, so the minister is seeking feedback from her counterparts on how initiatives in their jurisdictions will factor into Canada's overall commitment."[5] According to provincial officials no meaningful "consultation" ever occurred. Instead, a federal document was leaked in April 2015, accusing the provinces of dragging their feet on helping the federal government set a target for Paris. Less than a month later, the federal government released its poorly received INDC commitments.

Following the 2015 federal election, the newly elected Liberal government of Justin Trudeau made the trip to Paris. Despite considerable fanfare about the new "tone" in Canadian climate policy, the government ultimately chose to use the established playbook. While the government talked up the importance of international commitments at Paris, they adopted the targets proposed by the previous Conservative government – targets they had criticized. Defending this strategy, the government has argued that the difference in their approach is that they plan to actually meet those modest targets. While this process is still ongoing, it is important to note that the new government's plan is essentially the same as their predecessor's. The targets set for Canada at Paris will be achieved through provincial action. While the federal government plans to apply more pressure on reticent provinces to do "something," each province is free to pursue its own strategy on carbon pricing, and the details of what has been agreed after a year of complex negotiations has resulted in a considerable gap between the Paris commitments and Canada's actual policies.

The current struggle over climate policy, far from reflecting deep ideological divides we normally assume when we think of "polarization," is nonetheless beset by the challenges of an institutionalized polarization in which the federal government, if it hopes to meet its internationally agreed commitments, has to navigate a situation in which provinces have fundamentally different goals and ideas about climate policy.

Notes

1 This is one of the more mystifying aspects of Canadian climate policy. Many observers (including provincial officials) argue the federal government could unilaterally impose a "carbon tax" or a "cap and trade system" (the two most viable alternatives for dealing with Canada's emissions). Indeed, claims that the federal government cannot act without the support of the provinces are generally made by elected officials who have clear incentives to "pass the buck" on climate change. Regardless, the politics of climate change are such that it has become unthinkable that any federal government would act in this way – thus the belief that it must engage the provinces to come up with a collective response.
2 Unfortunately, as the David Suzuki Foundation points out, some projects supported by the Green Fund are incompatible with climate change mitigation goals. For example, spending such funds on highway expansion, which encourages urban sprawl, seems inconsistent with the intended goals of the fund (Holmes 2012, 58).
3 In "Kyoto terms," British Columbia's voluntary 2020 target is equivalent to 10 percent below 1990 levels – Canada's Kyoto target was 6 percent below 1990 levels by 2012 prior to withdrawing from the treaty (Government of British Columbia, 2014, 4).
4 The survey, completed in 2010, was directed at government policy analysts and administrators working in federal and provincial government policy analysis. Aside from examining the officials' knowledge of climate change adaptation challenges, it also sought information on their research experience, competencies, educational backgrounds and, most interestingly, the organization of their policy-related research activities in government. A total of 636 officials completed the survey, of which 185 (29 percent) worked for the federal government. Within the overall total, 15 percent of respondents self-identified as working in a "finance-related" agency.
5 Quoted from an email from Minister Aglukkaq's spokesperson on her behalf to media members about the Paris process. Aglukkaq refused to comment publicly on the process.

Bibliography

Angus Reid Institute. (2015, April 22). "Most Canadians Support Carbon Pricing; but Less Consensus on Effectiveness of Such Measures."
Barrett, Tom. (2011, December 5). "Why the Pacific Carbon Trust Draws Political Heat." Available at https://thetyee.ca/News/2011/12/05/CarbonTrustDrawsHeat.
Bernard, Jean-Thomas and Jean-Yves Duclos. (2009). "Québec's Green Future: The Lowest-Cost Route to Greenhouse Gas Reductions." C.D. Howe Institute.
Bickerton, James. (2010). "Deconstructing the New Federalism," *Canadian Political Science Review* 4 (2–3): 56–72.
Brown, Douglas. (2012). "Comparative Climate Change Policy and Federalism: An Overview." *Review of Policy Research* 29(1): 322–333.
Chalifour. Natalie J. (2008). "Making Federalism Work for Climate Change: Canada's Division of Powers over Carbon Taxes." *National Journal of Constitutional Law* 22: 121–214.

Damassa, Thomas and Taryn Fransen. (2015, May 15). "Canada's Proposed Climate Commitment Lags Behind Its Peers'." World Resources Institute.

David Suzuki Foundation. (2012). "All Over the Map 2012: A Comparison of Provincial Climate Change Plans." David Suzuki Foundation.

Dyment, David. (2006, August 11). "Foreign Policy and the Provinces." *Embassy*.

Environment and Climate Change Canada. (2014). "Canada's Emission Trends 2014." Government of Canada.

Environment Canada. (2012, August). "Canada's Emission Trends 2012," Table 16.

Flanagan, Eric. (2015). "Crafting an Effective Canadian Energy Strategy: How Energy East and the Oilsands Affect Climate and Energy Objectives." The Pembina Institute.

Gore, Christopher D. (2010). The Limits and Opportunities of Networks: Municipalities and Climate Change Policy. *Review of Policy Research* 27(1): 27–45.

Government of Alberta. (2002a). "Albertans & Climate Change: A Strategy for Managing Environmental and Economic Risks."

Government of Alberta. (2002b). "Albertans & Climate Change: Taking Action."

Government of Alberta. (2009). "Auditor General 2009 Report."

Government of Alberta. (2014a). "Alberta's Climate Change Regulations Extended."

Government of Alberta. (2014b). "Auditor General 2014 Report."

Government of British Columbia. (2013). "An Audit of Carbon Neutral Government." Office of the Auditor General of British Columbia.

Government of British Columbia. (2014). "Climate Action in British Colombia: 2014 Progress Report."

Government of Québec. (2012). "Québec in Action: Greener by 2020 Climate Change Action Plan 2013–2020."

Government of Québec. (2013a). "A Brief Look at the Cap-and-Trade System for Emission Allowances."

Government of Québec. (2013b). "Regulation Respecting a Cap-and-Trade System for Greenhouse Gas Emission Allowances: Technical Overview."

Green, Kenneth P. (2013, April 19). "Why 40/40 is Foolish/Foolish." Fraser Institute.

Handal, Laura. (2012). "Harper vs. Kyoto: Where Does That Leave Québec?" Behind the Numbers, Canadian Centre for Policy Alternatives.

Harrison, Kathryn. (2012). "The Political Economy of British Columbia's Carbon Tax." OECD Working Papers.

Harrison, Kathryn. (2013). "Federalism and Climate Policy Innovation: A Critical Reassessment." *Canadian Public Policy* 39: 95–108.

Harrison, Kathryn. (2016, November 30). "Pipelines are Not a Reconciliation of Canada's Environment and Economy." *Globe and Mail*.

Holmes, Miranda. (2012). "All Over the Map 2012: A Comparison of Provincial Climate Change Plans." David Suzuki Foundation.

Houle, David. (2011). "Understanding the Selection of Policy Instruments in Canadian Climate Change Policy." Ph.D. dissertation, University of Toronto.

Hunter, Justine. (2008, February 23). "How Beijing Set Off a Premier's Smoke Alarm." *Globe and Mail*.

Klinsky, Sonja. (2013). "Bottom-up Policy Lessons Emerging from Western Climate Initiative's Development Challenges." *Climate Policy* 13(2): 143–169.

Kukucha, Christopher. (2008). *The Provinces and Canadian Foreign Trade Policy*. Vancouver: UBC Press.

Lalonde, Michelle. (2011, December 16). "Québec Cap-and-Trade Follows Kyoto Reversal with Announcement, Arcand Slams Tories 'regrettable' move." *The Gazette*.

Macdonald, Douglas. (2001). "The Business Campaign to Prevent Kyoto Ratification." Paper presented at the Annual Meeting of the Canadian Political Science Association.

Macdonald, Douglas. (2013). "Allocating Canadian Greenhouse Gas Emission Reductions amongst Sources and Provinces." Executive Summary, University of Toronto.

Marshall, Dale, Ian Bruce, and Steven Guilbeault. (2011). "Ensuring the Environmental Integrity of Québec's Cap-and-Trade System for Global Warming Emissions." David Suzuki Foundation and Équiterre.

Meadows, Teresa and Tony Crossman. (2010). "A Tale of Two Provinces: Imposing Greenhouse Gas Emissions Constraints through Law and Policy in Alberta and British Columbia." *Alberta Law Review* 47(2): 421–456.

OECD. (2012). "The Political Economy of British Columbia's Carbon Tax." Working Party on Integrating Environmental and Economic Policies, Organisation for Economic Co-operation and Development.

Paris, Max. (2013, November 8). "Greenhouse Gas Reduction Called a Threat to Oil Industry." *CBC*.

Pembina Institute. (2000). "Provincial Government Performance on Climate Change: 2000."

Pembina Institute. (2009). "Highlights of Provincial Greenhouse Gas Reduction Plans."

Pembina Institute. (2013). "The B.C. Carbon Tax Backgrounder."

Rabe, Barry G. (2007). "Beyond Kyoto: Climate Change Policy in Multilevel Governance Systems." *Governance* 20(3): 423–444.

Séguin, Rhéal. (2009, November 23). "Québec Splits with Ottawa on Climate Change." *Globe and Mail*.

Stein, Janice G. (2006). "Canada by Mondrian: Networked Federalism in an Era of Globalization." The CIBC 2006 Scholar-in-Residence Lecture, Conference Board of Canada. Available at www.fafia-afia.org/files/CHAPTER1.pdf.

Stilborn, Jack. (2002). "The Kyoto Protocol: Intergovernmental Issues." Library of Parliament, Government of Canada.

Stilborn, Jack. (2003). "Canadian Intergovernmental Relations and The Kyoto Protocol: What Happened, What Didn't?" Canadian Political Science Association (CPSA) Conference Paper, Library of Parliament, Government of Canada.

Sustainable Prosperity. (2012). "British Columbia's Carbon Tax Shift: The First Four Years."

Williams, Russell Alan. (2013). "Climate Change Adaptation and Multilevel Governance – Challenges to Policy Capacity in Canadian Finance," in Denita Cepiku, David Jesuit and Ian Roberge (eds.), *Making Multi-Level Public Management Work: Cases from the EU and Beyond*, pp. 119–139. London: Taylor & Francis.

Williams, Russell Alan and Susan Morrissey Wyse. (2015). "The Road to Paris and Polarized Climate Policy in Canada." Paper Presented at the Annual Meeting of Atlantic Provinces Political Science Association, Halifax, Nova Scotia, September 25–27.

Wright, Ronald. (2005). "What Price Progress? The B.C. Government Doesn't Seem to Understand that Jobs Created at the Cost of Nature Are Stolen from the Future, Says Essayist." *Globe and Mail*.

6 Polarized business interests

EU climate policy-making during the "Great Recession"

Raffael Hanschmann

A prominent strand of literature builds upon values and beliefs to explain environmental policy (Dayton 2000; Elgin and Weible 2013). According to this view, belief systems are the decisive driver in all aspects of climate policy-making, be it collaboration (Ingold and Fischer 2014), conflict (Weible 2007) or framing of European Union (EU) environmental policies (Lenschow and Zito 1998). Political polarization in the field of climate change mitigation is usually understood as a paradigmatic tension between political actors subscribing to long-term sustainability transitions on the one hand, and short-term economic reliefs for regulated industries on the other hand. According to this view, polarization emerges from irreconcilable political beliefs and the corresponding political agendas. The recent economic crisis is assumed to have increased the belief-based political polarization by causing a "frame contest" between actors subscribing to different beliefs (Skovgaard 2014).

However, this view has some fundamental shortcomings. The focus on relatively stable belief systems ignores that, especially in EU politics, coalitions are frequently changing and formed ad hoc around specific issues. Likewise, it cannot explain why sometimes business actors prefer a costly regulatory tightening to maintaining the regulatory status quo. To explain this puzzle, this chapter highlights the redistributive aspects of political polarization in EU climate policy-making during the "Great Recession" after the economic crisis of 2009. It emphasizes that the relative gains and losses a regulatory initiative creates for firms are decisive for whether they support or oppose it, and that these gains and losses become more serious under tense economic conditions. If firms' gains and losses, caused by a regulatory initiative, vary markedly across member state industries an economic crisis can polarize a previously consensus-oriented policy venue. From that it follows that, in order to understand the effects of economic shocks on policy outcomes in specific regulatory sectors, scholars should focus less on competing beliefs at the macro-political level. Rather, it is necessary to scrutinize what an economic shock means for the interests and strategic choices of the actors involved in the policy network.

The "Great Recession" and its effect on EU environmental policy-making

After the global financial crisis in 2007 and 2008, the EU suffered from a significant downturn in economic activity and the consequences of the "Great Recession." Soon after, a government debt and banking crisis starting in late 2009 maneuvred the EU in a politically critical situation. Thus, "the crisis" is a complex multidimensional chronology of events that involves closely interlinked macroeconomic, sovereign debt and banking crises (Hodson and Puetter 2013; Walter 2013; Shambaugh et al. 2012). A crisis of such a magnitude impacts on EU policy-making in various policy fields.

Among the affected policy fields is climate and environmental policy, where decision-makers were facing a financial and climate change "double crisis" (Bina and La Camera 2011; Edenhofer and Stern 2009). EU environmental policy has generally leant toward expansion, deepening and institutionalization (Lenschow 2010), a development that gained momentum particularly after 2005 (Boasson and Wettestad 2013). The economic crisis put an end to this trend. Steinebach and Knill (2015) observed that the longest period of regulatory inactivity since the early 1980s was between 2011 and 2013. While policy-makers counteracted the economic downturn with "green growth" measures such as a car-scrap bonus in the immediate aftermath of the crisis outbreak (2008–2010), the recession later (from 2010) slowed down sustainability transitions (Geels 2013). Due to the urgency of economic hardship, "issues of climate change and the related challenges are deemed less urgent, and have slipped further down on the political agenda" (Boasson and Wettestad 2013: 2). This holds true also for the political agenda of the European Commission, which developed "from a supporter to a breakman" in defining renewable energy targets (Bürgin 2015; Steinebach and Knill 2016). Skovgaard (2014) asserts a political polarization along ideological lines within the policy field, finding that the crisis has deepened the division between those actors who consider climate change regulations to be beneficial for economic growth and those who believe them to be harmful. The increased polarization eventually caused a deadlock in EU emissions reduction target negotiations.

Despite growing consensus on the science of climate change, and although the "green growth" discourse propagates a win–win outcome for environmental and economic goals (Hajer 1995), political polarization in the policy field is usually explained as a cleavage between two irreconcilable policy agendas that give priority to either the mitigation of climate change or the preservation of economic wealth. While actors on the one side are willing to make economic concessions in order to reduce greenhouse gas emissions, other actors are much less willing to do so because they fear a decrease in economic wealth. Obviously, opponents of costly climate regulations are likely to be on the rise when economic shocks are endangering industries, causing mass layoffs and losses. According to this logic, all firms affected by an economic downturn, as well as by an economic shock, are expected to oppose costly regulatory initiatives.

However, this is not necessarily the case. Some firms support further regulatory tightening even if they are strongly affected by an economic shock. This insight has strong implications for the study of EU climate policy-making, given that large firms and business interest groups play a prominent role in the EU policy process and act with much political sophistication to gain access to policy fora (Coen 1997). Business and industrial actors are the "elephant in the room" in EU climate policy-making (Grant 2011). Climate policy is "more directly related to the economic interests of industries than are many other environmental policies" (Boasson and Wettestad 2013: 11). In a recent study on lobbying success in EU environmental policy, Bunea (2013: 566) found "additional evidence of the power of business over outcomes in a policy area where higher levels of regulation bring about concentrated costs on specific economic agents such as car producers." Business interests generally have good access to decision-makers in EU politics. They fruitfully apply inside lobbying strategies and by this means they profit from their strong resource endowment. Furthermore, issues such as emissions limitation policies require a high level of technological knowledge. The business lobby possesses a very high level of expertise and can best provide political actors with such information, which it would be too expensive for these actors to develop (Broscheid 2006: 93). This information is possibly exaggerated and misrepresentative, which is why decision-makers face a verification problem and should therefore treat it with caution (Grossman and Helpman 2001: 105). Nevertheless, relationships between interest groups and decision-makers are relatively stable and they exchange continually, which incentivizes lobby groups to create and maintain credibility (Grant 2013: 176). Business interest groups also profit from the relative strength of business-friendly actors within the Commission, such as DG Enterprise (Grant 2013: 176).

Given the pivotal role of business, it is insufficient to understand the polarizing effect of economic shocks on EU climate policy-making as a cleavage between competing political beliefs. Rather, it is more promising to analyze how an economic shock affects regulatory preferences and strategic choices within an industry, and how these changes translate into political polarization. A particular focus thus has to be put on how business shapes its regulatory preferences, and how these preferences may change during economic hardship. Also, it is important to see how member states adjust their preferences to those of crisis-shaken domestic industries, and how these changes aggregate and affect the decision-making process.

Why do some companies favour stricter regulatory standards while others don't?

Environmental regulations, such as process or product standards, bring about differential costs across firms within the same industry (Keohane et al. 1998 in Meckling 2015: 3). While some firms have to invest a lot of resources, for instance in research or technology, to meet the standards set by a regulation, others need to invest less or can already meet the standards. If a firm has to invest more than others, the regulation creates a competitive disadvantage and relative losses. If a firm needs to invest less or already complies with the proposed regulation, it has a competitive advantage and the regulation brings about relative gains.

Following Meckling (2015), the attitude of a firm towards a regulation is determined by relative gains and losses, as described above, but also by the degree of perceived regulatory pressure.[1] Firms facing relative losses will oppose any regulatory initiative if they perceive the regulatory pressure as low. In that scenario, a firm perceives the political demand for environmental regulation as low enough to have a chance to "get away" with no regulation. Under high regulatory pressure, however, they cannot demand the absence of any regulation. Instead, firms will "hedge" the regulatory initiative to minimize the compliance costs, or to level them across all firms that are subject to the regulation. This is achieved, for instance, by proposing regulatory measures themselves. Firms expecting relative gains from a regulatory initiative will not participate in the policy process if they perceive the regulatory pressure as low. They anticipate that the chances of passing the policy are low because potential "losers" of the initiative will oppose the regulation. Therefore, they abstain from investing resources in pro-regulatory advocacy. If firms expecting relative gains perceive the political demand for regulation as high, they will actively support the policy. If the chances of passing the regulation are good, firms will invest resources in advocating a policy design that is as advantageous for the business model as possible.

How does this typology of advocacy strategies change if an economic crisis puts industries in an economically more difficult situation? Due to the worsened business situation, relative losses caused by a regulatory initiative become even less bearable than before. By the same token, relative gains emerging from a regulation become more valuable if gains from business activity are less likely. In other words, the crisis "increased the stakes" (Clift and Woll 2012: 19) of business actors involved in the policy-making process. This has implications for the choice of strategy: the regulatory pressure and political demand for environmental regulation will decrease. During times of economic hardship, economic problems become more salient and urgent, while environmental problems slip down the political agenda. Firms that previously "hedged" a regulatory initiative will shift to a blunt opposition strategy. They will advocate that economic problems have become more salient and urgent. As they perceive less political demand for environmental regulation, they see a realistic chance to push the regulatory initiative off the decision-making agenda. Given that expected relative losses are more painful than before, firms are ready to invest more resources in anti-regulation advocacy. Indeed, Adelino and Dinc (2014) found that the more the crisis affected a firm's financial health, the more it increased its expenditure on lobbying. Firms that already opposed the regulatory initiative before the start of the crisis will continue to pursue this strategy.

Moreover, firms that previously supported the regulatory initiative will continue their pro-regulatory advocacy. They will intensify their lobbying in order to keep environmental issues high on the political agenda and keep regulatory pressure high. Also, firms that previously supported the regulatory initiative silently now have an incentive to invest resources in advocacy, because relative gains from an environmental regulation become more valuable for them as gains from business are more difficult to achieve during times of crisis.

Political polarization within the industry and the Council of the European Union

As established above, if firms within specific European policy sectors expect differential costs–benefit ratios to emerge from a regulatory initiative, an economic shock is likely to polarize the policy preferences within the industry. The advocacy strategies chosen by firms in the policy-making process lean toward stronger opposition by "losers" and stronger support by "winners" of a regulatory initiative. What implications does this polarization within an industry have for EU climate policy-making?

EU member states aggregate different domestic policy preferences, whereas economic interests are seen as prevailing (Moravcsik 1993). This applies also in the realm of environmental policy, where national governments attempt to shape regulations to the benefit of domestic industries. This phenomenon is known as "green protectionism", which has increasingly been observed in the EU (Steenblik 2009). It can be assumed that national governments will consider the concerns of business actors in the aggregation process even more than before the crisis outbreak. This is argued to be the case for two reasons. First, national governments have an interest in maximizing national welfare. National welfare is threatened if specific industrial sectors suffer from crisis-induced economic difficulties. Therefore, governments pay special attention to the political preferences of these industries. As argued above, industry preferences are hypothesized to vary more after the outbreak of the crisis than before. From that it follows that member state preferences also become more polarized. This assumption is confirmed by Bürgin (2015), who found that in the making of the 2030 renewable energy goals, policy preferences in the European Council were more heterogenous than they were when the 2020 goals were made. Second, business actors under economic pressure not only have more attention from the government, they also invest more resources in lobbying (Adelino and Dinc 2014) to advocate their policy preferences. Taken together, if the policy preferences of an industry are polarized, and if member state governments are more inclined to protect their domestic industries more decisively than before, a polarization of the policy debate among member states is the consequence.

Case study: carbon dioxide emission limits for passenger cars

The previous section demonstrated that an economic shock can polarize the regulatory preferences within a European industry, and that a polarization of intergovernmental bargaining is the consequence. These propositions are empirically illustrated using the case of carbon dioxide emission limits for passenger cars. The European automotive sector was one of the commercial and industrial sectors hit hardest by the economic crisis, with new passenger car registrations dropping from 4,185,273 in 2007 to 2,686,603 in 2012 (ACEA 2014). Emission limits regulation is an essential part of the EU's regulatory response to the "super wicked problem" of climate change (Levin et al. 2012). Road transport is responsible for 21 percent of the EU's carbon dioxide emissions. While emissions in other sectors decreased by 15 percent between 1990 and 2007, emissions from transport increased by 36 percent during the same period (European Commission 2014). The automotive sector was affected more severely by the crisis than any other business sector with the exception of housing and finance (Pavlinek 2012: 1). Apart from the banking sector, no policy field saw a larger amount of government intervention (Van Biesebroeck and Sturgeon 2010). The crisis affected all segments and regions of global vehicle production, mainly due to the automotive industry's sensitivity to business cycles (Pavlinek 2012: 1). Saturated vehicle markets of developed economies such as the EU were particularly affected, despite governmental efforts to stimulate demand for new vehicles. Since saturated vehicle markets are characterized mainly by replacement demand, consumers are likely to postpone purchases of new vehicles during periods of economic uncertainty (Dicken 2011). The drastic drop in new car registrations in the second half of 2008 (see Figure 6.1) resulted in temporary plant closures, layoffs and low rates of capacity utilization, while car producers reported problems with access to credit finance (Leheyda and Verboven 2013). The interim stabilization in 2009 was reached partly due to car scrapping schemes (Leheyda and Verboven 2013), but the decrease continued in 2010.

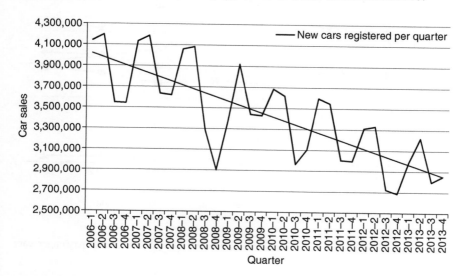

Figure 6.1 Passenger car registrations per quarter in the EU-27, 2006–2013.
Source: ACEA 2014.

As Figure 6.2 demonstrates, the ability of manufacturers to cope with the economic downturn varied across the European car industry. French and Italian carmakers, manufacturing mainly light cars with low pollutant emissions, lost ground in the European car market in the aftermath of the crisis. Most strikingly, the market share of PSA, which manufactures Peugeot and Citroën vehicles, decreased from 13.7 percent in 2010 to 11.1 percent in 2013. In contrast, manufacturers of heavy-engine cars such as Daimler, BMW and Porsche not only maintained but expanded their market share during the crisis. For instance, BMW expanded its market share from 5.1 percent in 2009 to 6.7 percent in 2013. As will be discussed below, these shifts are also expected to affect the political landscape.

Since 2000, the EU has monitored the average carbon dioxide emissions of all car manufacturers operating in the European internal market. Initially, the realization of reducing carbon dioxide emissions was left to the three main manufacturer's associations, European Automobile Manufacturers' Association (ACEA), Japanese Automobile Manufacturers Association (JAMA) and Korean Automobile Manufacturers Association (KAMA) through self-commitments and voluntary agreements (ten Brink 2010: 181). However, these efforts proved

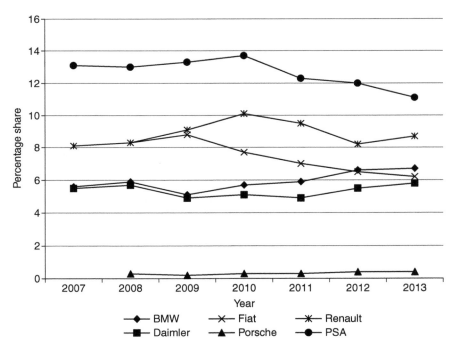

Figure 6.2 Market shares of selected manufacturers of light and heavy passenger cars (Western Europe).

Source: ACEA 2014.

Note
Compiled by the author.

inefficient, and it became apparent that more coercive measures would be neces-sary. Thus, the Commission's Directorate-General for the Environment and the Directorate-General for Enterprise and Industry began to push forward a pro-posal to introduce an emissions target of 120 grams per kilometer. Subsequently, the target of 120 grams per kilometer was softened (again) after the car industry proposed a so-called "integrated approach," that is, the combination of a (higher) emissions limit with technology-based instruments such as efficiency require-ments for air-conditioning systems, tyre pressure monitoring systems, low rolling resistance tyres, gear-shift indicators and increased use of bio-fuels (ten Brink 2010: 194). As a consequence, the Commission's final proposal set a 130 grams per kilometer carbon dioxide fleet average as the permitted threshold in 2009 (Regulation (EC) No 443/2009). The reduction of an additional ten grams per kilometer carbon dioxide was supposed to be achieved by the use of technology-based measures; this was thus left to the car industry (ten Brink 2010: 194). Regulation (EC) No 443/2009 had already set a limit of 95 grams per kilometer as a non-binding goal for 2020. However, in 2012 the Commission proposed a binding target. A deal between MEPs and member states was struck in June 2013, including the 95 grams per kilometer target and additional meas-ures that sought to soften the impact on car producers. Germany, however, unex-pectedly blocked the deal due to the upcoming domestic federal elections. The manner in which Germany cut the deal has frequently been described as unpre-cedented in the history of the EU. Finally, a slightly watered down agreement was reached early in 2014, with 95 percent of the 95 grams per kilometer target to be reached in 2020, and 100 percent in 2021.

Methodology

To determine the effect of the economic crisis on actor preferences and actor constellations in the policy field, the research design compares the decision-making processes of two subsequent regulations, each one being debated before and after the start of the economic crisis. Given that the analytical perspective is actor-centred and emphasizes the role of policy preferences, a longitudinal network approach is a reasonable choice. Within the family of longitudinal network approaches, discourse network analysis (DNA) is selected. DNA is an approach that combines "qualitative content analysis and quantitative social network analysis in order to conceptualize and measure the co-evolution of actors and concepts in a dynamic way" (Leifeld and Haunss 2012: 7). A DNA software tool is utilized to analyze the actor constellations, conflict structures and dynamics in the policy debate, based on their policy preferences. This makes the discourse network a good overall indicator of the empirical existence of coalitions, their between-group polarization and their within-group congruence in EU carbon dioxide emissions limits policy (Fisher et al. 2013).

Emissions regulations directly affect both the economic and environmental con-cerns of the stakeholders involved. If an organizational actor participates in the policy-making process, it is expected to utter its preferences directly or indirectly in political discourse. The discourse thus mirrors the preferences of actors, and unveils which actors commonly agree or disagree with a specific regulatory content. The software tool *Discourse Network Analyzer*[2] is used for importing text data, manual encoding of actor statements and the export of resulting concept and actor maps as several network types (Leifeld 2013: 173). An actor statement is "a text portion where an actor utters his or her policy preferences in a positive or a negative way" (Leifeld 2013: 173). Thus, a statement is a text portion that contains an actor, a concept and binary information about support or opposition.

Articles published in the newspaper *European Voice* and the online newspaper *EUobserver* are used as data sources. They constitute a common forum that makes all statements visible to all actors participating in the policy debate (Leifeld 2011: 164). Still, they have an entry barrier for individual citizens, though relevant political actors can disperse their statements at low cost (Leifeld 2011: 164). *European Voice* was widely considered the most important newspaper focusing on European affairs.[3] It was targeted at readers working in EU institutions and in the public sector. Since a major share of its 20,000 circulation was delivered gratis to EU institutions and policy-makers in Brussels, it is assumed that it served as a common platform for policy debates. However, since it was published weekly, the newspaper may have summarized and aggregated news too narrowly, while the statements of minor actors may have been missed. Therefore, the daily online newspaper *EUobserver* complements *European Voice* as a second source. The use of more than one source is a common strategy in discourse analysis (see, for example, Schneider and Ollmann 2013; Leifeld and Haunss 2012). With more than 3.5 million visits per year and 33,000 newsletter subscribers, *EUobserver* is among the most read media in Brussels. Eighteen percent of readers work in national or EU administrations, 17 percent in EU affairs consulting and business, and another 18 percent in think tanks and NGOS,[4] which makes the online newspaper suited to discourse analysis.

Analysis of the 130 grams per kilometer negotiations (Regulation (EC) No 443/2009)

The negotiations took place mainly in 2007 and 2008. A timeline of all major events during the negotiations is provided in Table 6.1. As becomes apparent, a short phase of the observation period (September 30, 2008 to December 12, 2008) falls within the period after the start of the economic crisis.[5] This is deemed unproblematic for two reasons. First, only 29 of 385 statements were coded after September 30, 2008. Second, Alexandrova et al. (2014) observe that "whereas the financial crisis was manifest from 2008, attention to the economy by the European Council did not peak before 2010." To structure the analysis, it can be divided into two phases, with the French–German agreement as a turning point in the negotiations.

Figure 6.3 shows the policy debate around the 130 grams per kilometer negotiations before the French–German agreement. It becomes apparent that the congruence network is most dense around the actor coalition favouring a

Table 6.1 Timeline of the 130 grams per kilometer negotiations

Date	Event/document	Main content
February 7, 2007	COM(2007) 19 final: Communication from the Commission to the Council and the European Parliament: *Results of the review of the Community Strategy to reduce CO$_2$ emissions from passenger cars and light-commercial vehicles.*	Integrated approach with a view to reaching the EU objective of 120 g CO$_2$/km by 2012, focusing on mandatory reductions of CO$_2$ emissions to reach the objective of 130 g CO$_2$/km for the average new car fleet and a further reduction of 10 g CO$_2$/km, or equivalent if technically necessary, by other technological improvements and by an increased use of biofuels.
December 19, 2007	COM(2007) 856 final: Proposal for a regulation of the European Parliament and of the Council: *Setting emission performance standards for new passenger cars as part of the Community's integrated approach to reduce CO$_2$ emissions from light-duty vehicles.*	Average new car fleet should achieve CO$_2$ emissions of 120 g CO$_2$/km. Average CO$_2$ emissions for new passenger cars at 130 g CO$_2$/km, complemented by additional measures corresponding to 10 g CO$_2$/km as part of the Community's integrated approach.
June 9, 2008	French–German agreement.	Both countries support 120 g CO$_2$/km goal; considering phasing in; agreement on weight-based limits; super-credits.
September 2, 2008	EP Industry Committee vote.	130 g CO$_2$/km by 2015; phasing in between 2012 and 2015; reduced fines.
September 25, 2008	EP Environment Committee vote.	130 g CO$_2$/km by 2012; additional 95 g CO$_2$/km by 2020.
October 1, 2008	French Council Presidency's proposal.	130 g CO$_2$/km by 2015, phasing in between 2012 and 2015; super-credits.
December 1, 2008	Agreement between member states and EP.	Agreement on the content of final proposal (130 g CO$_2$/km by 2015, phasing-in between 2012 and 2015, reduced penalties, super-credits and pooling).
April 23, 2009	Regulation (EC) No 443/2009 of the European Parliament and of the Council: *Setting emission performance standards for new passenger cars as part of the Community's integrated approach to reduce CO$_2$ emissions from light-duty vehicles.*	CO$_2$ emissions performance requirements for new passenger cars of 120 g CO$_2$/km as average emissions for the new car fleet. Average CO$_2$ emissions for new passenger cars at 130 g CO$_2$/km. From 2020, target of 95 g CO$_2$/km as average emissions for the new car fleet. Additional measures corresponding to a reduction of 10 g CO$_2$/km as part of the Community's integrated approach.

Note
Compiled by the author.

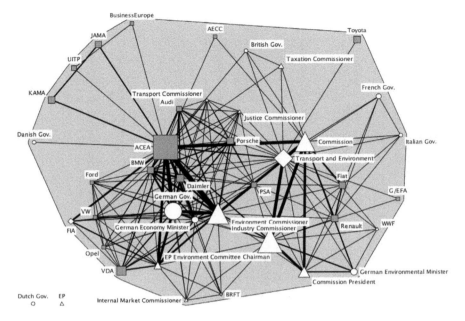

Figure 6.3 Congruence network of the 130 grams per kilometer negotiations before the
French–German compromise.

Notes
Grey rectangle: industry; white ellipse: member states; white triangle: EU institutions; white diamond:
environmental and consumer NGOs; grey triangle: European Parliament political groups; grey diamond:
other. ACEA: European Automobile Manufacturers' Association; AECC: Association for Emissions
Control by Catalyst; BRFT: Biodiversity Research and Training Forum; FIA: International Automobile
Association; G/EFA: The Greens/European Free Alliance; JAMA: Japanese Automobile Manufacturers
Association; KAMA: Korean Automobile Manufacturers Association; PSA: Peugot S.A.; VDA:
German Association of the Automotive Industry; VW: Volkswagen. Compiled by the author.

watered-down proposal, with German car manufacturers such as Daimler and
BMW at its core. Apparently, the preferences of the ACEA greatly overlap with
those of the German luxury brands, although it is supposed to represent the
entire European car industry. In contrast, the ACEA hardly shared any preferences with Renault and Fiat. For instance, it initially rejected any binding legislation, just as the German government, Daimler, BMW and the Industry
Commissioner did. Later in the negotiations, the ACEA also supported an
"integrated approach." In other words, Figure 6.3 suggests that the ACEA spoke
not only with a loud voice, but also with a strong German accent. Unlike their
German competitors, the French and Italian manufacturers did not form a coher-
ent coalition. The less dense ties between these actors (that is, less common preferences) and low node diameters (that is, fewer statements) show that they did
not have a common position and an insistent articulation in the policy debate,
leaving the dominating role for the "German" coalition.

The German government has a strong preference overlap with the German car industry. Initially, the German Chancellor, Angela Merkel, rejected a binding emissions limit generally, stating that "*it cannot possibly be that we create a general obligation under which all cars ... have to follow the same standards*" (EO January 31, 2007).[6] However, the German government's position was not always homogenous: while Merkel and the German Minister of Economic Affairs are closely related to the German car industry, the German Environment Minister, Sigmar Gabriel, "*support[ed] the Dimas camp*" (EO January 29, 2007) and embraced binding legislation from the beginning. The French government, in turn, protected its domestic industry in the early stage of negotiations, stating that "*nothing justifies giving a bigger right to pollute to the buyer of a bigger vehicle*" (EO November 15, 2007).

Like the ACEA, the Commission was split internally, as the dispute between the German Industry Commissioner, Günther Verheugen, and the Greek Environment Commissioner, Stavros Dimas, documents. Their publicly battled conflict dominated the negotiations and even found its way in policy-making textbooks as a showcase for turf battles within the Commission (see Lenschow 2010: 313). The Directorate General Enterprise and Industry is tightly embedded into the coalition of car manufacturers and the German government. Still in summer 2006, Verheugen's spokesman said that "*binding legislation is not on the agenda*" (EV July 27, 2006). When binding legislation turned out to be inevitable, Verheugen proposed a 130 grams per kilometer limit, while Stavros Dimas favoured 120 grams per kilometer by 2012 (EV December 7, 2006). In his call for binding legislation and, initially, for a 120 grams per kilometer target, Dimas was backed by the Commission President, Barroso, who clarified that "*there is a need for legislation to meet the [120 grams per kilometer] target set by the Commission*" (EV January 25, 2007). Accordingly, Commission officials commented that they are "*not happy with the phase-in*" rule of the final proposal (EO December 2, 2008). Unlike Dimas, Verheugen tried to shift responsibility away from car manufacturers, declaring that "*it is perhaps not possible or technically feasible to reach the carbon dioxide emission target by just looking at car engines and at the car industry*" (EV January 11, 2007). Verheugen clearly framed his position as economically reasonable, stating that "*our growth and jobs priority must not be endangered*" (EO January 23, 2007). Contrarily, Dimas insisted that "*we had an agreement that the car industry promised to fulfil and we now need legislation to keep that agreement*" (EV January 25, 2007). Since the opposition against a 120 grams per kilometer target did not abate, Dimas eventually had to accept the watered-down Commission Communication in February 2007.

The negotiations reached a turning point in Spring 2008, when the upcoming French Council Presidency led France to push the proposal and to make some concessions to its German counterpart. In doing so, the French government thus exerted the "true power of the chair" (Tallberg 2003: 8) of the Presidency by emphasizing an issue on the political agenda. France's behaviour can also be seen as supportive of Warntjen's (2007: 154) findings, suggesting that the

Presidency has a positive and statistically significant impact on environmental policies. While the French–German compromise supports the overall 120 grams per kilometer target envisaged by the Commission proposal, it suggests a substantial phase-in, weight-based limits and softer penalties for non-compliers. German Chancellor Merkel appraised the compromise as a "*giant step forward*" (EO June 10, 2008). Interestingly, both countries supported a long-term goal for 2020, which was opposed by the German car manufacturers.

The congruence network after the French–German agreement (Figure 6.4) is characterized by a lower number of participants and a lower density. The network graph clearly depicts the French–German collaboration: both actors are linked by a thick edge, indicating a high preference overlap. Eventually, Environment Commissioner Dimas also agreed on the deal struck by the French and German governments. With the legislative procedure proceeding, the role of the European Parliament, more precisely of the Industry and Environment Committees, became more prominent. As indicated in Table 6.1, the Industry

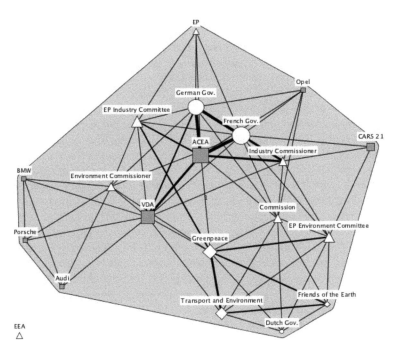

Figure 6.4 Congruence network of the 130 grams per kilometer negotiations after the French–German compromise.

Notes
Grey rectangle: industry; white ellipse: member states; white triangle: EU institutions; white diamond: environmental and consumer NGOs; grey triangle: European Parliament political groups; grey diamond: other. ACEA: European Automobile Manufacturers' Association; CARS 21: Competitive Automotive Regulatory System for the 21st Century VDA: German Association of the Automotive Industry. Compiled by the author.

Committee voted on changes to the proposal on September 2, 2008. The Environment Committee voted three weeks later, on September 25, 2008. Under the "enhanced cooperation procedure," the Environment Committee was responsible for the Parliament's response to the proposal. However, it had to accept amendments by the Industry Committee if these concerned industry competence. What, in turn, constitutes industry competence, must be agreed on by MEPs of both committees. The Industry Committee voted to accept a proposal drafted by the German MEP Langen, suggesting further watering down of the existing proposal with a less rigorous penalty scheme and more encompassing phasing-in, demanding that only 60 percent of a car fleet meet the emissions target by 2012. Although Langen's draft also included a 95 grams per kilometer target for 2020, environmental NGOs criticized the vote. When the draft was passed to the Environment Committee, its members voted against including the phasing-in and reduced penalties the Industry Committee had accepted, while the 95 grams per kilometer target for 2020 was accepted. Eventually, the draft by the European Parliament was even more environmentally ambitious than the Commission's proposal.

However, the French Council Presidency drafted a new proposal. This proposal suggested a phasing-in between 2012 and 2015 and a less rigorous penalty scheme, although the European Parliament Environment Committee had previously rejected both points. After three-way talks between the European Parliament, the Commission and the French Council Presidency during November 2008, representatives and negotiators from member states agreed on a compromise, including a target of 65 percent of a fleet to meet the emissions limit by 2012 and reduced fines. In return, opponents of the regulation accepted the inclusion of a legally binding 95 percent target for 2020. The proposal was approved by a plenary vote in the European Parliament and by member state governments and published as law in April 2009. Despite the adoption of a long-term target, environmental NGOs expressed contempt for the compromise, mainly because it did not allow for more than a 2 percent reduction in carbon dioxide emissions limits by 2015 compared to 2008. The Commission was also unhappy with the outcome of the negotiations: an anonymous Commission official admitted that *"we are not happy with the phasing-in"* (EO December 2, 2008). The environmental NGO Transport & Environment blamed lobbyists for the final outcome, stating that *"the story of this law is the story of special interests in industry and national governments preserving the status quo"* (EO December 2, 2008). These statements also indicate that environmental NGOs largely failed to influence Commission proposal COM(2007) 856 FINAL, as demonstrated by Klüver (2009).

The discourse network over the entire 130 grams per kilometer negotiations is illustrated in Figure 6.5. To conclude, the policy debate was dominated by an advocacy coalition around German premium manufacturers, the ACEA, the German government and the Industry Commissioner.

Why did no distinct antipole to the "German" advocacy coalition emerge in the policy debate? Manufacturers of light cars, predominantly from France and

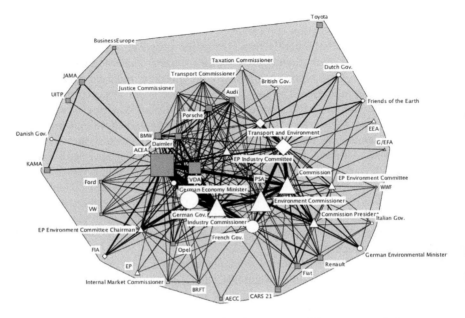

Figure 6.5 Congruence network of the entire 130 grams per kilometer negotiations.

Notes
Grey rectangle: industry; white ellipse: member states; white triangle: EU institutions; white diamond: environmental and consumer NGOs; grey triangle: European Parliament political groups; grey diamond: other. CEA: European Automobile Manufacturers' Association; AECC: Association for Emissions Control by Catalyst; BRFT: Biodiversity Research and Training Forum; CARS 21: Competitive Automotive Regulatory System for the 21st Century; EEA: European Environment Agency; FIA: International Automobile Association; G/EFA: The Greens/European Free Alliance; JAMA: Japanese Automobile Manufacturers Association; KAMA: Korean Automobile Manufacturers Association; PSA: Peugot S.A.; UITP: International Organization of Public Transport; VDA: German Association of the Automotive Industry; VW: Volkswagen. Compiled by the author.

Italy, were facing a more favorable cost–benefit ratio: meeting the proposed emissions targets was less costly for them as it was for manufacturers of heavy cars. They therefore had less incentive to spend resources on lobbying and convincing their national governments to take action. In addition, the French government had incentives to make concessions to Germany, that were unfavorable to French carmakers, because it was chairing the Council Presidency and wanted to successfully pass the legislation.

Analysis of the 95 grams per kilometer negotiations (Regulation (EU) 333/2014)

As in the previous discourse network, the analysis here is structured along two periods, before and after a turning point in the negotiations. In the 95 grams per kilometer negotiations, the turning point was the personal intervention by the

German Chancellor, Angela Merkel, on June 26, 2013, which broke a deal struck between member states and the European Parliament just one day earlier.

The discourse network before the German intervention is displayed in Figure 6.6. It becomes apparent that the network structure is clearly bipolarized into two distinct coalitions, as confirmed by the Girvan–Newman cluster analysis (light grey background).

The advocacy coalition around German car manufacturers and the German car manufacturers' association already observed in the previous discourse network persisted. Its adjacency to the European Parliament Environment Committee is surprising at first sight, but explicable because the Environment Committee voted for a proposal that included an expanded super-credits scheme – just as the German car lobby demanded (see Table 6.2 for an explanation of super-credits). While the ACEA is still participating in the "contra regulation" coalition, it has suffered from a substantial loss of power. Its members – among them French, German and Italian manufacturer associations – failed to agree on a common position, which is why the number of statements uttered by the ACEA decreased significantly as compared to the 130 grams per kilometer negotiations. The media reported "bitter exchanges at ACEA meetings" with strong tensions arising from "*declining sales that many French and Italian companies are suffering, while German luxury vehicle manufacturers are faring much better*" (EV July 19, 2012). The ACEA hence internalized the cleavage between "Northern" and "Southern" car manufacturers and their governments. This division is manifested also in the second advocacy coalition that emerged in the discourse. The network graph indicates that this advocacy coalition consists of a heterogenous and more encompassing set of actors, among them two environmental and two consumer NGOs, Italian and French car manufacturers, the French and Italian governments and Commission officials. In contrast to the German luxury brands, French and Italian carmakers supported stricter emissions regulations. In a speech at the European Parliament, the vice-president of Renault stated: "*Yes, we can reach 95 grams, there is no problem, we have the technology*" (EV July 12, 2012).

The publication of the Commission proposal in June 2012 was successfully delayed by German car lobbyists. They refused to accept a recalibration of the curve that indicates the permitted carbon dioxide output for a specific car, a change necessary for achieving the 95 grams per kilometer target (Figure 6.7). While manufacturers of small cars such as Fiat and Renault profit from a flatter slope than the existing one, the German luxury brands preferred a steeper slope gradient or, at least, maintaining the existing one. Also, the Commission proposed 2009 as the base year for the new slope, failing to take into account the efforts made by German car manufacturers between 2006 and 2009. In the end, the opponents agreed on setting the curve base back to 2006 instead of 2009. Also, the curve gradient was set to 0.0333, while the Germans preferred maintaining it at 0.0457. The Climate Action Commissioner, Connie Hedegaard, argued that the proposal was a compromise that asks "*all manufacturers to make the same relative effort to reduce their car emissions*" (EV July 12, 2012).

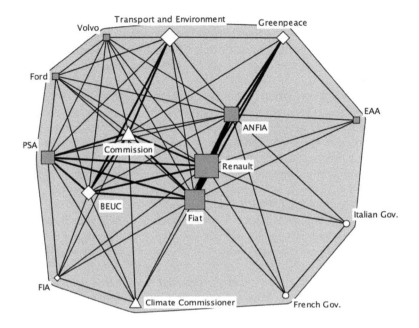

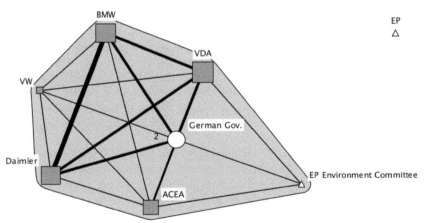

Figure 6.6 Congruence network of the 95 grams per kilometer negotiations before the German intervention.

Notes
Grey rectangle: industry; white ellipse: member states; white triangle: EU institutions; white diamond: environmental and consumer NGOs; grey triangle: European Parliament political groups; grey diamond: other. ACEA: European Automobile Manufacturers' Association; ANFIA: National Association of the Italian Automobile Industry; BEUC: The European Consumers' Organization; EAA: European Aluminium Association; EP: European Parliament; FIA: International Automobile Association; PSA: Peugot S.A.; VDA: German Association of the Automotive Industry; VW: Volkswagen. Compiled by the author.

Table 6.2 Timeline of the 95 grams per kilometer negotiations

Date	Event/document	Main content
July 11, 2012	COM(2012) 393 final: Proposal for a Regulation of the European Parliament and of the Council *amending Regulation (EC) No. 443/2009*	Maintain 95 g CO_2/km for 2020 target; maintain weight-based limit; maintain slope curve of 60% with 2006 as baseline fleet; super-credits for cars emitting <35 g/km CO_2 (factor 1.3; introduction between 2020 and 2023; limited to 20,000 vehicles/manufacturer); update of derogations for "niche" manufacturers; maintain eco-innovations; maintain 95 euros/km fine.
April 24, 2013	EP Environment Committee vote	Super-credits for cars emitting <50 g CO_2/km; 68–78 g CO_2/km for 2025 target.
June 7, 2013	German proposal submitted to the member states	"Banking" of super-credits earned before 2015 to use them after 2020.
June 24, 2013	Deal between Irish Council Presidency, member states and MEPs	Maintain 95 g CO_2/km for 2020 target; no 2025 target; super-credits factor raised to 2 instead of 1.3 and for cars <50 g CO_2/km instead of 35; no "banking" of super-credits.
June 24, 2013	Personal intervention by Merkel to undo June 24, 2013 deal	German government does not accept the rejection of super-credit "banking" and wants to postpone the target to 2024.
November 5, 2013	EP negotiators reject compromise proposal by Lithuanian Council Presidency	The compromise would have postponed the target to 2023; 95 g CO_2/km averaged across fleet; expansion of super-credits from 2023 to 2024 and "banking."
November 12, 2013	Counter-offer by EP negotiators	Expansion of super-credits to electric vehicles and/or phasing-in of penalties for non-compliance.
November 26, 2013	Deal between MEPs and member states	One year phase-in for 95 g CO_2/km; 95% until 2020, 100% until 2021; expansion of super-credits to electric vehicles.
February 25, 2013	EP votes for November 26, 2013 deal	
April 5, 2014	*Regulation (EU) No. 333/2014 of the European Parliament and of the Council of March 11, 2014 amending Regulation (EC) No. 443/2009*	95 g CO_2/km target for 2021, with 95% of a fleet to meet the target in 2020; weight-based limit; from 2019, 95 euros/g fine from the first grams of exceedance onwards; maintenance of eco-credits; maintenance of super-credits (from 2020 to 2023: factor 2 in 2020; 1.57 in 2021; 1.33 in 2022; 1 from 2023); derogations for "niche" manufacturers.

Note
Compiled by the author.

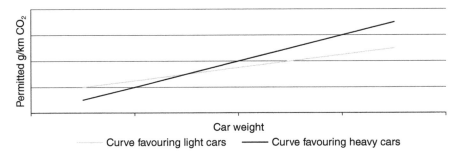

Figure 6.7 Schematic illustration of limit value curves.

Note
Compiled by the author.

From the beginning of the negotiations, the media described the lobbying by the German camp with terms such as "frantic" or "furious." German and Italian car manufacturers accused each other of being unfair, with the ANFIA president stating that the modifications would *"favour just one country"* (EV June 28, 2012). Contrarily, German voices described the Commission proposal as a *"gift to struggling French and Italian carmakers"* (EV July 12, 2013). As Figure 6.6 shows, Italian and French manufacturers were backed by environmental and consumer NGOs, with Greenpeace accusing BMW and Daimler of *"asking French and Italian carmakers to do the reductions in their place, instead of doing their fair share to move us on"* (EV June 28, 2012). Such statements underpin what becomes apparent in the congruence network: the actor structure in the policy debate is much more bipolarized than in the 130 grams per kilometer negotiations.

The reintroduction of a super-credit scheme was another "hot potato," discussed when the proposal was passed to the European Parliament. The German car lobby favoured an expansion of the previous scheme and found support among conservative German MEPs, who argued that larger cars should be politically favoured because *"larger vehicles ... generally play a pioneering role in vehicle technology"* (EV January 22, 2013). The Environment Committee voted to keep the existing super-credit scheme in April 2013. Environmentalists showed contempt for the decision, accusing Committee members of having fallen into a *"trap set by carmakers"* (EV April 24, 2013). Since the super-credit scheme proposal was less encompassing than the previous one, the German lobby pushed for even more concessions. In June 2013, the German government drafted a proposal that would allow car manufacturers to "bank" super-credits earned before 2015 and use them after 2020. The environmental NGO Transport and Environment evaluated the proposal as a *"desperate attempt by Germany to gain support for discredited banking proposals that have been rejected in the Parliament and by a large majority of member states"* (EV July 17, 2013). In fact, the deal reached by MEPs and member states on June 24, 2013, under the leadership of the Irish Council Presidency, did not contain the possibility of "banking" super-credits (see Table 6.2).

However, just one day after the deal was struck, German Chancellor Merkel personally approached the Irish Prime Minister, Enda Kenny, with the intention of undoing the deal. More precisely, Merkel tried to delay the vote by getting it off the agenda of the Council meeting and postponing it until after the Bundestag elections in late September 2013. Merkel justified the blockade with a phrase that summarizes nicely the main difference between the 130 and the 95 grams per kilometer negotiations: "*At a moment when we sit together for days to talk about employment, we also need to be careful not to weaken our own industrial base*" (EV June 28, 2013). The reason for the refusal is most likely that German manufacturers insisted on the inclusion of an even higher super-credit factor (3 instead of 2) and the "banking" option. Merkel's intervention can thus be seen as a protectionist move that was not observable before the crisis to such an extent.

Figure 6.8 shows the congruence network after Merkel's intervention, when the regulatory initiative was debated among member states. As becomes apparent, Germany gathered a large group of member states in order to prevent the law from passing at the Council. The media reported that Slovakia, the Czech Republic, Poland and Bulgaria could be won over by Germany, as well as the Netherlands, the UK, Portugal, Austria and Hungary. Many of these countries host large production plants of German car manufacturers. Eventually, Germany achieved a postponement of the vote. The German refusal caused irritation among environmental groups and French and Italian officials because taking back an already negotiated agreement is highly unusual in the EU. Transport & Environment stated that "*it's unprecedented in EU environmental policymaking that the pressure of one country delays a vote in an attempt to overturn a fairly-negotiated agreement*" (EV June 27, 2013). Similarly, Greenpeace accused Merkel of being "*not afraid of hijacking democratic processes and bully[ing] other governments to pamper a few high-end carmakers*" (EV June 27, 2013). When Germany again successfully delayed the vote at the next Council meeting on July 17, 2014, the Commission expressed concerns "*about the integrity of the Council's process*" (EV July 17, 2013).

After the Bundestag election in September 2013, the German government continued to refuse to accept the agreement. Instead, it came up with the entirely new suggestion of phasing-in the emissions limit stepwise between 2020 and 2024 because "*the issue of flexibility has not yet been sufficiently addressed*" (EV September 27, 2013). NGOs suspected Germany proposed the phasing-in because a change on the existing deal would require a second reading, which would be unlikely to take place before the European Parliament elections in May 2014. Such a substantial delay would give German car manufacturers even more time to work on their technology. The UK was reported to support Germany in exchange for Germany opposing the proposed cap on bankers' bonuses. France and Italy, in turn, kept on refusing any concessions to Germany. The Italian Environment Minister appealed to the German government, claiming that "*Italy too has had to accept outcomes as part of negotiations, our industry has*

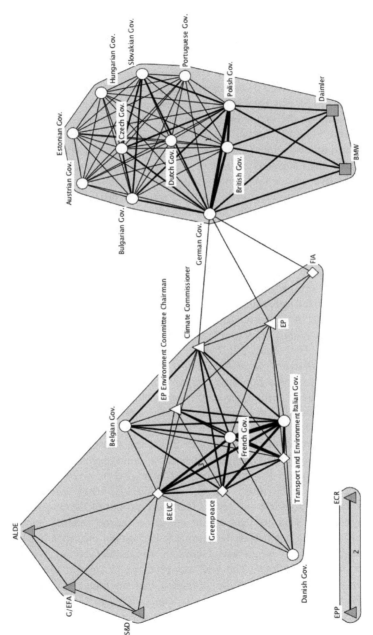

Figure 6.8 Congruence network of the 95 grams per kilometer negotiations after the German intervention.

Notes

Grey rectangle: industry; white ellipse: member states; white triangle: EU institutions; white diamond: environmental and consumer NGOs; grey triangle: European Parliament political groups; grey diamond: other. ALDE: Alliance of Liberals and Democrats; BEUC: The European Consumers' Organization; EP: European Parliament; FIA: International Automobile Association; G/EFA: The Greens/European Free Alliance; S&D: Socialists & Democrats. Compiled by the author.

had to sacrifice sometimes, too" (EV October 14, 2013). The Commission also rejected the phasing-in. Climate Action Commissioner Hedegaard stated that "*Germany's demand to delay the implementation [...] is not acceptable*" (EO October 15, 2013).

The deal was, however, eventually reopened in November 2013. Hoping to find a successful compromise, the Lithuanian Council Presidency suggested a phasing-in of two or three years, while Germany insisted on four years. In return, the Council Presidency's draft included an extension of the super-credit scheme to electric vehicles. These concessions resulted in environmentalists requesting the Presidency to "*come to their senses and stop trying to please Germany*" (EV October 29, 2013). Because of the phasing-in, the European Parliament promptly rejected the new proposal. An agreement was eventually settled in late November 2013, when MEPs and member states reached a compromise that included a minimal phase-in of 95 percent of a fleet meeting the emissions target in 2020 and 100 percent in 2021. On February 25, 2014, the European Parliament approved the legislation.

The congruence network illustrating the entire 95 grams per kilometer negotiations (Figure 6.9) is clearly divided into two clusters. The "contra regulation" coalition consists of two sub-groups: the German car industry as a domestic coalition on the one hand, and a group of fellow member states on the other. This division does not stem from diverging preferences; rather, it can be explained by different chronological stages of the policy-making process. Statements by industrial actors were aggregated in the media primarily during the early stages of the decision-making process, while statements uttered by member state officials and MEPs were recorded mainly during the turf battles within the Council.

The coalition of proponents of stricter emissions limits is gathered around manufacturers of light vehicles, such as Fiat, PSA and Renault. In contrast to the pre-crisis negotiations, Italy and France emerged as coequal opponents of the German government. The French–Italian coalition also had support from the Commission in general and Climate Action Commissioner Hedegaard in particular, as well as from consumer rights and environmental activists.

The economic crisis thus opened a previously latent cleavage within the car industry, as Figures 6.10 and 6.11 illustrate. As their declining market shares (Figure 6.2) indicate, Italian and French manufacturers suffered more during the crisis than their German competitors. The shift in market shares explains why these manufacturers, unlike in the previous negotiations, now form an advocacy coalition and behave in a more conflictive fashion. They also stood up for their interests within the ACEA, formerly dominated by German carmakers. This stalemate situation within the ACEA resulted in a marginalized role in the policy debate: the number of statements made by the ACEA declined from 35 before to five after the start of the crisis.

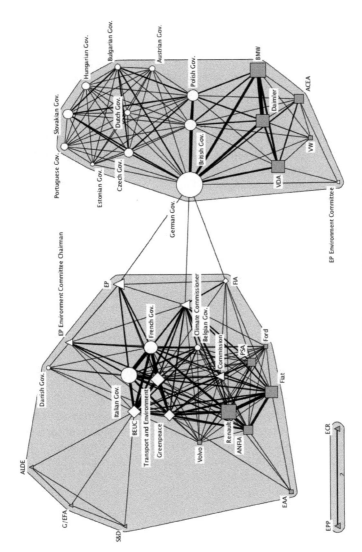

Figure 6.9 Congruence network of the entire 95 grams per kilometer negotiations.

Notes
Grey rectangle: industry; white ellipse: member states; white diamond: environmental and consumer NGOs; grey triangle: European Parliament political groups; grey diamond: other. ACEA: European Automobile Manufacturers' Association; ALDE: Alliance of Liberals and Democrats; ANFIA: National Association of the Italian Automobile Industry; BEUC: The European Consumers' Organization; EAA: European Aluminium Association; EP: European Parliament; FIA: International Automobile Association; G/EFA: The Greens/ European Free Alliance; PSA: Peugot S.A.; S&D: Socialists & Democrats; VDA: German Association of the Automotive Industry; VW: Volkswagen. Compiled by the author.

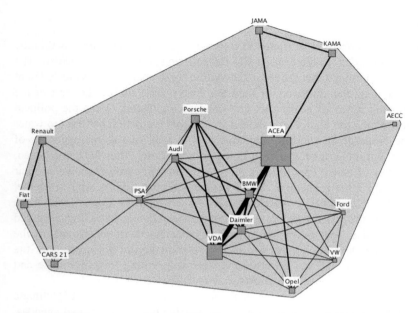

Figure 6.10 Congruence network of the European car industry during the 130 grams per kilometer negotiations.

Notes
Grey rectangle: industry. ACEA: European Automobile Manufacturers' Association; AECC: Association for Emissions Control by Catalyst; CARS 21: Competitive Automotive Regulatory System for the 21st century; JAMA: Japanese Automobile Manufacturers Association; KAMA: Korean Automobile manufacturers Association; PSA: Peugot S.A.; VDA: German Association of the Automotive Industry; VW: Volkswagen. Compiled by the author.

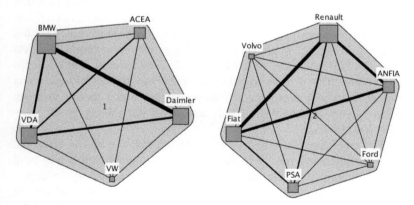

Figure 6.11 Congruence network of the European car industry during the 95 grams per kilometer negotiations.

Notes
Grey rectangle: industry. ACEA: European Automobile Manufacturers' Association; ANFIA: National Association of the Italian Automobile Industry; PSA: Peugot S.A.; VDA: German Association of the Automotive Industry; VW: Volkswagen. Compiled by the author.

Conclusion

Political polarization can be rooted in shifts in regulatory preferences within the regulated industries, as the case of EU car emissions regulations revealed. The case study highlighted that the recent economic crisis opened a previously latent cleavage among manufacturers of light and heavy cars. Before the start of the crisis, manufacturers of heavy cars first opposed regulation. When the political demands became too high, they reluctantly accepted regulation but tried to water down the proposal. In contrast, manufacturers of light cars were supportive of regulation, but remained rather tacit in the policy debate. After the crisis began, manufactures of heavy cars became more insistent and confrontational in their opposition to further regulation. As the personal intervention by Angela Merkel in June 2013 exemplifies, protectionist behaviour within the Council was more prevalent after the crisis began. In spring 2008, when Germany and France agreed on a compromise, both governments made considerable concessions against the wishes of their domestic industries. Such give-and-take did not occur after the crisis began, when national governments were less willing to compromise and more inclined to stay close to their domestic industries' preferences.

It has been claimed that political polarization in the realm of EU climate policy does not necessarily stem from irreconcilable policy beliefs and agendas. Rather, the redistributive effect of a regulatory initiative within the regulated industries needs to be taken into account. This holds particularly true in the institutional context of the EU, where actor constellations are best understood as ad hoc alliances that form around specific issues (Warleigh 2000). Taking into consideration the unsteadiness of policy coalitions in EU policy-making also reveals the weaknesses of analytical perspectives that emphasize stable common beliefs systems as "glue" that keeps coalitions together, such as the advocacy coalition framework (Sabatier 1988). Understanding EU environmental politics as a redistributive problem is promising as a growing body of literature indicates that decision-making in the EU is predominantly shaped by redistributive conflicts (Bailer et al. 2015; Hosli et al. 2011; Aksoy 2010; Zimmer et al. 2005; Kauppi and Widgrén 2004). This is especially the case as EU environmental regulations always had an underlying economic rationale: they serve as a tool to structure the Common Market (Jachtenfuchs 1996) and "level the playing field" (Lenschow 2010: 309) for trade.

There is an emerging consensus in the literature that the recent economic crisis had an abating effect on EU climate policy-making. While this may hold true for the bigger picture, the case study provides contradictory evidence. Because the difficult economic situation caused manufacturers of small cars to advocate a strict regulation more actively than before, opponents of more regulation watered down the proposal to a much lesser extent than they wanted. This reveals the need for more research on the mechanisms connecting economic trends and environmental policy.

What lessons can be drawn from the case study for policy-makers? It has been shown that regulations are likely to result in differential compliance costs across an industry. In the case presented here, manufacturers of heavy-polluting cars had to carry a higher burden than manufacturers of small cars. The acceptance of a regulatory initiative could be increased by levelling the compliance costs for all manufacturers. Such a move, however, would spare heavy polluters and thus come at the expense of a less environmentally ambitious regulation. It is here where the ideational aspect of environmental politics comes into play again.

Notes

1 Meckling (2015) describes perceived regulatory pressure as resulting from how a firm interprets its institutional environment and mixed signals with regard to demand for regulatory action on a given environmental issue.
2 https://github.com/leifeld/dna/releases.
3 *European Voice* was rebranded as *Politico Europe* in April 2015.
4 http://euobserver.com/mediakit.pdf.
5 It is difficult to determine one specific date when the crisis began in the EU. Here, September 30, 2008 is chosen as the date because the first EU member state, Ireland, promised to underwrite the entire Irish banking system.
6 For the sake of readability, statement citations from the newspaper *EUobserver* are referred to as "EO," while citations from the *European Voice* are referred to as "EV." References to articles from both media are included in the References under the full name of the publication.

References

ACEA. (2014). Consolidated Registration Figures. Retrieved September 13, 2014 from www.acea.be/statistics/tag/category/consolidated-figures.

Adelino, M., and I. S Dinc. (2014). "Corporate Distress and Lobbying: Evidence from the Stimulus Act." *Journal of Financial Economics*, 114(2), 256–272.

Aksoy, D. (2010). "Who Gets What, When, and How Revisited: Voting and Proposal Powers in the Allocation of the EU budget." *European Union Politics*, 11(2), 171–194.

Alexandrova, P., M. Carammia, S. Princen and A. Timmermans. (2014). "Measuring the European Council Agenda: Introducing a New Approach and Dataset." *European Union Politics*, 15(1), 152–167.

Bailer, S., M. Mattila and G. Schneider. (2015). "Money Makes the EU Go Round: The Objective Foundations of Conflict in the Council of Ministers." *JCMS: Journal of Common Market Studies*, 53(3), 437–456.

Bina, O. and F. La Camera. (2011). "Promise and Shortcomings of a Green Turn in Recent Policy Responses to the 'Double Crisis'." *Ecological Economics*, 70(12), 2308–2316.

Boasson, E. L. and M. J. Wettestad. (2013). *EU Climate Policy: Industry, Policy Interaction and External Environment*. Burlington, VT: Ashgate Publishing.

Broscheid, A. (2006). "Public Choice Models of Business Lobbying." In D. Coen and W. Grant (eds.), *Business and Government: Methods and Practice*. Opladen, Germany: Barbara Budrich.

Bunea, A. (2013). "Issues, Preferences and Ties: Determinants of Interest Groups' Preference Attainment in the EU Environmental Policy." *Journal of European Public Policy*, 20(4), 552–570.

Bürgin, A. (2015). "National Binding Renewable Energy Targets for 2020, but Not for 2030 Anymore: Why the European Commission Developed from a Supporter to a Brakeman." *Journal of European Public Policy*, 22(5), 690–707.

Clift, B. and C. Woll. (2012). "Economic Patriotism: Reinventing Control over Open Markets." *Journal of European Public Policy*, 19(3), 307–323.

Coen, D. (1997). "The Evolution of the Large Firm As a Political Actor in the European Union." *Journal of European Public Policy*, 4(1), 91–108.

Dayton, B. W. (2000). "Policy Frames, Policy Making and the Global Climate Change Discourse." In H. Addams and J. L. R. Proops (eds.), *Social Discourse and Environmental Policy: An Application of Q*, pp. 71–99. Cheltenham, UK: Edward Elgar Publishing.

Dicken, P. (2011). *Global Shift: Mapping the Changing Contours of the World Economy* (6th edn). New York: Guilford Press.

Edenhofer, O. and N. Stern. (2009). "Towards a Global Green Recovery: Recommendations for Immediate G20 Action." Report for the German Foreign Office, submitted to the G20 London Summit, April 2, 2009. Potsdam Institute for Climate Impact Research and Grantham Research Institute on Climate Change and the Environment.

Elgin, D. J. and C. M Weible. (2013). "A Stakeholder Analysis of Colorado Climate and Energy Issues Using Policy Analytical Capacity and the Advocacy Coalition Framework." *Review of Policy Research*, 30(1), 114–133.

EUobserver. (2007, January 23). "Commissioners Squabble over How to Make Cars Greener." Retrieved June 6, 2014 from http://euobserver.com/.

EUobserver. (2007, January 29). "German EU Presidency Struggles with Climate Change." Retrieved June 6, 2014 from http://euobserver.com/.

EUobserver. (2007, January 31). "Merkel Backs Car Lobby against EU Emissions Law." Retrieved June 6, 2014 from http://euobserver.com/.

EUobserver. (2007, November 15). "France at Loggerheads with Germany over Car Pollution." Retrieved June 6, 2014 from http://euobserver.com/.

EUobserver. (2008, June 10). "Germany, France Agree on Car Emissions." Retrieved June 6, 2014 from http://euobserver.com/.

EUobserver. (2008, December 2). "Car Companies Win Dilution of EU Emissions Law." Retrieved June 6, 2014 from http://euobserver.com/.

EUobserver. (2013, October 15). "Germany Gets Its Way on EU Car Emissions." Retrieved June 6, 2014 from http://euobserver.com/.

European Commission. (2014). "Reducing Emissions from Transport." Retrieved September 16, 2014 from http://ec.europa.eu/clima/policies/transport/index_en.htm.

European Voice. (2006, July 27). "Carmakers Risk Missing Greenhouse Gas Targets." Retrieved June 6, 2014 from www.politico.eu.

European Voice. (2006, December 7). "Europe Failing to Catch Up with US Car Emission Cuts." Retrieved June 6, 2014 from www.politico.eu.

European Voice. (2007, January 11). "Commission Set to Confirm CO_2 Legislation for Carmakers." Retrieved June 6, 2014 from www.politico.eu.

European Voice. (2007, January 25). "Commission Heads for Compromise over Car Emissions." Retrieved June 6, 2014 from www.politico.eu.

European Voice. (2012, June 28). "Germany Fights against Italy over Car Emissions." Retrieved June 6, 2014 from www.politico.eu.

European Voice. (2012, July 12). "Commission Proposes Vehicle Emissions Limits for 2020." Retrieved June 6, 2014 from www.politico.eu.

European Voice. (2012, July 19). "Concessions and exemptions." Retrieved June 6, 2014 from www.politico.eu.

European Voice. (2013, January 22). "MEPs Clash over Car Emissions." Retrieved June 6, 2014 from www.politico.eu.

European Voice. (2013, April 24). "MEPs Vote to Extend 'Supercredits' for Car Emissions." Retrieved June 6, 2014 from www.politico.eu.

European Voice. (2013, June 28). "Germany Blocks Car CO_2 Limit Deal." Retrieved June 6, 2014 from www.politico.eu.

European Voice. (2013, July 17). "Germany Continues to Block Emissions Deal." Retrieved June 6, 2014 from www.politico.eu.

European Voice. (2013, September 27). "Germany Tries New Objection as Car CO_2 Vote Returns." Retrieved June 6, 2014 from www.politico.eu www.politico.eu.

European Voice. (2013, October 14). "Car CO_2 Vote Delayed." Retrieved June 6, 2014 from www.politico.eu.

European Voice. (2013, October 29). "Lithuania Pushes Car CO_2 Compromise." Retrieved June 6, 2014 from www.politico.eu.

Fisher, D. R., P. Leifeld and Y. Iwaki. (2013). "Mapping the Ideological Networks of American Climate Politics." *Climatic Change*, 116(3–4), 523–545.

Geels, F. W. (2013). "The Impact of the Financial–Economic Crisis on Sustainability Transitions: Financial Investment, Governance and Public Discourse." *Environmental Innovation and Societal Transitions*, 6, 67–95.

Grant, W. (2011). "Business: The Elephant in the Room?" In R. K. W. Wurzel and J. Connelly (eds.), *The European Union as a Leader in International Climate Change Politics*. New York: Routledge.

Grant, W. (2013). "Business." In A. Jordan and C. Adelle (eds.), *Environmental Policy in the EU* (3rd edn), pp. 170–188. London; New York: Routledge.

Grossman, G. M. and E. Helpman. (2001). *Special Interest Politics*. Cambridge, MA: MIT Press.

Hajer, M. A. (1995). *The Politics of Environmental Discourse: Ecological Modernization and the Policy Process*. Oxford: Oxford University Press.

Hodson, D. and U. Puetter. (2013). "The European Union and the Economic Crisis." In M. Cini and N. Pérez-Solórzano Borragán (eds.), *European Union Politics* (4th edn). Oxford: Oxford University Press.

Hosli, M. O., M. Mattila and M. Uriot. (2011). "Voting in the Council of the European Union after the 2004 Enlargement: A Comparison of Old and New Member States." *JCMS: Journal of Common Market Studies*, 49(6), 1249–1270.

Ingold, K. and M. Fischer. (2014). "Drivers of Collaboration to Mitigate Climate Change: An Illustration of Swiss Climate Policy over 15 Years. *Global Environmental Change*, 24, 88–98.

Jachtenfuchs, M. (1996). "Regieren durch Überzeugen." In M. Jachtenfuchs and B. Kohler-Koch (eds.), *Europäische Integration*, pp. 429–454. Opladen, Germany: Leske + Budrich.

Kauppi, H. and M. Widgrén. (2004). "What Determines EU Decision Making? Needs, Power or Both?" *Economic Policy*, 19(39), 222–266.

Keohane, N. O., R. L Revesz and R. N. Stavins. (1998). "The Choice of Regulatory Instruments in Environmental Policy." *Harvard Environmental Law Review*, 22, 313.

Klüver, H. (2009). "Measuring Interest Group Influence Using Quantitative Text Analysis." *European Union Politics*, 10(4), 535–549.

Leheyda, N. and F. Verboven. (2013). "Scrapping Subsidies during the Financial Crisis – Evidence from Europe." Discussion Paper No. 13–079, ZEW (Centre for European

Economic Research). Retrieved March 22, 2017 from http://ftp.zew.de/pub/zew-docs/dp/dp13079.pdf.

Leifeld, P. (2011). "Discourse Networks and German Pension Politics." (Ph.D. thesis). University of Konstanz, Konstanz.

Leifeld, P. (2013). "Reconceptualizing Major Policy Change in the Advocacy Coalition Framework: A Discourse Network Analysis of German Pension Politics." *Policy Studies Journal*, 41(1), 169–198.

Leifeld, P. and S. Haunss. (2012). "Political Discourse Networks and the Conflict over Software Patents in Europe." *European Journal of Political Research*, 51(3), 382–409.

Lenschow, A. (2010). "Environmental Policy." In H. Wallace, M. A. Pollack and A. R. Young (eds.), *Policy-Making in the European Union* (6th edn), pp. 307–330. Oxford: Oxford University Press.

Lenschow, A. and A. R. Zito. (1998). "Blurring or Shifting of Policy Frames?: Institutionalization of the Economic–Environmental Policy Linkage in the European Community." *Governance*, 11(4), 415–441.

Levin, K., B. Cashore, S. Bernstein and G. Auld. (2012). "Overcoming the Tragedy of Super Wicked Problems: Constraining Our Future Selves to Ameliorate Global Climate Change." *Policy Sciences*, 45(2), 123–152.

Meckling, J. (2015). "Oppose, Support, or Hedge? Distributional Effects, Regulatory Pressure, and Business Strategy in Environmental Politics." *Global Environmental Politics*, 15(2), 19–37.

Moravcsik, A. (1993). "Preferences and Power in the European Community: A Liberal Intergovernmentalist Approach." *Journal of Common Market Studies*, *31*(4), 473–524.

Pavlinek, P. (2012). "The Impact of the 2008–2009 Crisis on the Automotive Industry: Global Trends and Firm-Level Effects in Central Europe." *European Urban and Regional Studies*, 22(1), 20–40.

Sabatier, P. A. (1988). "An Advocacy Coalition Framework of Policy Change and the Role of Policy-Oriented Learning Therein." *Policy Sciences*, 21(2–3), 129–168.

Schneider, V. and J. Ollmann. (2013). "Punctuations and Displacements in Policy Discourse: The Climate Change Issue in Germany 2007–2010." In S. Silvern and S. Young (eds.), *Environmental Change and Sustainability*. Rijeka: InTech.

Shambaugh, J. C., R. Reis and H. Rey. (2012). "The Euro's Three Crises." Brookings Papers on Economic Activity, 157–231, Brookings Institution.

Skovgaard, J. (2014). "EU Climate Policy after the Crisis." *Environmental Politics*, 23(1), 1–17.

Steenblik, R. (2009). "Green Growth, Protectionism, and the Crisis." In S. J. Evenett, B. M. Hoekman and O. Cattaneo (eds.), *Effective Crisis Response and Openness: Implications for the Trading System*, pp. 249–262. Washington, DC: Centre for Economic Policy Research.

Steinebach, Y. and C. Knill. (2015). "The Impact of Economic Trends on Environmental Policy-Making." *Ökologisches Wirtschaften*, 30(3), 41–45.

Steinebach, Y. and C. Knill. (2016). "Still an Entrepreneur? The Changing Role of the European Commission in EU Environmental Policy-Making." *Journal of European Public Policy*, 24(3), 429–446.

Tallberg, J. (2003). "The Agenda-Shaping Powers of the EU Council Presidency." *Journal of European Public Policy*, 10(1), 1–19.

ten Brink, P. (2010). "Mitigating the CO2 Emissions from Cars in the EU (Regulation (EC) No 443/2009)." In S. Oberthür and M. Pallemaerts (eds.), *The New Climate*

Policies of the European Union – Internal Legislation and Climate Diplomacy, pp. 179–209. Brussels: Brussels University Press.

Van Biesebroeck, J. and T. J. Sturgeon. (2010). "Effects of the 2008–09 Crisis on the Automotive Industry in Developing Countries: A Global Value Chain Perspective." In O. Cattaneo, G. Gereffi and C. Staritz (eds.), *Global Value Chains in a Postcrisis World: A Development Perspective*, pp. 209–244. Washington, DC: The World Bank.

Walter, S. (2013). *Financial Crises and the Politics of Macroeconomic Adjustments*. Cambridge: Cambridge University Press.

Warleigh, A. (2000). "The Hustle: Citizenship Practice, NGOs and 'Policy Coalitions' in the European Union – The Cases of Auto Oil, Drinking Water and Unit Pricing." *Journal of European Public Policy*, 7(2), 229–243.

Warntjen, A. (2007). "Steering the Union – The Impact of the EU Presidency on Legislative Activity in the Council." *JCMS: Journal of Common Market Studies*, 45(5), 1135–1157.

Weible, C. M. (2007). "An Advocacy Coalition Framework Approach to Stakeholder Analysis: Understanding the Political Context of California Marine Protected Area Policy." *Journal of Public Administration Research and Theory*, 17(1), 95–117.

Zimmer, C., G. Schneider and M. Dobbins. (2005). "The Contested Council: Conflict Dimensions of an Intergovernmental EU Institution." *Political Studies*, 53(2), 403–422.

Part III
Potential remedies to polarized policymaking

7 Comparative national energy policies and climate change actions in countries with divided and unified governments

Reflections, projections and opportunities for improved pedagogy

Thomas Rohrer and Pamela S. Gates

Introduction

The global climate destabilization brought about largely by combustion of fossil fuels (coal, petroleum hydrocarbons and natural gas), increasing the concentration of greenhouse gases such as carbon dioxide and methane in the atmosphere, is one of the most significant ecological issues facing the planet (Pachauri et al. 2015). The most productive way in which nations that are significant emitters of carbon dioxide, methane and other greenhouse gases can address this problem is by the development and implementation of progressive, sustainable energy policies with decreasing reliance on combustion of "fossil fuels" (Pew Environment Group 2010). Most developed nations are now pursuing national policies to transition from antiquated fossil fuel energy economies to systems with a significant proportion of sustainable alternative energy production in recognition of the importance of this issue in the twenty-first century (Sovacool and Brown 2010).

National energy policies vary widely from country to country based on the economic needs of the nation and the perspective that is held regarding the national responsibility for protection of the local, regional and global environment. Different types of governments may be expected to formulate different energy policies based on the type of government in place and the number of political factions participating in the development of national policies.

In this chapter, we compare the energy policies of developed nations with differing governmental structures. The energy policy of the United States of America, with a two-party democratic republican government, the Kingdom of Denmark with a multi-party democratic coalition government and the People's Republic of China, a totalitarian government, are compared and contrasted. China and the United States were selected as they are the biggest carbon emitters and the world's two largest economies. Their political approaches to greenhouse gas control policy vary widely and are molded by their differing political systems. Denmark has been a leader in environmental issues in Europe since the 1980s and stands out as a global leader in alternative energy installation.

The Danish political system is one that involves building a coalition government from multiple political parties and so a broad consensus must be built to implement national policies. Despite the limited economic influence of Denmark in the global economy, the country has had a significant role as a leader of environmental and energy policy in the Nordic countries and in the European Union.

Within these countries, the public understanding of the science behind global climate change and the acceptance of the need to develop political policies to address the issue vary widely. Countries relying on democratic political systems require an electorate with an accurate understanding of an issue if sound policies are to be implemented. Robbins (2016) has discussed how understanding the science and policy of global greenhouse gas management is a critical public health issue, in addition to the broader ecological concerns. In the United States, there has been a deep division in public acceptance of the need to take action to resolve climate issues. Citizens are divided both on the issue of whether global climate destabilization is real and what needs to be done to address it. Suggestions for developing improved public understanding of energy and climate issues via improved pedagogy need to assure better systems for teaching and learning about the climate change issue and ensure sound energy policy development.

Energy policy in the United States

Energy independence has been the holy grail of American policy since the mid-1970s and has been addressed in major speeches by presidents Nixon, Carter, Clinton, G. H. W. Bush, G. W. Bush and Obama (Ydstie 2012). Virtually every administration over the past fifty years has seen this issue as a high priority and publicly declared it to be so. But rather than articulating a clear and focused mission and objectives to achieve this goal, American energy policy has often been a confused mixture of regulations and incentives that pander to the vested interests of multinational corporations and established energy systems instead of dedicating sufficient resources to new, innovative, sustainable power generation programs (Evans 1988).

Energy independence requires a forward-looking approach based on sustainable energy systems. There is a clear recognition that current national energy policies focused on fossil fuel extraction are neither sustainable nor in the best interests of the United States. The growing recognition of the devastating impacts of global climate destabilization on the infrastructure and agriculture of the United States, as well as the rest of the world, are rather more contemporary issues which are further driving the move away from fossil fuel combustion. Sustainable alternative energy systems are becoming a key component of sustainable energy policy in the United States (USEIA 2014).

The national energy policy of the United States is driven by a complex framework of national laws and regulations and implemented by numerous regulatory agencies. In this century, at least four major pieces of legislation have been enacted, which set a course for national energy policy. These include:

- The Energy Policy Act, 2005
- The Energy Independence and Security Act, 2007
- The Emergency Economic Stabilization Act, 2008
- The American Recovery and Investment Act, 2009.

The last two statutes relate more specifically to economics than to energy, but they contain significant sections that will shape national energy policy, including directing the creation of a national smart energy grid, providing renewable energy tax credits and developing a national home weatherization program to effect energy conservation. The statutory provisions in this legislation will provide a framework for the construction and implementation of national energy policy well into the future. These four statutes serve as the basis for the United States' twenty-first century energy policy and will encourage a more prospective approach to the transition from fossil fuels to sustainable energy systems.

The federal Energy Policy Act of 2005 and the Energy Independence and Security Act of 2007 set out, in over 1,000 pages of law, the basis for actions and policies of the U.S. federal government on future energy policy. From these laws, it is clear that the United States Congress feels that energy policy should be established at the federal level and that state and local energy policies should follow the federal lead. These statutes have been criticized for their lack of strong, specific mandates and deadlines but they do set out a framework for a number of important actions to promote energy conservation and move the country forward into more sustainable energy systems.

The current United States Energy Policy Act of 2005 (USEPA) does not establish a clear and powerful national program to promote sustainable energy systems. Instead, it adopts a piecemeal approach in several areas to improve the country's energy status. Title One of the law focuses on conservation and retrofitting of government buildings and individual residences to save energy. Various consumer education and certification programs are included (e.g., Energy Star appliance labeling). A clear and comprehensive prospective policy is lacking.

USEPA Title Two, which covers renewable energy, provides for a national assessment of renewable energy resources, funding for research and additional evaluation of the suitability of federal lands for geothermal or solar projects. It lays out a more prospective policy than Title One. While both these sections of the statute may provide some movement toward a more sustainable energy infrastructure, they lack the firm directives that the current energy and climate situation demands.

The Act also opens up millions of acres of additional public land for hydrocarbon leasing, including substantial offshore areas. Production incentives in the form of billions of dollars of tax credits are provided to fossil hydrocarbon producers. Increased access to federal lands for exploration and drilling is given, along with an expansion of coal leases on federal lands and funding for research and demonstration projects related to the "clean coal" program. There is also support for expansion of nuclear power facilities. Again, these sections offer encouragement and incentives to private sector development but lack any mandates to force movement in the direction of sustainable alternative energy systems.

Public records show that the U.S. federal government provided substantially larger subsidies to fossil fuel industries than to renewable resource development during the 2002–2008 period reviewed for this chapter. Subsidies to companies involved in fossil fuels totaled approximately $72 billion over the study period, representing a direct cost to taxpayers. Subsidies for renewable fuels totaled $29 billion over the same period (Adeyeye et al. 2009).

A recent report by the International Monetary Fund (IMF 2015) found that post-tax energy subsidies globally are much higher than previously estimated, totaling $4.9 trillion, equivalent to 6.5 percent of global gross domestic product. Their evaluation also noted that energy subsidies impose large fiscal costs on governments which need to be financed by some combination of higher public debt, increased tax burdens and diversion of spending from other public needs such as health care, education and improved infrastructure. They found that fossil fuel subsidies damaged the environment and human health by causing more premature deaths from local air pollution, exacerbating urban congestion and increasing global greenhouse gas emissions (IMF 2015).

State-specific energy efficiency incentive programs also play a significant role in the overall energy policy of the United States. The American Council for an Energy Efficient Economy (ACEEE 2016) notes that about half of the states have energy efficiency programs which provide subsidies for reduced electrical use from traditional generation sources such as coal-fired power plants. These subsidies lock the United States into a future that is still heavily invested in fossil fuel development and extraction. In order to assure sustainable energy sources for the long term, the government should consider prospective fiscal policies that support renewable energy systems at a higher level and gradually reduce support for fossil fuel companies.

The discovery of new methods of extracting natural gas from large shale formations under the continental United States may provide hope for reaching the elusive goal of energy independence. Energy economist Phil Verleger has predicted that, within less than a decade, the United States would no longer need to import crude oil and will become a net exporter of natural gas (Verleger 1990). Both large and small energy companies are now using controversial techniques such as hydraulic fracturing combined with horizontal drilling to unlock vast oil and natural gas deposits trapped in shale formations in several states including Pennsylvania, North Dakota, Oklahoma and Texas. North Dakota, for instance, now produces half a million barrels of crude oil per day, and production of oil, coal and natural gas is rising (Hook 2009). The Antrim and Utica shale formations in Michigan are also currently being targeted for development by this process (Curtis 2002; Jenkins and Boyer 2008).

The hydraulic fracturing boom has brought with it a number of significant environmental concerns. The process is currently suspected of causing problems with water supply contamination in both the eastern and western United States (Osborn et al. 2011). The U.S. Environmental Protection Agency and the U.S.

Geological Survey have conducted studies linking contamination of drinking water aquifers to hydraulic fracturing for hydrocarbon extraction (Osborn et al. 2011). The process has also been linked to earthquakes in normally stable geological areas (Vermylen and Zoback 2011; Tucker 2012).

While this new technology may provide a supply of new natural gas reserve resources that will alleviate some of the short-term concerns about energy supplies, continued reliance on non-renewable fossil fuel sources is not sustainable in the long run. In fact, focusing resources on natural gas extraction will likely diminish support for alternative, sustainable energy systems as gas prices drop. Wiseman has also noted the dearth of regulations in this arena and the likelihood that there will be widespread harm to environmental quality and human health as the industry rushes to extract hydrocarbons by expanded horizontal fracturing operations (Wiseman 2009). A viable prospective energy policy needs to be combined with environmental regulations that also have a forward-looking view of resource management and protection.

The global moral and ethical reason to shift from fossil fuel consumption is the aggregate impact of releases of greenhouse gases such as carbon dioxide and methane into our atmosphere and subsequent climate destabilization (Gore 2006; Pachauri et al. 2015). The United States took a leadership position under the administration of then Vice-President Albert Gore in the 1990s but has never followed up with a strong regulatory program to control emissions. Attempts to have the Kyoto Protocol on greenhouse gas reduction ratified by the U.S. Congress have failed. Congress has resisted full endorsement and ratification of the protocol, preferring to allow voluntary actions and the free-market system to control carbon dioxide emissions with no national commitment to a prescribed limit on greenhouse gas emissions. Current federal legislation relies upon a "cap and trade" program focused on letting the free market play a major role in regulating emissions.

Despite thousands of pages of laws and regulations, the United States' energy policy is surprisingly weak in practice. While recognizing the critical issue of energy supply and using the "Bully Pulpit" to declare that the nation must become energy self-sufficient and remedy its "addiction to oil," the federal government has done little to mandate a program which would ensure the availability of sustainable energy resources in the future. The current Congress favors programs that rely on the private sector to resolve the energy crisis and is reluctant to take a firm stand in the public administration of energy resources. Both Congress and regulatory agencies are focused more on tax incentives and voluntary mechanisms than on any strong regulatory instruments to compel the transition to sustainable energy systems.

One reason for this approach may be the influence that major energy production corporations have on national politics (Evans 1988). Another may be the fact that the United States has less than 5 percent of the world's population but uses 26 percent of world energy resources (United States, Department of Energy 2011). This energy consumption results in the production of more than one-quarter of all finished goods produced worldwide. With such a high-calorie energy diet feeding the world's largest economy, it is difficult from a public management perspective to direct a rapid change to a sustainable energy economy when traditional fuel sources are still available at relatively low cost.

Energy policy in the United States thus remains conflicted, with legislators maintaining strong support for traditional fuel sources while recognizing the need for energy independence and sustainable, renewable energy production in the future. The potential to develop a sustainable energy future exists, but the political influences pushing billions of dollars in federal financial support to the fossil fuel industry will slow the transition and may cause the United States to be adversely positioned in the future (Rosenberg 2008). Other nations may outpace the United States in the installation of clean, renewable energy infrastructure, resulting in economic and strategic disadvantage for the country (Rohrer and Kurtz 2014; White House 2015).

Energy policy in the People's Republic of China

Totalitarian regimes such as the People's Republic of China place strict controls on the release of information from government ministries. Thus, it is difficult to ascertain what the formal energy policy of the nation actually is. Government officials may also present an exaggerated scenario of progress in the energy sector in situations where data are not freely available to validate or refute their claims.

Despite this, a number of "think tanks" and government research organizations have compiled relevant information in an attempt to clarify the true energy policy of the People's Republic of China (PRC) (Pew Environment Group 2010; USEIA 2014).

The PRC is well known for being the world's largest emitter of carbon dioxide and other greenhouse gases. The country's economic growth in the manufacturing sector and abundant fuel reserves have resulted in combustion of fossil fuels at an accelerated rate with expectations of continued growth at an average of 8 percent per annum. China continues to build new fossil fuel generation plants with as many as fifty new facilities coming online each year (Yeoh and Rajaraman 2004).

The electricity generation sector, with its coal-dominated fuel mix and high proportion of inefficient, antiquated generating units, is a key contributor to China's significant environmental problems. Seven out of ten of the world's most polluted cities are in China, with urban pollution levels greatly exceeding World Health Organization standards (Hertsgaard, 1997). China is coming under increasing international pressure to control its emissions as the global impact becomes more evident. Pollution control of emissions sources is very weak in China, with industrial output being of greater concern than environmental quality. Pollution from largely unregulated coal plant emissions have darkened the skies of major industrial areas and caused acute and chronic human health impacts. Acid rain damage to crops and forests has affected more than one-third of the land in China, and economic losses approach 2 percent of the country's gross domestic product (Yeoh and Rajaraman 2004). The energy demands of a growing manufacturing economy are expected to keep demand for electricity high in the foreseeable future.

In addition to being a major consumer of fossil fuels, the country has also supported energy production from renewable sources. The PRC has had some national support for generation of electricity from sustainable sources for over twenty years. In 1994, the Ministry of Electric Power issued a regulation requiring provincial authorities to connect wind farms with the grid at the nearest point and to purchase all the electricity generated (Cherni and Kentish 2007). China currently has a target of 15 percent renewable power generation by 2020.

Current growth in sustainable energy production systems provides some hope for the future. In addition to promoting energy efficiency, the PRC is actively pursuing alternative energy development as a strategy to reduce energy demand, provide for energy security and reduce greenhouse gas emissions and other pollutants (Zheng and Fridley 2011). China has also become the world's largest investor in sustainable power generation systems with expenditure of $84 billion in 2010. This compares to $18.6 billion in expenditure by the United States during the same period. With successful alternative energy development, some 32 percent of China's electricity and 21 percent of its total primary energy will be supplied by sustainable alternative energy systems by 2030 (Zheng and Fridley 2011).

In November 2014, U.S. President Barack Obama and PRC President Xi Jinping announced a joint agreement on actions to mitigate global climate destabilization. This agreement commits both countries to achieving a protocol or other legal instrument for reducing greenhouse gas emissions as part of the United Nations Climate Conference in Paris in December 2015. The United States agreed to targeted emission reductions of 26 to 28 percent below 2005 levels by 2025, while China was allowed to make its best efforts to control emissions such that peak carbon dioxide emissions will begin to decline by 2030. Both countries also agreed to work cooperatively on a number of other projects including:

- establishing a United States–China Climate Change Working Group
- phasing out production and release of other potent greenhouse gases such as hydrofluorocarbons (HFCs)
- creating a United States–China Clean Energy Research Center
- examining inefficient fossil fuel subsidies under the G-20 meetings
- promoting trade in "green goods"
- pilot projects to demonstrate clean energy production and storage
- convening a "Climate Smart/Low-Carbon Cities Initiative" to develop new model infrastructure.

This agreement established the foundation for a comprehensive multi-national climate agreement on a global scale for the Paris climate talks in 2015.

Within China there is growing realization of the need to reduce fossil fuel emissions and invest in a sustainable power industry infrastructure to ensure that the PRC maintains its position as a major global manufacturing center (Wang et al. 2010). In 2010, the National People's Congress laid out plans for significant energy conservation programs, investment in new energy technologies and environmental protection initiatives funded by an outlay of over $20 billion dollars in government funding (Xin and Stone 2010).

Unlike the United States, where major shifts in energy and environmental policy must be developed incrementally through a partisan legislative process, the PRC government can act rapidly once the country's leaders have decided upon a necessary course of action. Pew Research Center estimated that there would be expenditure totaling one trillion U.S. dollars on sustainable energy infrastructure from 2010–2015, with China leading the way (Pew Environment Group 2010). This investment in renewable energy has resulted in moving the peak carbon emissions date estimated for China back by five years (Green and Stern 2015) from 2030 to approximately 2025. Improvements recorded in the level, rate, structure and energy efficiency of China's economic growth and national policy developments in recent years have led to a remarkably rapid shift in greenhouse gas emissions from the PRC (ibid.).

Energy policy in the Kingdom of Denmark

In contrast to the United States and the PRC, Denmark has a much more limited fossil fuel resource base. The North Sea hydrocarbon fields have some reserves of crude oil and natural gas, and Denmark is actually a net exporter of crude oil. Coal reserves are all but absent, and any coal consumed is imported from other European countries, primarily Germany. This lack of fossil fuel security has prompted the Kingdom of Denmark to take a comprehensive approach to assuring its future energy supply via an aggressive program to install sustainable, renewable energy systems throughout the country. Similar actions are being implemented in other European nations such as Germany and the United Kingdom.

Like other Western nations, Denmark has suffered the economic costs of increasing prices for crude oil and refined petroleum products. Over a decade ago, the national government began a dialogue with the citizens of Denmark on the development of a national energy policy. This resulted in the publication in February 2012 of "Energy Strategy 2050" by the Danish Ministry of Climate and Energy (Ministry of Climate and Energy 2012). Under this strategy, the country aims to be 100 percent energy self-sufficient by 2020 and free of hydrocarbon consumption by 2050. The nation had previously committed to a portfolio standard for renewable energy systems of 30 percent by 2020.

The goals in Denmark's energy strategy have led to a comprehensive program of energy conservation, utilization of waste materials for energy production and a national program to install a large base of wind power and solar systems. That the Ministry is named "Climate and Energy" indicates that the Danish government recognizes the link between fossil fuel consumption and climate change.

This understanding also drives the need to develop sustainable, non-polluting energy systems. The country has a clear and focused energy strategy which moves it away from dependence on fossil fuels and into a strong program of sustainable energy systems. Like Canada, Denmark has committed to meet or exceed the goals of the Kyoto Protocol (Ministry of Climate and Energy 2012). The citizenry strongly support this program thanks to years of citizen involvement and engagement in the policy development process.

As of 2010, Denmark met 22 percent of its national electrical energy demand with wind power systems (United States, Energy Information Administration 2011). The Danish company, Vestas, is one of the world's largest manufacturers of wind turbine generators for both land and offshore applications. While advances in the sustainable generation of electricity are noteworthy, the country still relies on coal for 21.6 percent of its overall energy consumption (United States, Energy Information Administration 2011).

In tax-heavy Denmark, the federal government encouraged private investment in commercial wind farms by offering tax exemptions for revenues generated by wind power industries. Corporations, citizens and municipal governments were given opportunities to invest in a turbine outright or buy shares in wind turbine cooperatives. Governmental support to build facilities that use animal waste and household refuse to generate electricity have also contributed to the Danish quest for energy self-sufficiency (Ministry of Climate and Energy 2012). In addressing carbon emissions, Denmark also passed legislation to tax the energy industry with a structure that encouraged conservation and also allowed other taxes to be reduced (Harrison 2010).

In Denmark, the government, private industry and the citizenry are all united in working toward the common goal of energy self-sufficiency. Its educated citizenry accepts the science of global climate change and the moral imperative to take the actions necessary to combat climate destabilization and become carbon neutral by 2050. United States citizens would benefit from the same form of pedagogy that produces the scientific understanding and critical thinking exhibited by the Danes.

The commitment to sustainable energy systems in Denmark has required some government resources but the shift is resulting in economic benefits to the country (Ewing et al. 2007). These benefits are expected to increase as fossil fuel costs accelerate due to declining reserves and increased demand. Costs for alternative energy systems such as wind and solar power continue to decline worldwide.

Policymaking in the Kingdom of Denmark will be driven by these factors to favor sustainable, renewable energy systems and will make the country energy independent earlier than many larger industrial nations. Other western European countries such as Germany, Sweden, Finland, Spain and the United Kingdom are following similar paths. It has been noted that Europeans accept the science of global climate change and recognize that it is driven by combustion of fossil fuels.

Improving environmental pedagogy

The relatively slow transition from fossil fuels to sustainable energy systems in the United States may be attributed to a number of factors. The severe economic recession of 2008–2012 caused a shift in investor funding away from new technologies such as wind and solar power. Also, the United States' policies described earlier, which favored exploration and extraction by American companies via government subsidies and favorable tax treatment, did work to increase the supply of traditional hydrocarbon sources. Combined with reduced fuel demand due to the economic stagnation of the recession, domestic prices for coal, liquid petroleum and natural gas fell to levels not seen for several years. These economic factors coupled with confusing media messages and political posturing has caused American concern about climate change to decline in recent years (Scruggs and Benegal 2012).

At present, less than half (47–49 percent) of adult Americans believe that global climate change is real (Leiserowitz et al. 2013). Only 42 percent of adults in the United States know that the vast majority (97 percent) of climate scientists agree that global climate destabilization is occurring and that it is primarily caused by human activities (Melillo et al. 2014). Personal concerns about the impact of global warming on the planet have actually decreased over time, dropping from 33 percent in 2001 to 28 percent in March 2010 (Gallup 2010), with the most recent Gallup polls putting the figure at 25 percent (Carmichael et al. 2017). These statistics may explain the differences between American political parties on issues relating to the problem of global climate destabilization.

A common explanation for rising doubts, at least in the United States, about the reality of climate change and its global impact is the belief that there are coordinated efforts by industry and media outlets to downplay the issue and criticize the data and scientists conducting the work (McCright and Dunlap 2011; Scruggs and Benegal 2012). Climate change skeptics often receive as much attention in the media as published scientific studies with little critical thinking being applied to news reports. Conflicting opinions on climate change, as well as other scientific issues, tend to generate more media interest than consensus. Public opinion research suggests that people with the least grounded opinions are most susceptible to manipulation by the media resulting in fluctuating opinions on an issue (Zaller 1992).

Western European countries and the PRC have established themselves as leaders in combating global climate destabilization by moving away from fossil fuels and developing a sustainable energy economy. The Unites States, in contrast, has done relatively little, even with a large suite of regulatory agencies and statutory authority to move in this direction.

Part of the problem is the lack of majority public support among voters for these changes. The opinions of the electorate are formed by their knowledge of the issue, whether it is based on sound science or exaggerated rhetoric. Reforming the pedagogy of climate change needs to be done purposefully and over a long period of time to change current perspectives in American society.

As a start, the following steps can be taken.

1   Establish **environmental studies** (science and policy) as part of the core K–12 (kindergarten through to twelfth grade) curricula for all students. Integration of environmental issues into basic sciences such as biology, chemistry and physics and into the humanities and social sciences would improve understanding of complex environmental issues.

2   **Improve communication by climate scientists.** Support media programming which clearly explains the causes and consequences of global climate change. Use the internet and other multi-media sources to serve as an easily accessible repository for climate change facts.

3   **De-politicize** global climate destabilization. Make environmental quality, a stable planet and environmental health **non-partisan** issues that all can support. Once the economic benefits of alternative energy systems are compared to the fossil fuel economy, public understanding of the benefits of supporting clean energy will spread.

4   **Empower youth** to take an active role in "saving the planet" – model on established recycling education programs and other pro-environment campaigns that are already in place.

5   Develop **social media tools to advance understanding** of climate change and the mitigating actions that can be taken by all members of society. Modeling a challenge such as the one done on social media with the "ice bucket challenge" can be key in spreading information about climate change and encouraging commitment by participants.

6   Recruit people and businesses to be partners in the "**war on climate change,**" similar to the war on drugs or the war on terrorism.

7   Develop "**critical thinking**" skills in earlier grades and have students use those skills to evaluate news reports and industry propaganda. By providing systematic K–12 initiatives, young people can become engaged in ways to "save the world" for themselves and generations that will follow.

8   Develop **faith-based initiatives** to encourage people of various faiths to see the religious component of caring for the natural world of their Creator. There have been a variety of Judaic, Christian and Muslim sects which have addressed this issue. No less of an authority than the current Pope of the Roman Catholic Church, Francis I, has issued an encyclical calling for swift action on the problem of global climate destabilization. In "Laudato Si'" (Francesco 2015), Pope Francis warned of the dangers to creation of the impact of the fossil fuel industry and urged developed nations to take action to protect the planet and to ease the suffering of those underprivileged countries who bear the brunt of the negative effects of climate change.

Advancing the education of the populace via the means listed above is a vital and necessary component of assuring public support for the necessary advances and investments to transition to sustainable energy systems. A better educated public (whether via secular education or religious instruction) is clearly the key to improved understanding of the critical issue of global climate destabilization. With a clearer understanding of the negative planetary effects of fossil fuel combustion and the benefits, both economic and environmental, of sustainable energy systems, one should expect broader support for progressive energy policies in any political system.

References

ACEEE. 2016. "Energy Efficiency Resource Standard." American Council for an Energy Efficient Economy. Available at http://aceee.org/policy-brief/energy-efficiency-resource-standard-eers (accessed April 3, 2017).

Adeyeye, Adenike, James Barrett, Jordan Diamond, Lisa Goldman, John Pendergrass and Daniel Schramm. 2009. "Estimating U.S. Government Subsidies to Energy Sources: 2002–2008." Environmental Law Institute, Washington, DC. Available at www.elistore.org/reports_detail.asp?ID=11358&topic=Energy_and_Innovation (accessed March 23, 2017).

Carmichael, J. T., R. J. Brulle and J. K. Huxster. 2017. "The Great Divide: Understanding the Role of Media and Other Drivers of the Partisan Divide in Public Concern over Climate Change in the USA, 2001–2014." *Climatic Change* 141: 599. doi:10.1007/s10584-017-1908-1.

Cherni, Judith A. and Joanna Kentish. 2007. "Renewable Energy Policy and Electricity Market Reforms in China." *Energy Policy* 35: 3616–3629.

Curtis, John B. 2002. "Fractured Shale-Gas Systems." *American Association of Petroleum Geologists Bulletin* 86 (11): 1921–1938.

Daly, Herman E. 2006. "Sustainable Development – Definitions, Principles, Policies." In *The Future of Sustainability*, edited by Marco Keiner, pp. 33–54. Dordrecht, The Netherlands: Springer Press.

Evans, Diana. 1988. "Oil PACs and Aggressive Campaign Contribution Strategies." *Journal of Politics* 50 (4): 1047–1056.

Ewing, B. T., R. Sari and U. Soytas. 2007. "Disaggregate Energy Consumption and Industrial Output in the United States." *Energy Policy* 35: 1274–1281.

Francesco. 2015. "Laudato Si – Encyclical Letter of the Holy Father Francis on Care for Our Common Home." The Vactican.

Gallup. 2010, March 11. "Americans' Global Warming Concerns Continue to Drop." Available at www.gallup.com/poll/126560/Americans-Global-Warming-Concerns-Continue-Drop.aspx?version=print (accessed April 3, 2017).

Gore, Al. 2006. *An Inconvenient Truth: The Planetary Emergency of Global Warming and What We Can Do About It.* New York: Rodale Press.

Green, F. and N. Stern. 2015. "China's 'New Normal': Structural Change, Better Growth, and Peak Emissions." Policy Brief, Grantham Research Institute on Climate Change and the Environment, London School of Economics.

Harrison, Kathryn. 2010. "The Comparative Politics of Carbon Taxation." *Annual Review of Law and Social Science* 6: 501–529.

Hertsgaard, Mark. 1997, November. "Our Real China Problem." *The Atlantic.*

Hook, Mikael. 2009. "Historical Trends in American Coal Production and a Possible Future Outlook." *International Journal of Coal Geology* 78 (3): 201–216.

IMF. 2015. "How Large are Global Energy Subsidies?" Working Paper WP/15/105, International Monetary Fund, Washington, DC.

IPCC. 2007. "Climate Change 2007: The Physical Science Basis." Contribution of Working Group I to the Fourth Assessment Report of the Intergovernmental Panel on Climate Change, edited by S. Solomon, D. Qin, M. Manning, Z. Chen, M. Marquis, K. B. Averyt, M. Tignor and H. L. Miller. Cambridge and New York: Cambridge University Press.

Islam, M., A. Fartaj and D. S.-K. Ting. 2004. "Current Utilization and Future Prospects of Emerging Renewable Energy Applications in Canada." *Renewable and Sustainable Energy Review* 8: 493–519.

Jenkins, C. D. and C. M. Boyer, 2008. "Coal-bed and Shale-gas Reservoirs." *Journal of Petroleum Geology* 60 (2): 92–99.

Leiserowitz, A., E. Maibach, C. Roser-Renouf, G. Feinberg and P. Howe. 2013. "Climate Change in the American Mind: Americans' Global Warming Beliefs and Attitudes in April 2013." Yale University and George Mason University: Yale Project on Climate Change Communication, New Haven, CT.

McCright, A. M. and R. E. Dunlap. 2011. "The Politicization of Climate Change and Polarization in the American Public's Views of Global Warming, 2001–2010." *The Sociological Quarterly* 52 (2): 155–194.

Melillo, J. M., T. C. Richmond and G. W. Yohe (eds.). 2014. "Highlights of Climate Change Impacts in the United States: The Third National Climate Assessment." U.S. Global Change Research Program, Department of Energy, Washington DC.

Ministry of Climate and Energy. 2012. "Danish Energy Strategy 2050: From Coal, Oil and Gas to Green Energy." Copenhagen: Danish Ministry of Climate and Energy.

Osborn, S. G., A. Vegnosh, N. R. Warner and R. B. Jackson. 2011. "Methane Contamination of Drinking Water Accompanying Gas Well Drilling and Hydraulic Fracturing." *Proceedings of the National Academy of Sciences* 108 (20): 8172–8176.

Pachauri, R. K., L. Meyer, G. K. Plattner and T. Stocker. 2015. "Climate Change 2014: Synthesis Report." Contribution of Working Groups I, II and III to the Fifth Assessment Report of the Intergovernmental Panel on Climate Change. IPCC, United Nations, New York.

Pew Environment Group. 2010. "Who's Winning the Clean Energy Race?" Pew Charitable Trust, Washington, DC.

Rhodes, Christopher J. 2016. "The 2015 Paris Climate Change Conference: COP21." *Science Progress* 99 (6): 97–104.

Robbins, Anthony. 2016. "How to Understand the Results of the Climate Change Summit: Conference of Parties 21 (COP21) Paris 2015." *Journal of Public Health* 37 (2): 129–132.

Rohrer, Thomas K. and Rick S. Kurtz. 2014. "Public Management of Sustainable Energy Development: How National Policies Help or Hinder Future Energy Security." In *Governance and Public Management: Strategic Foundations for Volatile Times*, edited by Charles Conteh, Thomas J. Greitens, David K. Jesuit and Ian Roberge, pp. 63–75. London and New York: Routledge.

Rosenberg, R. 2008. "Diversifying America's Energy Future: The Future of Renewable Wind Power." *Virginia Environmental Law Journal* 26 (3): 505–544.

Scruggs, Lyle and Salil Benegal. 2012. "Declining Public Concern about Climate Change: Can We blame the Great recession?" *Global Environmental Change* 22 (2): 505–515.

Senter, Mary M. and T. K. Rohrer. 2013. "Citizen Attitudes and Opinions on Large Scale Wind Turbine Installations in the Northwest Lower Peninsula of Michigan." Center for Applied Research and Rural Studies, Central Michigan University, Mount Pleasant, MI.

Smith, G. G. 1989. *Coal Resources of Canada.* Ottawa: The Geological Survey of Canada.

Soderbergh, B., F. Robelius and K. Aleklett. 2007. "A Crash Programme for the Canadian Oil Sands Industry." *Energy Policy* 35 (3): 1931–1947.

Sovacool, Benjamin K. and Marilyn A. Brown. 2010. "Competing Dimensions of Energy Security: An International Perspective." *Annual Review of Environment and Resources* 35: 77–108.

Tucker, Charlotte. 2012. "Health Concerns of 'Fracking' Drawing Increased Attention: EPA Conducting Studies on Health Effects." *The Nation's Health* 42 (2): 1–14.

United States, Department of Energy. 1988. "25th Anniversary of the 1973 Oil Embargo." Washington, DC: U. S. Government Printing Office.

United States, Energy Information Administration. 2009. "International Energy Data and Analysis for Denmark." Available at www.eia.gov/countries/country-data.cfm?fips=DA (accessed March 1, 2012).

United States, Energy Information Administration. 2011. "International Energy Outlook 2011: World Energy Demand and Economic Outlook." Washington, DC: U.S. Department of Energy.

UNFCC. 2015a. "United Nations Framework Convention on Climate Change." Available at http://unfccc.int/2860.php (accessed May 27, 2015).

UNFCC. 2015b. "Lima Call for Climate Action." Draft report. Available at http://unfccc.int/files/meetings/lima_dec_2014/application/pdf/auv_cop20_lima_call_for_climate_action.pdf (accessed May 27, 2015).

USEIA. 2014. "International Energy Outlook 2014: World Petroleum and Other Liquid Fuels." U.S. Energy Information Administration, Washington, DC.

USEPA. 2008. "National Action Plan for Energy Efficiency – Vision for 2025: A Framework for Change." U.S. Department of Energy and the Environmental Protection Agency. Available at https://energy.gov/sites/prod/files/edg/images/Action_Plan_for_EE_1118.pdf (accessed April 3, 2017).

Verleger, Phillip. 1990. "Understanding the 1990 Oil Crisis." *The Energy Journal* 11: 15–33.

Vermylen, John P. and Mark D. Zoback. 2011. "Hydraulic Fracturing, Microseismic Magnitudes and Stress Evaluation in the Barnett Shale, Texas, USA." Paper presented at the Society of Petroleum Engineers Hydraulic Fracturing Conference, January 24–26, 2011, The Woodlands, Texas.

Wang, F., H. Yin and S. Li. 2010. "China's Renewable Energy Policy: Commitments and Challenges." *Energy Policy* 38 (4): 1872–1878.

White House. 2015. "The National Security Implications of a Changing Climate: Findings from Select Federal Reports." Washington, DC.

Wiseman, Hannah J. 2009. "Untested Waters: The Rise of Hydraulic Fracturing in Oil and Gas Production and the Need to Revisit Regulation." *Fordham Environmental Law Review* 20: 115–158.

Xin, H. and R. Stone. 2010. "The 2010 Budget: China Amasses War Chest to Confront Its Environmental Nightmares." *Science* 327 (5972): 1440–1441.

Ydstie, John. 2012, March 7. "Is U.S. Energy Independence Finally Within Reach?" *National Public Radio.* Available at www.npr.org/2012/03/07/148036966/is-u-s-energy-independence-finally-within-reach (accessed March 23, 2017).

Yeoh, B. and R. Rajaraman. 2004. "Electricity in China: The Latest Reforms." *The Electricity Journal* 17 (3): 60–69.

Zaller, John. 1992. *The Nature and Origins of Mass Opinion.* New York: Cambridge University Press.

Zarnikau, J. 2003. "Consumer Demand for 'Green Power' and Energy Efficiency." *Energy Policy* 31: 1661–1672.

Zheng, Nina and David G. Fridley. 2011. "Alternative Energy Development and China's Energy Future." Lawrence Berkeley National Laboratory Report, Berkeley, CA.

8   Exploring the mediating effects of institutions on polarization and political conflict

Evidence from Michigan cities

Nathan Grasse, Thomas Greitens, David Jesuit and Lawrence Sych

Thriving city governments depend on public managers with sufficient leadership credibility to mobilize effective organizational responses to political challenges. Today, a city's council members, employees, citizens and interest groups expect city leaders to exercise foresight and practice strategic management that effectively manages political conflict. An organizational culture and structure that engenders change and innovation underlies a city government's ability to adapt its behaviors, practices and policies in ways that effectively address pressures such as political conflict and polarization.

As political polarization among residents of local communities increases, credible leaders managing strategically will presumably shape organizational responses to maintain stability and movement toward attaining their goals. Nonetheless, polarization and political conflict increases workforce pressures on staff and generates heightened conflict among city council members and mid-level managers. Sustaining balanced organizational responses to political conflict challenges the abilities of city managers as leaders and the outcomes usually remain obscured for long periods of time.

This study develops a model that examines the potential influences of different institutional structures and management strategies on political conflict in polarized and, for the sake of comparison, non-polarized municipalities. Based on previous streams of research discussed below, we posit that both institutional structures and management tools, such as the use of strategic planning, can influence conflict in polarized municipalities, controlling for other factors such as local government fiscal stress and the socioeconomic levels of individuals within the local government.

Literature review

One of the fundamental questions in the study of urban politics relates to how different forms of government affect policy outcomes. During the Progressive Era, a model of urban governance emerged that emphasized non-politicized management principles such as the council-manager form of government. This type of government is in direct contrast to the strong mayoral systems that had developed in most major American cities in the nineteenth and early twentieth centuries, in which politics and partisanship played an essential role in running the city machine. Today, we can observe three forms of municipal government in Michigan: council-manager, strong mayor and weak mayor (Cekola 2011). Additional Progressive reforms called for holding non-partisan elections with municipal governments electing candidates at-large rather than in individual districts. Many of these reforms continue to influence current good governance reform efforts with proponents typically advocating against strong mayoral systems and instead emphasizing the council-manager reformed model of governance. However, there is little research that examines how polarization interacts with these different forms of government to influence conflict in cities.

City managers today may find themselves in somewhat awkward leadership situations. Inside city hall, managers must mediate public distrust and sometimes outright hostility toward government as well as respond to public demands for services (Meier and Bohte 2006; Terry 2003). On the one hand, the manager is expected by many residents to lead city efforts to, among other things, sustain a quality of life that attracts residents, grow the local economy and nourish downtown businesses, promote citizen engagement and help create a vision of the future in the short and long run. On the other hand, the manager's tenure rests in the hands of the elected council (and perhaps even a mayor) who individually or collectively may instead see themselves as political leaders and the manager as but a hired hand (Svara 1991).

The concept of strategic planning and its forward-looking approach can be linked with a more pragmatic focus on implementation given the criticisms by scholars such as Mintzberg (1994) who note that planning alone lacks mechanisms for evaluation and adjustment. In reaction to these criticisms, strategic management as conceptualized here includes a broader array of practices beyond planning alone, that collectively fosters organizational outcomes including increased effectiveness, adaptation to environment changes, implementing successful reforms, enhancing employee satisfaction and establishing positive working environments (Bryson 1995; Mercer 1991; Poister and Streib 2005). Adding implementation and evaluation components completes the planning process (Halachmi et al. 1993; Steiss 2003). Planning in this way is tied to strategic management, the "all-encompassing process of developing and managing a strategic agenda" (Mercer 1991; Poister and Streib 2005, 46), and has also been theoretically tied to employee performance and well-being, allowing them to better fulfill their roles and responsibilities while also strengthening employees' teamwork and expertise (Bryson 1995).

Various environmental influences might also be expected to drive local government conflicts. The variables included in this analysis all represent pressures faced by local governments that are traditionally held to make governing more difficult. The first of these factors represents the homogeneity and racial composition of communities. Traditionally, the diversity of a community was used by researchers to help explain the growth of council-manager forms of government in the twentieth century under the assumption that more homoge-nous, suburbanized communities typically implemented these types of reforms in their local government (Lineberry and Fowler 1967). However, new research indicates that economic factors within a community may play a more significant role in the adoption of these reforms than community diversity (Choi et al. 2013). Consequently, for this study it is hypothesized that homogeneous com-munities will have more cooperative rather than conflictual relations within their governments (Svara 1991). Similarly, per capita income should influence organ-izational outcomes, with governments serving more affluent constituencies likely to have more resources and success and thus being better able to provide ser-vices. This should affect both service provision and employee attitudes.

Levine (1980, 4) defines fiscal stress as

> this gap between the needs and expectations of citizens and government employees for government services and benefits and the inability of the economy to generate enough economic growth to expand (or even sustain, in some places) tax-supported programs without putting unacceptable demands on taxpayers' take-home pay.

A seemingly rational and responsive management strategy would include a long-range, multi-year revenue and expenditure forecast, prioritized program rank-ings, integrated new revenue resources, workforce productivity improvements and rationed services to attain budget balance and stability. In reality, Levine argues that an inherently politicized environment of powerful and influential interests instead produces disjointed management responses that are short-ranged, incremental and undertaken with an assumption that the fiscal stress will be temporary.

Under conditions of long-term fiscal stress, Levine (1980, 6) suggests leaders "need to develop a middle course for strategic planning that combines a manage-rial disposition to make government more cost-effective with a realistic accept-ance of the political forces that constrain comprehensive policy making." Leadership, he notes, is critical to restore fiscal stability for "… [w]ithout able leadership the process of guiding a government through a fiscal squeeze may turn out to be hazardous and self-defeating" (Levine 1980, 7). Their strategic response should include smoothing its negative effects over time and making tar-geted and deep cuts earlier in the process. Levine (1980, 310) leaves the trade-off between efficiency and equity, "the most difficult strategic choice," to managerial and political discretion.

Bozeman (2010, 561) argues that a longer perspective with broader implica-tions for a post-decline environment offers public managers "the potential to give us insights not revealed when focusing on an isolated episode, no matter how salient the events seem at the time" resulting in greater theory development. Pandey (2010) argues that a durable sense of recession demands more extreme actions from leaders than they would otherwise take in a more "normal" cutback episode which in turn create three "paradoxes" for managers. These are:

- Public organizations possess limited means to alter often ambiguous goals as part of managing cutbacks which results in a complex set of trade-offs given time, strength of public support and prior resource commitments.
- The focus on employment, compensation and other personnel matters leads to voiding the social contract between a public organization and its workforce.
- Innovative efforts, work and performance are threatened during cutback periods and it is not clear how these can be continued while cutting back service levels.

Convincing solutions to these dilemmas for public organizations will elude their leaders and managers, according to Pandey, who suggests that a strategic perspective can lengthen the horizon and open up more opportunities in a recession-shaped environment.

Models and data

Our model hopes to identify factors that influence conflict in polarized cities, in order to help leaders better manage and make governance work. The model employs multiple variables measuring the key influences outlined in the literature review. Some relate to organizational characteristics, while others represent environmental factors that influence local governments. Organizational characteristics that might be expected to influence outcomes are the use of management tools such as strategic planning and the institutional structure of government. Possible environmental influences that might influence outcomes are the racial composition of populations and per capita income.

This study utilizes a path analysis model in order to examine the potential influence of institutional reforms and strategic management in polarized municipalities. Path analysis allows the estimation of the mediating effect of variables as well as the potential for non-recursive relationships. Path regressions rely on simultaneous equations in order to identify these associations. Path analysis also clearly has limitations; for instance, it can only assess whether or not the hypothesized relationships fit the data – it cannot predict whether other better-fitting models exist (Kline 2005).

The primary source of the data used in this study is a survey of 1,430 municipal officials representing the 92 Michigan municipalities with populations in excess of 10,000. The survey collected data from department heads, council members, city managers and mayors. A total of 1,272 individuals were surveyed with 466 returning survey materials, resulting in a 36.64b percent response rate. Using secondary data sources, from the Bureau of the Census, the Citizens Research Council of Michigan and the State of Michigan Treasury Department, we included a number of important contextual variables in our models.

Independent variables

We are particularly interested in the ways in which communities might be able to overcome some of the obstacles posed by ideologically polarized residents. Accordingly, we emphasize factors that are more readily adapted by leadership. First, we use Frederickson et al.'s (2004) five-point scale that we termed "administrative city." This variable captures the extent to which a municipality's institutions have been reformed to reflect scientific management principles. Cities are categorized from highly "political" to highly "administrative" based on the extent to which they display political or administrative characteristics. This scale allows us to capture the diverse nature of municipal structures utilized by local governments in Michigan (Carr and Karuppusamy 2009, 2010).

Our measure of strategic planning is derived from our survey and uses the index proposed by Ihrke et al. (2003). The items in the index include:

1   "This local government engages in regular goal setting strategies for policy making."
2   "This local government has utilized strategic planning to frame its mission."
3   "This local government has a clear mission statement."
4   "This local government has a strategic plan that includes both short- and long-term priorities."
5   "This local government has conducted a stakeholder analysis and thorough environmental scan of its strengths, weaknesses, opportunities and threats (SWOT)."

The five-item index ranges from a 5, indicating council members do not feel these tasks are going on in their communities, to 25, indicating council members feel these tasks are being carried out regularly in their communities.

We measure fiscal stress in a community as the change in State of Michigan shared revenue. Reductions in shared revenue are expected to create additional pressure on organizations as they struggle with fewer resources. Local governments continue to fight a losing battle when it comes to matters of intergovernmental revenues. Intergovernmental transfers between federal and local governments and between state and local governments have been diminishing for nearly four decades. This problem is particularly acute in Michigan due to the significant cuts in shared revenue initiated by the state legislature in the late 1990s. In fact, available state shared revenue declined from 1.3 billion dollars in fiscal year 2003–2004 to 1.1 billion dollars in fiscal year 2005–2006. This variable measures change in shared revenue from 1999 to 2006.

The Introduction to this volume offers several insights into ways of measuring political polarization. In this chapter, we operationalize polarization using the level of partisan competition within the municipality, which is consistent with the notion that the electorate in the U.S. has become more ideologically unified into opposing political parties. Specifically, we use the two-party vote total for the Michigan State Board of Education within each community in the 2006 election.

Contests in these "second-order" elections are less likely to be influenced by the personal characteristics of the candidates and thus more accurately assess partisanship. We then sort municipalities by their party competitiveness, which is simply the difference in the vote share between the Democratic and Republican parties. Those that are in the top third in terms of their competitiveness are considered polarized. We construct two models: one that includes only polarized communities and one that examines only those that are non-polarized. This resulted in data from 126 respondents in the polarized communities.

Finally, we include two demographic variables that are hypothesized to be related to our dependent variables: the average per capita income of a municipality's residents and the homogeneity of a community, measured as the percentage of the population identified as White.

Dependent variables

This study uses Jehn's schema of conflict. Among others, Svara (1990) suggests that conflict affects organizational effectiveness, so it is reasonable to expect that increased levels of conflict will be associated with an inability to make governance "work." This schema of conflict guided the creation of the two conflict indices we use in this study, one capturing "process conflict," the other assessing "policy conflict." We develop each index using responses from six questions, three each, from our survey. These questions are reported in Table 8.1.

Results

When examining three outcomes in polarized municipalities, it is clear that institutional form has the potential to have both direct and indirect effects on the success of these local governments. The path regression found in Table 8.1 displays the standardized coefficients for the associations between exogenous and endogenous variables. The headings in bold in Table 8.2 represent the outcomes

Table 8.1 Council conflict indices

	N	Mean
Process conflict		
How much friction is there on the council about task responsibilities?	455	2.380
How frequently do you have disagreements on the council about tasks?	453	2.433
How often are there disagreements about who should do what on the council?	452	2.272
Policy conflict		
How much conflict over ideas is there on the council?	455	2.967
How often do people on the council have conflict of opinions about the problems you are working on?	452	2.978
How often do you disagree about resource allocation on the council?	452	2.644
Valid *N* (listwise)	451	

Table 8.2 Parameter estimates for path model of institutional form and fiscal stress, policy conflict and process conflict in polarized cities

Parameter	Standardized coefficient	Standard error
Fiscal Stress 2009		
Fiscal Stress 2006	0.841***	0.031
Mean Income	0.0169**	0.002
Policy Conflict		
Administrative City	−0.303***	0.079
Strategic Planning	0.161*	0.083
Process Conflict	0.290***	0.079
Process Conflict		
Strategic Planning	−0.159*	0.087
Strategic Planning		
Administrative City	0.218**	0.085
Fiscal Stress 2006		
Administrative City	−0.170**	0.062
Percent White	−0.828***	0.038
Mean Income	0.095	0.065
Administrative City		
Percent White	−0.297***	0.081
Mean Income	0.460***	0.074

Notes
RMSEA = 0.027.
CFI = 0.996.
TLI = 0.992.

for our polarized communities, reporting the parameter estimates for fiscal stress, policy conflict, process conflict and institutional form. Examining the standardized coefficients reveals the association between independent variables and these outcomes. The presence of reformed government structures, as represented by the variable "administrative city," has a significant direct effect on reducing the level of policy conflict in polarized municipalities, as demonstrated by the standardized coefficient of −0.303. Beyond this direct effect on policy conflict, institutional structure also demonstrates significant indirect effects on both fiscal stress (in 2009) and process conflict. These are revealed by examining the product of the coefficient from the variables "administrative city" to "fiscal stress 2006" and the coefficient from "fiscal stress 2006" to "fiscal stress 2009" ($-0.170*0.841 = -0.143$) in Figure 8.1, as well as the product of the coefficient from the variables "administrative city" to "strategic planning" and the coefficient from "strategic planning" to "process conflict" ($0.218* - 0.159 = -0.035$). Even when controlling for a number of other factors, reformed institutional structures are clearly associated with desired outcomes in these polarized Michigan communities.

Beyond institutional form, the management tool strategic planning also directly reduces conflicts over who should do what within the municipality

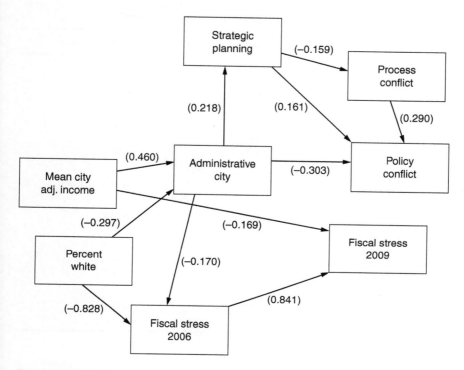

Figure 8.1 Path model of polarized municipalities – institutional form and outcomes.

(process). However, it also corresponds with greater policy conflict. It may be that strategic planning helps to raise critical issues and therefore acts to increase the importance of these issues, serving as a catalyst for policy disagreements that might otherwise remain dormant.

The strong fit of these refined path models (fitted by examining modification indices) is evidenced by three goodness-of-fit statistics, the Root Mean Square Error of Approximation (RMSEA), the Comparative Fit Index (CFI) and the Tucker-Lewis Index (TLI). Each of these statistics indicates that the specified model is a strong fit for the data, as RMSEA <0.05, CFI>0.93 and TLI>0.90 (Byrne 1994; Hu and Bentler 1995; MacCallum et al. 1996).

Table 8.3 reports the results of our model that examined non-polarized municipalities in Michigan. The fit of the model is mediocre, at best, in the model examining the non-polarized municipalities. None of the goodness-of-fit statistics meets the minimum criteria and we cannot reject the null hypothesis for the model. Nonetheless, there are a few important differences in the coefficients that are worth noting. Of course, we must treat findings from this model with a great deal of caution. First, reformed institutional structures, represented by the variable administrative city, are no longer directly related to reductions in policy conflict. This suggests that in communities where there is a wider consensus

Table 8.3 Parameter estimates for path model of institutional form and fiscal stress, policy conflict and process conflict in non-polarized cities

Parameter	Standardized coefficient	Standard error
Fiscal Stress 2009		
Fiscal Stress 2006	0.671***	0.04
Mean Income	0.055	0.05
Policy Conflict		
Administrative City	−0.064	0.058
Strategic Planning	0.122*	0.06
Process Conflict	0.330***	0.057
Process Conflict		
Strategic Planning	−0.280***	0.056
Strategic Planning		
Administrative City	0.205***	0.058
Fiscal Stress 2006		
Administrative City	−0.099*	0.053
Percent White	−0.384***	0.05
Mean Income	−0.247	0.052
Administrative City		
Percent White	0.256***	0.058
Mean Income	0.160***	0.06

Notes
RMSEA=0.088.
CFI=0.917.
TLI=0.850.

over policy, there is less need for institutional reform. In other words, institutions matter most in polarized contexts. Second, we also find that management tools such as strategic planning remain important in reducing conflicts over process, but also continue to promote conflicts over policies.

Conclusions

The findings presented here indicate that both institutional structure and the use of strategic planning help to influence, and perhaps even ultimately moderate, political conflicts in polarized communities. These findings, although exploratory in nature, highlight the potential for complex interdependencies between environmental pressures, institutional forms, strategic management tools and polarization and seem to offer possible solutions for local communities polarized by political conflict.

Our study, however, has some limitations. For instance, this analysis relies exclusively on survey data and relies on the opinions of respondents for both measures of strategic planning and conflict. Despite this potential flaw, the consistent results may lend some credence to our findings. The data for this analysis is also limited to one state. Clearly expanding this analysis to a national sample of municipalities would enhance the generalizability of these findings. Despite these limitations, this analysis suggests that the administrative city, strategic management tools and fiscal stress may condition organizations' capacity to manage conflict in polarized communities. Case studies on the effective use of these tools in cases of extreme polarization may have the capacity to generate critical best practices for practitioners who might otherwise struggle to use these tools effectively.

References

Backoff, Robert, Barton Wechsler and R.E.J. Crew. 1993. "The Challenge of Strategic Management in Local Government." *Public Administration Quarterly* 17(2):127–145.

Bozeman, Barry. 2010. "Hard Lessons from Hard Times: Reconsidering and Reorienting the 'Managing Decline' Literature." *Public Administration Review* 70(4):557–563.

Bryson, John. 1995. *Strategic Planning for Public and Nonprofit Organizations.* San Francisco, CA: Jossey-Bass.

Bryson, John and Barbara Crosby. 1992. *Leadership for the Common Good: Tackling Public Problems in a Shared Problem World.* San Francisco, CA: Jossey-Bass.

Bryson, John and Barbara Crosby. 1995. "Leadership Roles in Making Strategic Planning Work." In *Strategic Planning for Public and Nonprofit Organizations,* John Bryson (ed.). San Francisco, CA: Jossey-Bass.

Bryson, John and W.D. Roering. 1988. "Initiation of Strategic Planning by Governments." *Public Administration Review* 48(6):995–1004.

Bryson, John and W.D. Roering. 1989. "Mobilizing Initiation Efforts: The Case of Government Strategic Planning." In *Research on the Management of Innovation,* Andrew Van de Ven, Harold Angle and M. Scott Poole (eds.). New York: Harper Business.

Byrne, B.M. (1994). *Structural Equation Modeling with EQS and EQS/Windows.* Thousand Oaks, CA: Sage Publications.

Carr, Jered B. and Shanthi Karuppusamy. 2009. "Beyond Ideal Types of Municipal Structure: Adapted Cities in Michigan." *American Review of Public Administration* 39:304–321.

Carr, Jered B. and Shanthi Karuppusamy. 2010. "Reassessing the Link between City Structure and Fiscal Policy: Is the Problem Poor Measures of Governmental Structure?" *American Review of Public Administration* 40:209–228.

Cekola, Kim. 2011, March/April. "Mayors Have a Direct Link to Voters." *The Review: The Official Magazine of the Michigan Municipal League.*

Chambers, Lance and Michael Taylor. 1999. *Strategic Planning: Processes, Tools and Outcomes.* Aldershot, UK: Ashgate.

Choi, Cheon, Richard C Feiock and Jungah Bae. 2013. "The Adoption and Abandonment of Council-Manager Government." *Public Administration Review* 73(5):727–736.

Denhardt, Robert B. 1985. "Strategic Planning in State and Local Government." *State and Local Government Review* 17(4):174–179.

Feiock, Richard. C., Moon-Gi Jeong and Jaheon Kim. 2003. "Credible Commitment and Council-Manager Government: Implications for Policy Instrument Choices" *Public Administration Review* 63(5):616–625.

Frederickson, George, Gary Johnson and Curtis Wood. 2004. *The Adapted City: Institutional Dynamics and Structural Change.* Armonk, NY: M.E. Sharpe.

Halachmi, Arie, William P. Hardy and Bernie L. Rhoades. 1993. "Demographic Data and Strategic Analysis." *Public Administration Quarterly* 17(2):159–174.

Hendrick, Rebecca. 2003. "Strategic Planning Environment, Process, and Performance in Public Agencies" *Journal of Public Administration Research and Theory* 13(4):491–519.

Hu, L.T. and P.M. Bentler. (1995). "Evaluating Model Fit." In *Structural Equation Modeling: Concepts, Issues, and Applications*, R.H. Hoyle (ed.), pp. 76–99. Thousand Oaks, CA: Sage.

Ihrke, Douglas, Rick Proctor and Jerry Gabris. 2003. "Understanding Innovation in Municipal Government: City Council Member Perspectives." *Journal of Urban Affairs* 25(1):79–90.

Kearney, Richard and Evan Berman. 1999. *Public Sector Performance: Management, Motivation, and Measurement*. Boulder, CO: Westview Press.

Kline, Rex B. 2005. *Principles and Practice of Structural Equation Modeling*. New York: Guilford.

Levine, Charles H. 1980. *Managing Fiscal Stress: The Crisis in the Public Sector*. Chatham, NJ: Chatham House.

Lineberry, Robert and Edmund Fowler. 1967. "Reformism and Public Policies in American Cities." *American Political Science Review* 61(3):701–716.

Lyons, William. 1978. "Reform and Response in American Cities: Structure and Policy Reconsidered." *Social Science Quarterly* 59(June):18–132.

MacCallum, R.C., M.W. Browne and H.M. Sugawara. 1996. "Power Analysis and Determination of Sample Size for Covariance Structure Modeling." *Psychological Methods* 1:130–149.

Meier, Kenneth J. and Bohte, John. 2007. *Politics and Bureaucracy: Policymaking in the Fourth Branch of Government*, 5th edn. Belmont, CA: Wadsworth/Cengage Learning.

Mercer, James. 1991. *Strategic Planning for Public Managers*. New York: Quorum Books.

Mintzberg, Henry. 1994. *The Rise and Fall of Strategic Planning: Preconceiving Roles for Planning, Plans, Planners*. New York: Free Press.

Newcomer, Kathryn, Edward T. Jennings, Cheryle Broom and Allen Lomax. 2002. "Meeting the Challenges of Performance-Oriented Government." Center for Accountability and Performance, American Society for Public Administration, Washington, DC.

Osborne, David and Ted Gaebler. 1992. *Reinventing Government: How the Entrepreneurial Spirit is Transforming the Public Sector*. Reading, MA: Addison-Wesley.

Pandey, Sanjay K. 2010. "Cutback Management and the Paradox of Publicness." *Public Administration Review* 70(4):564–571.

Poister, Theodore and Gregory Streib. 1994. "Municipal Management Tools from 1976 to 1993: An Overview and Update." *Public Productivity and Management Review* 18(2):115–125.

Poister, Theodore and Gregory Streib. 2005. "Elements of Strategic Planning and Management in Municipal Government: Status after Two Decades." *Public Administration Review* 65(1):45–56.

Radford, K.J. 1980. *Strategic Planning: An Analytical Approach*. Reston, VA: Reston.

Steiss, Alan Walter. 2003. *Strategic Management for Public and Nonprofit Organizations*. New York: Marcel Dekker.

Streib, Gregory. 1992. "Applying Strategic Decision Making in Local Government." *Public Productivity and Management Review* 15(3):341–355.

Svara, James. 1990. *Official Leadership in the City: Patterns of Conflict and Cooperation*. New York: Oxford University Press.

Svara, James H. 1991. "Council and Administrator Perspectives on the City Manager's Role: Conflict, Divergence, or Congruence?" *Administration & Society* 23(2):227–246.
Swanstrom, Todd. 1987. "The Limits of Strategic Planning for Cities." *Journal of Urban Affairs* 9(2):139–157.
Terry, Larry D. 2003. *Leadership of Public Bureaucracies: The Administrator as Conservator*. Armonk, NY: M.E. Sharpe.

9 Political polarization, fiscal stress and financing public universities

A comparative analysis of the Ontario and Michigan public policy experience

Lawrence Sych and Marcy Taylor

Introduction: political polarization and higher education finance

How well has the public university fared financially over the last ten years as its provincial or state government grew more politically polarized and fiscally stressed, its public subsidy slowly diminished, and its student/parent base grappled with economic uncertainty? Formal analysis of the financial condition by government leaders took on greater importance with the onset of the 2008 Great Recession and the consequent need to ensure sustainable policies and services. States and provinces in particular experienced more severe stress as compared to their local governments (Mikesell and Ross 2014). However, the experiences of public universities, which are particularly reliant on their state/provincial governments for financial support, remain largely unexplored.

Moreover, the polarization of the American and Canadian electorate poses yet another challenge to governance at the state/provincial levels by compounding fiscal stress pressures and struggles to develop effective responses. The U.S. has historically experienced higher polarization levels when compared to Canada (Baumer and Gold 2010). Yet Canada's national party system since the 1993 election "constituted the most regionalized and ideologically polarized party system in Canadian history" (Baumer and Gold 2010; Bickerton 2014: 273). Polarization inhibits elected leaders seeking to organize broad coalitions of cross-party support which prove useful when crafting budgetary plans. Polarization "encourages confrontation over compromise" as "the parties today are becoming less diverse, more ideologically homogeneous, and less inclined to pursue reasonable agreements" (Brownstein 2007: 11–12).

Some observers argue that federalism could insulate states and provinces from nationally polarized politics (Brownstein 2007; Simeon et al. 2014). It is now clear that these constituent units are not immune from polarization. Michigan's legislature progressively acquired polarizing positions in response to a series of increasingly partisan governors, and by one account is now the third most polarized state legislature in the U.S. (Shor 2014; Shor and McCarty 2011). Ontario's electoral results over the last three election cycles reveal steadily increasing political polarization, founded in part on the geographic and demographic basis of party coalitions (Anderson and Coletto 2014; Cain and Paperny 2014; Coletto 2011; Ibbitson 2015).

For the public higher education policy arena, polarization contributes to a weakening of the public good argument. Dar and Lee (2014: 475) describe the effects of political polarization on higher education: "Given the susceptibility of higher education spending to political and business cycles, we argue that the effect of partisanship on higher education spending is contingent upon the degree of polarization between the two parties and state economic conditions." They go on to explain that when there is low political polarization, we can expect "that the collective-benefit dimension of higher education will take precedence and that both Democrats and Republicans will be more likely to support higher education spending.... [W]ith increasing degrees of polarization, the collective-benefit argument will become less salient" (Dar and Lee 2014: 476). Political gridlock takes place, and partisans are more likely to shift their focus to other policy areas that provide more targeted benefit to their base. The highly polarized situations in Michigan and Ontario leave higher education without an advocate; they create competition (rather than collaboration) among the state/provincial institutions for resources.

Still, higher education occupies a precarious position. Although universities produce highly educated graduates, engage in basic and applied research, and attract business and industry to a region, higher education remains a merit good. It is a good that while possessing characteristics of a private good is nonetheless worthy of public subsidy to enhance its social benefits. Public subsidies to provincial or state universities, however, come at the expense of other public services, or alternatively, tax cuts. Moreover, subsidized public benefits of the university also accrue to students and their parents who gain personal benefits at a cost lower than the private market would provide. Recognizing who benefits most intensely, more polarized legislatures can instead steer funding toward alternative favored programs and let universities raise revenue from students and parents to make up the difference. No other state or provincial program can raise such revenues in response to subsidy cutbacks. The result is steady erosion in legislative financial support for provincial and state universities.

While others have studied the effects of polarization on higher education at the macro level, this chapter explores how these effects play out at the institutional level. In particular, we hypothesize that public institutions will respond to a polarized political environment by playing to the middle: promoting the social efficiency agenda of providing accessibility to job training and regional economic development that has become the default policy position for both sides of the aisle. To test this question, we use two samples of public universities drawn from Michigan, U.S. and Ontario, Canada in a two-stage approach. In the first stage, we employ a model of financial condition analysis (FCA) using a set of ten indicators applied to annual audited financial statements to determine university solvency over a ten-year period and a summary score to reveal relative university rankings within each sample. Financial trends and scores are assumed to be partly the consequences of university leadership decisions taken to address

environmental changes that include increasing legislative political polarization
and fiscal stress. In the second stage of the analysis, we use these same financial
statements, or reports, to construct rhetorical analyses of university decision-
making. Based on these findings, we address several questions. How well is
FCA narrated by a university's financial officers? What can we say about the
quality of its financial leadership? In this way, we seek to address FCA in light
of the stories leaders tell to gain insight into their policy decisions in response to
fiscal stress and increasingly polarized politics.

FCA can highlight changes in conditions over time within and across universities. While institutional performance on key indicators illustrate recession and
recovery effects on financial condition, they are also presumed to be a result of
university administrators who reacted to environmental and competitive pressures by making key policy decisions. That is, the policy space for decisions,
while constricted by stress, would still allow some range of action on meaningful decisions intended to improve conditions (Justice and Scorsone 2013). Using
FCA and rhetorical analysis to understand university decision-making, we hope
to interpret this institutional policy space in ways that would permit universities
to better address financial stability and public accountability in response to
polarization.

The concept of financial condition

Scholars and practitioners enjoy a consensus on four core dimensions, or solven-
cies, of financial condition as a concept. These include cash solvency focusing
on the short term, budgetary solvency with its focus on annual budget balance, a
service-level solvency centered on service provision adequate to meet constituents' needs, and long-run solvency, or the long-run balance between spending
needs and revenue resources. FCA advocates encourage visioning a future
extended out to ten years, and as long as forty (Kavanagh 2007). For example,
university planners routinely consider elementary and secondary student populations to project college enrollments ten to fifteen years in the future.

Other foresight advocates seek to determine long-term trends to develop
probable policy futures over ten, twenty, and even fifty years (Roberge 2014).
Habegger (2009: 51) explains that organizations practicing foresight exercises
find "it informs policy by providing more systematic knowledge about potentially relevant trends and developments in the perceptible political, economic,
social, or technological environments" facing the organization. Moreover, foresight becomes a driver of organizational learning with "reflexive mutual social
learning processes among policy-makers that stimulate 'the emergence of
common visions' ... because it enables learning, creates linkages, networks, and
knowledge flows between people and organizations, and generates knowledge,
ideas, and visions" (Habegger 2009: 52). In taking these factors into account,
financial condition as a concept represents a dynamic and fluid process shaped
by external factors such as fiscal stress and political polarization as well as by
internal policy decisions.

Cases and methods

FCA relies on longitudinal assessment of key indicators over a period of time and compared among a set of peer units. The Michigan set includes all fifteen universities and thirteen governing boards. The University of Michigan's Board of Regents also governs two branch campuses at Flint and Dearborn. Its financial statements do not break down by branches, and so it is treated as one case. The Ontario set initially included nineteen of twenty-three public universities. The Dominican University College and St. Paul University were excluded because of exceptionally small enrollments (244 and 780 respectively). Two other speciality schools, the Royal Military College of Canada (1,700 enrolled) and the Ontario College of Art and Design (3,450 enrolled) were excluded because no comparable Michigan universities exist.

For each case, annual financial statements were collected from each university's website. Given the need to assemble a set of observations to construct and evaluate ten years of annual changes, we set a base year of 2005 and an end year of 2014. Financial statements for this period were collected for all thirteen Michigan universities. Among the nineteen selected Ontario universities, Algoma University was removed because it was officially created in 2007. We excluded other universities failing to post annual financial reports from 2005 onward on their websites (Laurentian University, Trent University, the University of Windsor, and the University of Ontario Institute of Technology). The final Ontario set included fourteen universities.

Our measurement of FCA begins with Brown's (1993) ten indicators found in his "10-point test." Mead (2006) modified Brown's test to balance short term, liquidity measures, with longer-term pressures and liabilities based on accrual methods of accounting for long-term liabilities employed as a consequence of the Governmental Accounting Standards Board Standard 34 adopted in the U.S. in 1999. KPMG LLP and Prager, McCarthy and Sealy, LLC (1999) developed a Composite Financial Index (CFI) for universities by combining four "core" financial ratios found in Mead's work in a formula to produce a summary performance measurement. We included these four indicators in our measure.

In his analysis of Southern Utah University, Vice President for Finance and Government Relations Dorian Page (n.d.) employed a host of indicators which included the CFI index and several others which collectively reflect much of Mead's index. We modified Page's work to create a ten-point index by first, removing indicators incorporating student enrollments given the exceptional volatility of annual enrollments among Michigan and Ontario universities, and second, retaining one "demand" indicator (Student Financial Aid) and one "contribution" indicator (Tuition and Fee Revenue) to reflect an institutional reaction to competition among peer universities. Table 9.1 displays the ten selected indicators, a brief description, and calculation formulas.

Annual values for each indicator were calculated for each university over the ten-year study period. Mead's scoring rubric was then used to develop summary scores for each university indicator for each year. The ratios for each indicator

Table 9.1 Financial condition analysis indicators

Ratio	Description	Formula
Current	Measure of liquidity	Current Assets/Current Liabilities
Primary Reserve	Measure of financial strength; expendable resources that may be used to satisfy ongoing obligations	Unrestricted Net Assets + Expendable Restricted Net Assets/ Total Operating Expenses
Return on Net Assets	Economic return on investment	Increase (Decrease) in Net Assets/ Net Assets at Beginning of Year
Viability	Relative liquidity; availability of assets that may be used to pay obligations (e.g., long-term debt)	Unrestricted Net Assets + Expendable Restricted Net Assets/ Total Non-Current Liabilities
Net Operating	Compares net operating income or (loss) to total operating revenues	Income/(Loss) Before Other Revenues/Total Operating Revenues + Non-operating Revenues
Contribution	Measures given revenue source (tuition/fees) share of total revenues	Tuition and Fees/Total Operating Revenues + Non-operating Revenues
Demand	Measures a given category of expense as a percentage of total expenses	Student Aid/Total Operating Expenses
Debt Burden	Compares debt service (principal + interest) payments to total operating expenses	Principal + Interest Payments/Total Operating Expenses
Debt Coverage	Measures the excess income available for covering annual debt service payments	Changes in Unrestricted Net Assets + Interest Expense + Depreciation Expense/Principal + Interest Payments
Capital Related Debt to Net Capital Assets	Measures the extent to which facilities and other capital assets have been financed by debt	Capital Related Debt (Long-term Liabilities)/Net Capital Assets

for each year were ranked by quartiles. Ratios falling in the bottom quartile were scored −1, those in the second quartile were scored 0, ratios in the third quartile scored 1, and those in the top quartile were scored 2. Totaling a university's ten ratios each year produced a possible score ranging from −10 (assuming each ratio fell in the lowest quartile that year) to +20 (assuming each ratio fell in the highest quartile). For the decade, the possible range was −100 to +200. Table 9.2 displays the summary scores for each set of universities.

The scores reveal significant variation among universities in each sample. This suggests that even the high performing universities are not consistent across time and/or indicators. Moreover, there is vast room for improvement at the top of the scale (a maximum of 200) as well as room for yet more degradation of FCA at the bottom of the scale (a minimum of −100).

Table 9.2 Summary financial condition scores for Ontario and Michigan universities

Ontario		Michigan	
Queen's	107	University of Michigan	134
McMaster	95	Ferris State	96
Waterloo	92	Michigan State	96
Ryerson	78	Central Michigan	89
Carleton	71	Northern Michigan	58
Guelph	68	Oakland	58
Nipissing	52	Grand Valley State	35
Brock	42	Wayne State	22
Western Ontario	41	Michigan Tech	20
Lakehead	39	Saginaw Valley State	13
Ottawa	38	Lake Superior State	7
Toronto	12	Western Michigan	−12
York	−4	Eastern Michigan	−27
Wilfred Laurier	−31		

FCA offers one lens through which to view the strategic decision-making of higher education institutions. However, the summary scores beg interpretation (if not a clear causality). We used annual financial reports as a means to uncover a sense of the intra- and inter-institutional narratives these trends reveal. What elements of the higher education policy environment – which Dar and Lee (2014: 471) describe as a "hybrid" policy area "characterized by complex partnerships between the public and private sector and by party-based coalitions that often shift or split across different issues" – are salient? How do institutions frame their actions with regard to their public missions? At the very least, financial reports serve as key policy documents that universities use to communicate to a variety of constituents the assumptions or values underlying strategic priorities and institutional identity. What are the stories these documents tell?

Analyzing financial reports rhetorically

We approached the examination of financial documents rhetorically, that is from a close analysis of the textual elements that mediate or construct the social reality – or story – presented. As a qualitative, case-study based approach, rhetorical analysis uses induction and interpretation that focus on the *effects* of textual representation on one policy area: institutional budgets and planning. Coming from a policy perspective, such a qualitative, poststructuralist approach is natural. It also aligns with recent work on narrative research and public policy that identifies elements of narrative and assigns meaning to the objects and processes of policy discussions. For example, Michael D. Jones and Mark K. McBeth (2010: 334) review the work of Frank Fischer and Deborah Stone, who advocate "a more interpretive policy analysis where analysts take seriously the discursively subjective nature of public policy." This post-positivist approach recognizes the importance of language to public policy.

While we did not undertake a systematic coding of elements, we did follow an interpretive approach similar to what Matthew Hartley and Christopher C. Morphew describe as *content analysis*. In their study of institutional mission statements and college viewbooks (Hartley and Morphew 2008; Morphew and Hartley 2006), they systematically identified, classified, and then compared the symbols, images, and messages of documents across a range of institutional types, focusing on key themes by which to categorize. Coding across a large sample like ours tends to produce aggregate interpretations (patterns), which are useful for comparison. Assuming, for instance, that institutions within a state or province offer competing narratives (i.e., they are competing for a larger percentage of the state appropriation or a larger market share of students from the state/province), such a comparison helps us to understand the narrative strategies they deploy to make short- and long-term decisions, to justify those decisions in terms of their missions, and to persuade their stakeholders – governing boards, state and provincial governments, and even parents and students – to take certain future actions. They may also allow us to see key policy differences between states or between the U.S. and Canada in terms of the larger narrative surrounding higher education policy. To represent the potential of combining FCA with narrative policy analysis, our approach includes a focus on four representative cases, the top and bottom two performers in each sample. A case study approach is in keeping with the literature on the rhetoric of financial reporting, particularly in cases of public sector or university accountability (see Chariri and Ekonomi 2007; Coy and Pratt 1998; Coy et al. 2001).

Purpose and audience of financial reports

Peter J. Hager and H.J. Scheiber (1990) describe the elements of the annual corporate financial report as fairly uniform, and the assumption is that the concept and format of the annual report has been translated, unchallenged, from private sector corporate reporting into the public sector (Mack and Ryan 2007). The research agrees that audiences for annual reports are multiple, but the primary audience must be seen as external: those elected politicians whose job it is "to ensure that accountability is exercised by those to whom assets are entrusted to be managed on behalf of the public good" (Coy and Pratt 1998: 541). However, universities, to varying degrees, at least implicitly assume other audiences. Coy et al. (2001: 14) describe a larger range of internal and external stakeholders, "considered to be all those with a legitimate economic, social or political interest in the organization." Considering how audience needs and power shape the message in the report, we considered the role of the following potential constituents (taken from Coy et al. 2001: 15):

- *internal campus-based citizens*: senior managers, support staff, academics, student service recipients;
- *sister organizations/competitors*: employees of other tertiary education institutions;

- *elected and appointed representatives*: parliamentarians (legislators), institution councils or senates, trustee board members, government and regulators, advisory committee members;
- *resource providers*: suppliers and lenders, donors and sponsors, investors and partners, professional associations;
- *external citizens*: voters and taxpayers, other pressure groups, non-student service recipients, advisers and consultants, alumni;
- *analysts and media*: researchers, journalists, librarians.

The annual report is "widely regarded as the main accountability mechanism, reporting on the governance and performance of an institution" (Mack and Ryan 2007: 134). *Accountability*, then, serves as one conceptual framework for analyzing the audiences and purposes of annual reports. The audiences above imply layers of "publics" to whom institutions must account, and annual reports function variously as public documents. As such, annual reports perform a key function in legitimizing one's institutional identity, particularly in terms of aligning the corporate ethos of the university to prevailing narratives about the purposes of public higher education. As we will see in a moment, those purposes can be seen in the language and images of the annual reports to various degrees, but all the samples are artifacts of a larger narrative of accountability that has dominated educational policy since at least the mid-1980s. David A. Tandberg and Nicholas W. Hillman (2014: 223) describe the shift in public policy dubbed the "new accountability" in public higher education:

> In many states [in the U.S.], the state oversight and accountability environment for public colleges and universities underwent a significant shift during the 1990s, from one that concentrated on regulatory compliance, rudimentary reporting of inputs, and accounting for expenditures to one that focused on measuring performance and accounting for outcomes or results.

We see in policies such as performance funding for higher education that as the political environment has grown increasingly polarized, accountability has replaced such key policy terms as "opportunity," "accessibility," and "democratic citizenship" as the primary lens through which to understand the goals of higher education (see, for example, Kelderman 2015; for an analysis of the shift in key policy terms in education reform over time, see Asen 2012).

It is fair to say that all university financial reports, regardless of financial condition, serve both normative and strategic purposes that rest on certain assumptions about the wider goals of higher education. David F. Labaree (1997: 42) argues that U.S. educational policy has involved a struggle over three competing goals:

- *democratic equality*: the perspective of the citizen, from which education is seen as a public good, designed to prepare people to play constructive roles in a democratic society;

- *social efficiency*: the perspective of the taxpayer and employer, from which education is seen as a public good designed to prepare workers to fill structurally necessary market roles;
- *social mobility*: the perspective of the individual educational consumer, from which education is seen as a private good designed to prepare individuals for successful social competition for more desirable market roles.

Like university mission statements, annual reports express priorities that reflect these purposes, and thus they can serve a strategic and instrumental purpose; that is, they can provide evidence of decision-making and "inspire organizational members to conform to shared goals and communicate the institution's characteristics, values and history to key external constituents" (Morphew and Hartley 2006: 457). Annual reports also serve a legitimating function that can be seen as more ritualistic than instrumental. They are normative in the sense that public institutions are expected to reflect their public purposes through their financial stewardship. We argue that the need for institutional transparency and careful shaping of a university's ethos becomes increasingly important as the effects of polarization on the higher education policy arena are manifested.

The narratives of financial condition: four cases from Michigan and Ontario

We now present and discuss four narratives of financial condition drawn from Michigan and Ontario. Given their polarized politics, we can use the top and bottom performers from each region to comparatively assess the narrative effects of financial reporting in relation to polarization, enrollment, revenue, and peer competition in the state or province.

The University of Michigan

The University of Michigan (UM), by all accounts, lives up to its flagship status by attaining the top summary score on the indicators of financial condition (shown in Table 9.2), so it serves as a model for comparison. In some ways, because of its strong financial performance, it could choose to allow the standard forms of the financial statements to speak for themselves. In its 2014 *Annual Report*, the image of a campus building with massive Doric columns rising into a bright UM blue sky on the second page suggests traditional academic values, strength, and the optimism of both future growth and innovation. The image reifies UM's identity and serves as a strong enough symbol to frame the financial documents without much comment. However, the report is much more of an annual report (the title UM chose for this document) than simply a year-end financial statement, as is the case with the other three institutions presented here.[1] The production values alone signal that the university is positioning itself differently than its Michigan or Ontario peers – as opposed to merely fulfilling its reporting obligations to the state (and, perhaps, to its elected board of trustees);

this document is clearly speaking to a larger public audience whose interests go beyond purely economic ones. In this sense, the UM annual report is more like private corporate annual reports than those of its peers. It is a marketing document, selling the value of its own status as an elite institution.

As a way of asserting the institution's distinctiveness, the opening half (forty-one pages out of eighty-eight) is devoted to performance on a range of topics, starting with opening letters from the president, interim chief financial officer, and vice president for development, followed by a narrative organized by topic. The letters are typical in their assertions of financial stability, but they are unique in their emphases and use of graphics. For example, the president's letter, showing a picture of Mark S. Schlissel in a book-lined office inset within a larger image of a traditional Gothic campus building, asserts the university's "vast strengths" in terms of its "tremendous intellectual assets" and its purpose to "better society and to improve the world through research and education." Although their official mission statement includes service to the people of Michigan, this report is less about service to the state than it is about its global position. UM is definitely preparing students for citizenship, but as citizens of the world and not just the state. The image of the old campus building, solidly representing academic pursuits, reinforces the message that UM is about producing knowledge, not about preparing a workforce for the state.

Still, although the size of its endowment and the sizeable revenues generated by clinical patient care mean that it does not have to compete for performance funding to the same degree as other Michigan public universities, UM management still wants to convince its elected board and the citizens of the state that they are reasonable team players, so they discuss state appropriations gingerly and have kept their tuition increases within the caps set by the governor's performance funding policy. The letter from the chief financial officer includes a section on the financial stability afforded by the university's strategy to diversify revenue – the balance it achieves here is unique, as will be seen in the other cases described below – that then glides gracefully into a section titled "General Fund Operating Budget Challenge." Here, the writer manages to assert UM's important partnership with the state ("support from the state of Michigan remains a key part of our strength") while also emphasizing that state appropriations have declined 23 percent since financial year 2003.

Considering the branch campuses in the mix, UM's enrollments have been very solid in the ten-year period, with 7 percent and 9 percent growth at UM-Dearborn and UM-Ann Arbor, respectively, and 31 percent at UM-Flint. To maintain this growth, the university must appeal to students through the idea of "value," both in the sense of actual costs and in the sense of value-added – what they get here they can't get anywhere else: the status that is University of Michigan (that status is conferred on the branch campuses as well, as the report does not distinguish the branch campuses from the main Ann Arbor campus except in a one-page highlight of each campus). In this sense, the report subtly promotes Labaree's (1997) social mobility agenda throughout, one that speaks to students as consumers of education as a private good. Clearly, UM goes to great lengths to assure those consumers that they can access this commodity. Perhaps because affordability is a key policy term in the higher education conversation nationally, it is emphasized in the messages of both the president and the chief financial officer in the pull-out quotes. The chief financial officer emphasizes that priority in his message as well, with the pull-out quote focusing on tuition fees: "In FY 2015, for the sixth year in a row, there will no increase in the cost to attend U-M for the typical Ann Arbor campus undergraduate resident student who has financial need." The range of qualifiers in the statement are explained in the fine print of the Management's Discussion and Analysis, where indeed we see that tuition rate increases actually *did* occur, ranging from 1.1 percent for resident undergraduates at Ann Arbor to 3.5 percent for undergraduates at the UM-Dearborn and UM-Flint campuses, offset by modest increases in need-based financial aid. Scholarships and fellowships make up only 2 percent of the total operating expenses.

This contradiction aside, the overall message is one of accessibility, and in both form and substance, the report represents a fairly robust example of what Coy et al. (2001: 14) call a "public accountability model" of annual reporting. "The value of the annual report," they assert, "rests in the provision of a wide range of summarized, relevant information in a single document, which enables all stakeholders to obtain a comprehensive understanding of a university's objectives and performance in financial and non-financial terms." We posit that UM's financial strength and reputation allow it to remain somewhat aloof from the competition for resources created by the defunding of higher education. Still, one might conclude that the institution both reflects and constructs that reputation by providing at least the appearance of full transparency and accessibility in their comprehensive annual report.

Eastern Michigan University

In contrast, and perhaps because Eastern Michigan University (EMU) has elements of financial condition it would prefer to hide, it has chosen a minimalist rhetorical strategy "in its 2014 *Financial Statements and Supplemental Information.*" As many institutions do, EMU uses a solid and traditional campus building to grace its cover, but it quickly moves to the auditor's report and the Management's Discussion and Analysis with no introductory elements to set the context. This low level of disclosure could signal an effort to avoid bad news, but it also misses an opportunity to control the interpretation. As we saw with the case of UM, offering more details of performance builds credibility, while a lack of disclosure may result in even more intense scrutiny of the financials, especially given the financial condition trends. Here, management's decision-making is completely obscured, even in terms of those initiatives that one might claim as winners. Despite the claims toward openness and shared governance in its university mission and values, including a commitment to "participatory decision-making," "open communication," "financial and operational integrity," and "accountability," it fails to use this document to provide access to stakeholders.

In the 2014 report, the section titled "Financial Highlights" illustrates a strategy that we see throughout EMU's presentation – what Coy et al. (2001: 8) call "opportunities for massaging, which may exaggerate strengths and understate weaknesses." The section opens with net position, but before we see the Statement of Net Position, the document asserts, "The University's financial position remained strong at June 30, 2014, with assets of $565 million, liabilities of $337 million, and deferred inflows of $13 million." The single sentence is followed by a graphical representation of changes in net position.

Because of the statement of strength, with assets exceeding liabilities, and because the bar chart does not provide fine enough distinctions to interpret variation between years, one reads this section as positive. Yet the actual Statement of Net Position shows a *decline* in net position since 2012, a trend that is supported by the summary financial condition scores.

A similar kind of messaging appears in the interesting example of the value of derivative instruments. The 2012 report includes the following disclosure in the "Financial Highlights" section: "Due to fluctuation in interest rates, the fair value of the derivative liability increased by $30.8 million in 2012, followed by a decrease of $6.7 million in 2011, and an increase of $7.1 million in 2010." First of all, the *cause* of the change is assigned to the market, not to internal decision-making – no agency is assigned to management, thereby absolving them from potential criticism. Second, the choice to describe an "increase in fair value liability" is similar to a double-negative – overall, net assets *decreased* in 2012 by almost the same amount as the *increase* in derivative liability. The notes that all financial reports use to explain the various elements of the financial picture are not readily accessible to a lay reader in this regard, due to the technical language. Interestingly, by 2014, EMU was no longer recording these interest rate swaps under non-operating revenue in the Statement of Revenues, Expenses and Changes in Net Assets. Why? "Due to the reassignment of interest rate swaps to the refinanced debt in 2013." One has to read the fine print under Note 5 to see that all hedging relationships were terminated in 2013 and designated into new hedging relationships that are presumably reported differently (in accordance with Governmental Accounting Standards Board Statement No. 53). The lengthy and highly technical note on interest rate swaps ends with the statement: "For fiscal year ending June 30, 2014, the fair value of hedging derivative instruments increased $4,232,890." It is difficult to tell whether that is a positive or negative effect, since it is now hidden in the balance sheets and is easily missed at the end of a long note in the back of the document. At the very least, it remains uninterpreted, which is risky when the indicators of financial health appear so fragile.

The latest EMU financial report reviewed here focuses whatever rhetorical energy it can muster to promote its student-centeredness. In the section titled "Funding for a Successful Future," the report boasts:

Through diligent efforts at fiscal stewardship and strategic cost containment measures, the University has been able to set the standard for tuition restraint in the state of Michigan, while still continuing to invest in facilities and programs that help EMU students succeed in today's economy.

In keeping with a social efficiency agenda (preparing students for the workforce) that reinforces the state's priorities, EMU legitimates its public stewardship role. Tuition and fees make up approximately 50 percent of all revenues and 74 percent of the operating revenues (without state appropriations of 20 percent of total revenues). It is also not liquid: it scores in the bottom quartile in current ratio, primary reserve ratio, and viability ratio, and its latest report shows an unbalanced net position, with 86 percent in capital assets, 4 percent in restricted assets, and 9 percent in unrestricted net assets. Jeff Denneen and Tom Dretler (2012: 3) describe the liquidity crisis in higher education as follows: "Many institutions have operated on the assumption that the more they build, spend, diversify and expand, the more they will persist and prosper. But instead, the opposite has happened: Institutions have become overleveraged." This seems to be the case with EMU, despite management's assertion of strong fiscal stewardship.

By our measures, EMU is heavily dependent on tuition revenues, and while meeting state performance funding requirements has meant an increase in state appropriations since 2011, enrollments have fallen 2.5 per cent since 2006, with a sharp decline since 2012. For financial year 2016, EMU responded by flouting the tuition restraint cap of 3.2 percent set by the state performance formula, instead raising tuition 7.8 percent – effectively contradicting its 2014 statement regarding the "University's commitment to helping students and their families

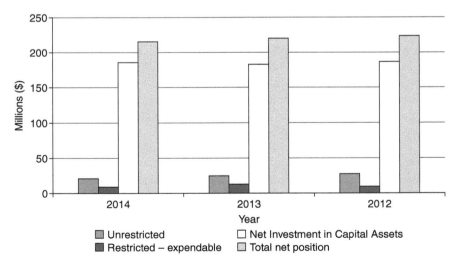

Figure 9.1 Sample graph from EMU's 2014 financial statement.

deal with the increasing costs of attending college." Former president Susan Martin claims that the $10 million in additional funds will go toward capital investments:

> 'We have a very tight balance sheet,' Martin said. 'Our balance sheet is too thin. We need to improve our reserves and use the money to help with needed capital improvements. We never have enough money for what we need to do. We've tried to manage as best we can, but this step was needed.'
>
> (Jesse 2015)

EMU's low level of disclosure masks the true thinness of its balance sheet, and it remains to be seen how its tuition strategy will play out with the legislature and the public. We suggest that both tactics are risky in a polarized environment where accountability and transparency are critical to an institution's ethos as a responsible steward of public resources. Is EMU's response to fiscal stress typical of public higher education institutions?

Wilfrid Laurier University

One way to answer that question is to compare it to the low performer in the Ontario sample. Like Eastern Michigan, Wilfrid Laurier University (WLU) is at the bottom of its respective group of institutions according to our FCA and, like EMU, WLU chooses a minimalist approach to its financial report, with an extremely sparse presentation devoid of any context or interpretation. Laurier approaches the financial report in a standard way, implying that the management does not envision the document as functioning beyond its obligation to the board of trustees and the province. Coy et al. (2001: 13) review the literature on reporting by U.S. colleges and universities in the mid-1990s and produce three conclusions:

- Reporting is dominated by information that was seen as useful to users making economic decisions and evaluating management's effectiveness in fulfilling its stewardship responsibilities.
- Overall, the level of disclosure is low.
- Reporting about service and performance is particularly undeveloped.

WLU's approach reflects these qualities in the extreme. The 2015 *Financial Statements of Wilfrid Laurier University* includes no cover art to attempt to symbolize institutional identity. In fact, there is no graphical information outside of the balance sheets, and even the Management's Discussion and Analysis is missing. The overwhelming language of the document is the language of accountancy, emphasized by placing the Independent Auditors' Report first with no introductory remarks or background (in sharp contrast to the prominent example of UM and, to a lesser degree, the other institutions' reports). There is no attempt to explain or justify decision-making, with the notes to the financial statements written in highly technical language for the purpose of defining practice or clarifying terms only. The sparseness of the presentation impedes readers from assessing the credibility of the information and the people presenting it. Is this minimal disclosure an attempt to deflect agency for what is essentially bad news?

Not necessarily. If we look beyond the financial statements at WLU, we find other means of communicating financial information to internal and external audiences, that reflect both the shared governance within the institution and the constraints of the provincial government. These documents work with the FCA to fill in some of the blanks left by the financial statements. For instance, in analyzing performance indicators relative to the other thirteen Ontario universities in our study, we find that while overall WLU ranks at the bottom in financial strength – in particular it lacks liquidity and maintains a high debt ratio – the financial picture is trending upward. In its latest financial statement, WLU shows that net position has improved by $66.3 million, with a positive change in net assets of $14.1 million. Likewise, management was able to improve the deficit in unrestricted net assets by $30.5 million. The financial outlook remains challenging, however.

Our analysis shows that of the Ontario universities, WLU is most dependent on tuition (revenues from student tuition and fees and provincial operating grants represent 93 percent of the total operating revenues) and thus is the most affected by enrollment declines, which began in 2014 and are expected to continue through 2021. Likewise, the university remains overleveraged due to substantial building and growth in the period between 1997–2004. In order to move from a primarily undergraduate institution to a more "comprehensive" university with increased graduate programs and research activity, it may have overbuilt based on the expectation that undergraduate enrollments would continue to grow. Finally, like other Ontario institutions, the pension liability remains a cause of structural deficit in the unrestricted net assets. The 2015–2016 Budget (produced through a shared governance process and communicated with the university throughout the budget development cycle) provides a glimpse as to WLU's strategies for improving its financial outlook amid fiscal stress:

- shifting to a responsibility-centered budgeting model to provide "greater alignment of resources to activities, allow greater budget flexibility within units, and incent faculties to generate revenue and reduce costs";
- integrating program prioritization and budget development to focus on high-priority initiatives;
- implementing multi-year planning and recovery strategies;
- suspending some debt service payments or extending the time window for reaching pension deficit solvency; and
- institutionalizing multi-year departmental budget cuts (2015–2016 Budget: 13).

The sixty-nine-page budget report provides a remarkable level of transparency while maintaining a tone of calm but very serious resolve. There is little attempt to color the currently dark financial picture with either offsetting positive strengths or subterfuge, as EMU does. WLU clearly uses the budget report as a *prospective* document – it opens with "This report contains forward-looking information" – and their budget development process is a vehicle for strategic planning. This may suggest why the financial statements – which are reports on past performance – are not invested with the same level of detail. Coy et al.'s "public accountability model" (2001: 14) suggests the value of aligning multiple levels of transparency within annual reports, something that WLU may recognize as necessary, especially in light of tighter governmental controls. The budget report describes the Broader Public Sector Accountability Act, under which universities must publish annual business plans. In addition, according to the report, the government is currently considering requiring universities to:

(1) Publish their mandate and strategic direction; (2) Publish current and future plans and key activities; (3) Publish performance targets; (4) Publish annual reports that provide a description of key activities over the previous year, an analysis of operational performance, a discussion of performance targets achieved and actions taken if not achieved, and a copy of the audited financial statements.

We argued earlier that one effect of polarization in the higher education policy arena is a retreat to greater accountability as a social efficiency agenda is pursued, illustrated well by the legislation described here. In a polarized environment combining dwindling public subsidies with an increasingly competitive market as the number of students decline, transparency and performance become important capital.

Queen's University

Queen's University (QU), the strongest performer in the group of Ontario institutions in our sample, moves toward a public accountability model in its various reporting strategies, but falls short of a fully integrated annual report that could serve to emphasize how performance on its mandate and strategic directions aligns with financial performance. Perhaps because of QU's status as a large research university (currently serving 22,000 students), that, according to its vision, is "the Canadian research-intensive university with a transformative student learning experience," the management has gone to some lengths to project an image of solid stewardship and transparency for its primary audience, the provincial government. Like UM, QU uses the opening section of the *13–14 Financial Statements*, here called "The Year in Review," to describe its solid management of funds, opening the section with very good news: "In 2013–2014, the university completed the year with a $45.6 million surplus." While acknowledging briefly the "challenges" that remain – including "uncertainties around government funding, a prolonged period of low interest rates, a pension plan that is not financially sustainable, and $242 million of deferred maintenance" – the first page of the document is dominated by a consolidated statement of operations balance sheet that reveals growth in net position of almost $200 million. It scores in the top of the Ontario universities on primary reserve ratio, return on net assets ratio, viability ratio, and net operating ratio. While capital debt to capital assets is relatively high (ranking third behind Toronto and Wilfrid Laurier), QU continues to grow in enrollments when others are declining, so investment in building seemed warranted through the current year. In the *Budget Report 2015–2016*, management states that the university is looking at fully-funded enrollment growth through 2018, but the institution is wary about the volatility of enrollments due to the fact that over 90 percent of its operating revenues come from tuition and provincial grants.

Even with its many strengths, QU fails to take rhetorical advantage of the reporting mechanisms to fully leverage its considerable assets in legitimating its image as *the* leader in the province. In *Public No More*, Gary C. Fethke and Andrew J. Policano (2012: 7) describe the "new reality" to which public universities must adapt. This reality includes: (1) more focused strategic vision; (2) financial transparency; and (3) increased external accountability. A truly integrated planning process – involving key internal and external stakeholders – would bring these elements together and communicate them in accessible ways to the various audiences. In QU's case, we see three limitations.

First, while the financial statements include some context-setting elements that make them accessible to a lay audience, much planning and performance information is reported elsewhere. For example, the opening letter from the Vice-Principal for Finance and Administration includes three links to annual budget reports, quarterly financial updates, and rating agency reports. However, the information is not integrated into the Management's Discussion and Analysis and it remains solely focused on financial information. QU does post an "annual report" on its website (www.queensu.ca/annualreport2014/content/home) that documents a range of achievements stemming from its strategic plan, including a section on financial sustainability and planning for the future. This report could serve to replace stand-alone financial statements within a fully-integrated public accountability approach. Second, QU enjoys what appears to be a robust shared governance system, but decision-making remains blurred in the financial statements. Established by royal charter in 1841, QU has a large Board of Trustees (44 members) plus a Senate, both of which include budget and finance committees. QU includes these budget review committees in the process of planning, but their roles are obscured in the reports, particularly in terms of program prioritization. Finally, QU fails to provide what we call symbolic framing. Its reports lack visuals and interpretations of the financial data that are so critical in interpreting performance relative to mission. Such framing, as we see in the UM example, can link decision-making to the core identity of the institution and help to legitimate the university's public purposes.

QU should look to another Ontario neighbor, McMaster, for an exemplar of an integrated report that makes effective use of symbolic framing to create an ethos of confidence, creativity, and transparency. McMaster's 2013–2014

Annual Financial Report combines striking graphics and student art revolving around a theme – of *mosaic* – that reflects the university's efforts "to bring together several strategic plans" that are then either described in the document or hyperlinked. The table of contents shows the elements of the report, which include more than simply financial data. The Management's Discussion and Analysis is organized by topic, each with its own image and caption to introduce it, which provides incredible detail (both visually and in writing) well beyond most financial statements. Like UM, McMaster uses high production values and accessible language to reify its image (as a creative, student-centered, and forward-thinking institution), while the integration of student art and captions reinforces the lofty goals of higher education as a public good that comes from careful attention to financial stewardship in the service of the academic mission. For instance, the image at the top of the "By the Numbers" page, titled *Spies on the Beach*, is described in the caption box:

> The integration of figures in an enigmatic space through the process of collage is reflective of the mosaic initiative that aims to apply innovative processes and practices to encourage student growth and success. The images function as a reflection of very human encounters of confidence, inspiration, vulnerability, and strength through experience; all feelings we encounter on our journey toward higher learning.

QU is on the way toward this kind of transparent and fully integrated annual report, something that all the public institutions in our sample should embrace as they adapt to the erosion of government support for higher education.

Conclusion

University leaders who recognize political constraints in the environment can begin to focus attention on taking steps to build realistic and sustainable futures. Political polarization will continue to exert its effects on state and provincial government, and their public universities, for the foreseeable future until such time voters enact changes through the electoral process. Universities, in turn, cannot grow out of their present financial conditions through enrollment increases because it has either plateaued (in Ontario) or declined (in Michigan). Nor can public universities impose large tuition and fee increases in the face of government and competitive market pressures. These constraints, coupled with regular economic cycles including recessions, will sustain fiscal stressors that demand the kind of integrated university response illustrated by McMaster.

Decision-makers from the president down to academic department level should avail themselves of the integrated system and use it first, to recognize the institution's broader trajectories, and second, to determine how their organizational unit fits into these trajectories. At a minimum, the system should include a variety of "portals" for leaders interested in budgets, financial statements, strategic plans, capital plans, performance results, and program prioritization plans. Familiarity with such an integrated system will sensitize users to financial and budgetary conditions, the practice of foresight and strategic thinking, external as well as internal competitive pressures, and programmatic needs, demands, and subsidies. A system of this kind, as shown by the McMaster experience, complements traditional "programmatic" thinking common among education leaders with a more pragmatic financial way of thinking about the enterprise. This should facilitate the building of organizational coalitions around exceedingly difficult decisions required in times of political polarization and fiscal stress.

For purposes of shared governance and fuller public accountability, we are looking for richer descriptions of institutions' distinctiveness and their ability to adjust to the demands of a range of constituents.

> Since the environment is driving the demand for increased accountability, higher education can best protect its interests by becoming actively involved in dictating the types of information that best portray the wide range of benefits that emanate from higher education. Otherwise, a bottom-line economic perspective might be externally applied and would, in the long run, lead higher education away from many of its real societal responsibilities (Lawrence, 1978, p. 176).
>
> (Coy et al. 2001: 26)

Judging the health of an institution goes beyond its financial condition to the quality of the leadership's decision-making, and an integrated, more robust, and transparent reporting system can allow for more informed judgments. Moreover, in polarized politics, the best strategic option for an institution's leadership rests on an integrated and comprehensive system that simultaneously blunts adversarial attacks while effectively conveying the institution's rich potential to fulfill its stakeholder needs. The leadership can employ its mosaic system to attract, convince, and mobilize its stakeholders and constituents to forge a protective shield against polarized politics and thereby broaden awareness of its mission, vision, and accomplishments.

Note

1 Please contact Lawrence Sych if you would like a copy of this or any of the other reports examined in this chapter: lawrence.sych@cmich.edu.

References

Anderson, Bruce and David Coletto. 2014. "Ontario Election: Too Close to Call." *Abacus Data*. Available at http://abacusinsider.com/ontario-election-2/close-call-liberals-tories-tied-36-voters-ndp-22/ (accessed May 3, 2015).

Asen, Robert. 2012. "Lyndon Baines Johnson and George W. Bush on Education Reform: Ascribing Agency and Responsibility through Key Policy Terms." *Rhetoric and Public Affairs* 15, no. 2: 289–317.

Baumer, Donald C. and Howard J. Gold. 2010. *Parties, Polarization, and Democracy in the United States*. Boulder, CO: Paradigm Publishers.

Bickerton, James. 2014. "Competing for Power: Parties and Elections in Canada." In *Canadian Politics*, James Bickerton and Alain-G. Gagnon (eds.), pp. 249–279. Toronto: University of Toronto Press.

Brown, K.W. 1993. "The 10-point Test of Financial Condition: Toward an Easy-To-Use Assessment Tool for Smaller Cities." *Government Finance Review* 9, no. 6: 21–26.

Brownstein, Ronald. 2007. *The Second Civil War: How Extreme Partisanship Has Paralyzed Washington and Polarized America*. New York: Penguin Press.

Buddy, Nancy J. 2014. "Analyzing the Financial Condition of Higher Education Institutions Using Financial Ratio Analysis. University of North Texas Digital Library, Denton, TX. Available at http://digital.library.unt.edu/ark:/67531/metadc2194 (accessed November 16, 2014).

Cain, Patrick and Anna Mehler Paperny. 2014, June 24. "Your Guide to Ontario's Political Polarization (Have Fun Governing That)." *Global News*. Available at http://global-news.ca/news/1407504/your-guide-to-ontarios-political-rifts-have-fun-governing-that/ (accessed May 25, 2015).

Chariri, Anis and Fakultas Ekonomi. 2007. "Rhetoric in Financial Reporting: A Case Study." Paper presented at the Eighth Asian Academic Accounting Association Conference, August 19–20. Available at http://core.ac.uk/download/pdf/11702265.pdf (accessed March 25, 2017).

Coletto, David. 2011. "Ontario Political Party Brand Analysis." *Abacus Data*. Available at http://abacusdata.ca/wp-content/uploads/2011/09/Party-Branding-Sept-18-2011-FINAL.pdf (accessed May 3, 2015).

Coy, David and Michael Pratt. 1998. "An Insight into Accountability and Politics in Universities: A Case Study." *Accounting, Auditing & Accountability Journal* 11, no. 5: 540–561.

Coy, David, Mary Fischer, and Teresa Gordon. 2001. "Public Accountability: A New Paradigm for College and University Annual Reports." *Critical Perspectives on Accounting* 12: 1–31.

Dar, Luciana and Dong-Wook Lee. 2014. "Partisanship, Political Polarization, and State Higher Education Budget Outcomes." *The Journal of Higher Education* 85, no. 4: 469–498.

Denneen, Jeff and Tom Dretler. 2012. "The Financially Sustainable University: A Focused Strategy Can Help Colleges and Universities Reinvent Their Industry and Stop Spending Beyond Their Means." *Bain & Company*. Available at www.bain.com/publications/articles/financially-sustainable-university.aspx. (accessed June 15, 2015).

Fethke, Gary C and Andrew J. Policano. 2012. *Public No More: A New Path to Excellence for America's Public Universities*. Stanford, CA: Stanford University Press.

Habegger, Beat. 2010. "Strategic Foresight in Public Policy: Reviewing the Experiences of the UK, Singapore and the Netherlands." *Futures* 42, no. 1: 49–58.

Hager, Peter J. and H.J. Scheiber. 1990. "Reading Smoke and Mirrors: The Rhetoric of Corporate Annual Reports." *Journal of Technical Writing and Communication* 20, no. 2: 113–130.

Hartley, Matthew and Christopher C. Morphew. 2008. "What's Being Sold and To What End? A Content Analysis of College Viewbooks." *The Journal of Higher Education* 79, no. 6: 671–691.

Ibbitson, John. 2015, May 22. "Alberta's Political Polarization Should Worry Justin Trudeau." *The Globe and Mail*. Available at www.theglobeandmail.com/news/alberta/

albertas-political-polarization-should-worry-justin-trudeau/article24574701/ (accessed June 14, 2015).

Jesse, David. 2015, June16. "Tough Choice? EMU Hikes Tuition, Forfeits $1M in State Aid." *Detroit Free Press.* Available at www.freep.com/story/news/local/michigan/2015/06/16/eastern-michigan-tuition-increase/28811079/ (accessed June 17, 2015).

Jones, Michael D. and Mark K. McBeth. 2010. "A Narrative Policy Framework: Clear Enough to Be Wrong?" *Policy Studies Journal* 38, no. 2: 329–353.

Justice, Jonathan B. and Eric A. Scorsone. 2013. "Measuring and Predicting Local Government Fiscal Stress: Theory and Practice." In *Handbook of Local Government Fiscal Health*, Helisse Levine, Jonathan B. Justice, and Eric A. Scorsone (eds.), pp. 43–74. Burlington, MA: Jones and Bartlett Learning.

Kavanagh, S.C. 2007. *Financing the Future: Long-Term Financial Planning for Local Government.* Chicago, IL: Government Finance Officers Association.

Kelderman, Eric. 2015, March 5. "Republican Governors' Shared Goals for Higher Ed: Accountability and Work-Force Preparation." *The Chronicle of Higher Education.* Available at http://chronicle.com/article/Republican-Governors-Shared/228227/. (accessed May 22, 2015).

KPMG LLP and Prager, McCarthy & Sealy, LLC. 1999. "Ratio Analysis in Higher Education: Measuring Past Performance to Chart Future Direction," 4th edn. Available at www.prager.com/Public/raihe4.pdf (accessed April 14, 2015).

Labaree, David F. 1997. "Public Goods, Private Goods: The American Struggle over Educational Goals." *American Educational Research Journal* 43, no. 1: 39–81.

Lambert, Lance. 2015, June 17. "Performance-Based Funding Can Be Fickle, One University's Close Call." *The Chronicle of Higher Education.* Available at http://chronicle.com/article/Performance-Based-Funding-Can/230943/ (accessed June 17, 2015).

Lawrence, B. 1978. "The Outcomes of Higher Education: To Measure or Not to Measure." In *Research and Planning for Higher Education*, R.H. Fenske and P.R. Staskey (eds.), pp. 175–178. Tallahassee, FL: Association for Institutional Research.

Mack, Janet and Christine Ryan. 2007. "Is There an Audience for Public Sector Annual Reports: Australian Evidence?" *International Journal of Public Sector Management* 20, no. 2: 134–146.

Mead, D.M. 2006. "A Manageable System of Economic Condition Analysis for Governments." In *Handbook of Public Financial Management*, H.A. Frank (ed.), pp. 383–417. New York: Taylor & Francis.

Mikesell, John L and Justin Ross. 2014. "State Revenue Forecasts and Political Acceptance: The Value of Consensus Forecasting in the Budget Process." *Public Administration Review* 74, no. 2: 188–203.

Morphew, Christopher C. and Matthew Hartley. 2006. "Mission Statements: A Thematic Analysis of Rhetoric across Institutional Type." *The Journal of Higher Education* 77, no. 3: 456–471.

Page, Dorian. n.d. "Southern Utah University – Financial Indicators (2011)." Available at www.suu.edu/ad/finance/pdf/financial-indicators-2012.pdf (accessed March 31, 2017).

Roberge, Ian. 2014. "Foresight: Transforming Government." In *Governance and Public Management: Strategic Foundations for Volatile Times*, Charles Conteh, Thomas J. Greitens, David K. Jesuit, and Ian Roberge (eds.), pp. 25–38. New York: Routledge.

Saichaie, Ken and Christopher C. Morphew. 2014. "What College and University Websites Reveal about the Purposes of Higher Education." *The Journal of Higher Education* 85, no. 4: 499–530.

Shor, Boris. 2014, January 14. "How U.S. State Legislatures Are Polarized and Getting More Polarized (in 2 Graphs)." *Washington Post*. Available at www.washingtonpost.com/blogs/monkey-cage/wp/2014/01/14/how-u-s-state. (accessed November 17, 2014).

Shor, Boris. 2014. "How U.S. State Legislatures Are Polarized and Getting More Polarized (in 2 Graphs)." www.washingtonpost.com/blogs/monkey-cage/wp/2014/01/14/how-u-s-state (accessed November 17, 2014).

Shor, Boris and Nolan McCarty. 2011. "The Ideological Mapping of American Legislatures." *American Political Science Review* 105, no. 3: 530–551.

Simeon, Richard, Ian Robinson, and Jennifer Wallner. 2014. "The Dynamics of Canadian Federalism." In *Canadian Politics*, James Bickerton and Alain-G. Gagnon (eds.), pp. 65–91. Toronto: University of Toronto Press.

Tandberg, David A. and Nicholas W. Hillman. 2014. "State Higher Education Performance Funding: Data, Outcomes, and Policy Implications." *Journal of Education Finance* 39, no. 3: 222–243.

10 The silence is deafening

A look into financial services sector policymaking in Canada

Ian Roberge

This volume analyzes polarization from multiple angles, including its causes and effects. The opposite of polarization is silence, or apathy. There are many policy fields where popular engagement is limited. Among other reasons, there may be few mechanisms in place to encourage participation. Policymakers may also be minimally interested in popular input, or may just pay lip service to it. Citizens themselves may not always be interested in participating. This silence is just as troubling as polarization. The policymaking process in these fields is often left to experts who yield great influence. Their decisions may not always reflect the broadly defined public good. How is participation to be facilitated in policy fields where involvement is limited? How are barriers to participation to be overcome? How is policymaking to be more inclusive, most importantly in fields where citizens are not currently heard, or where there is a dearth of interest, but where their input would be beneficial? In the financial services sector, policymaking is expert-led and there are few opportunities for citizens to engage. Popular input is rarely solicited. There are, though, good reasons to encourage greater participation; among them, is that citizens are also consumers of financial products. Finance plays a central role in the economy of a country, yet citizens have almost no say in decision-making. This chapter considers ways of facilitating citizen participation in financial services sector policymaking.

More precisely, this chapter focuses on Canada where popular participation is circumscribed. The Canadian case is an interesting one because the country's apparent good fortunes during the 2007–2008 global financial crisis has generated a feeling of false security anchored in the belief that the system is immune from major turbulence. Canadian success, though, has been overblown. Canada went through the worst financial crisis of its history in 2007 – the asset-backed commercial paper crisis (Harris 2010). During the global crisis, three of the country's "big five" banks would have gone under without government support (Macdonald 2012). The global financial crisis helped generate polarized politics in the United States and in Europe (Funke et al. 2015). Canadians, for their part, have generally remained nonchalant. The country's political and economic elites have claimed that the country was a model to emulate, which the public has accepted. While the United States and Europe adopted financial services sector reforms, the Canadian government did not push forward any substantive policy change. The population, in turn, has not been particularly interested in financial services sector policy. Livesey (2012) highlights many reasons why Canadians should be wary of the country's big banks, yet there is popular apathy. The problem in Canada is that policymaking is fairly closed or opaque, that it is hard for citizens to participate and that despite the field's significance citizens are genuinely not interested in getting involved. How is this apathy to be explained, and how to overcome it? How is popular participation to be encouraged? How is consumer interest to be accounted for and integrated into the policymaking process? Faced with multiple challenges, Canada would surely profit from a robust conversation about finance policy.

In this chapter we explore two interrelated arguments. First, polarization and the lack of participation has the same remedy – increased politicization. The concept of politicization, in this case, refers to the institutionalization of mediated sites of engagement to facilitate and encourage participation. Politicization allows for the expression and inclusion of diverse voices in a structured environment and can serve as a mechanism to manage conflict. In the Canadian case, there is limited politicization and the sector is, largely, governed in a technocratic fashion. There are few avenues for participation into financial services sector policymaking. The second argument is that policymakers need to strike the right balance between opacity and transparency to allow for politicization and to facilitate the inclusion of a diversity of voices in the policy process. In Canada like elsewhere, policymaking in the financial services sector too often leans toward the opacity side of the spectrum to the detriment of transparency. Regulatory decision-making, in particular, tends to be done without much public scrutiny. Citizens are excluded on the justification that they do not possess the requisite technical knowledge to participate effectively in decision-making. There is no reason to believe, however, that under the right circumstances citizens could not make a valuable contribution to policymaking in finance. Politicization, as such, gives users a chance to have a voice in the decision-making process.

The first part of this chapter considers the equilibrium needed between politicization, citizen engagement, opacity, and transparency. The second part analyzes the Canadian case in some detail. We also consider one particular way in which to increase participation in financial services sector policymaking – a regulatory users' committee. The proposal is not put forward as a panacea. However, the committee represents a form of politicization that can account directly for the interests of consumers in the policymaking process.

The research for this chapter results from a literature review that includes publicly available grey literature sources, as well as primary and secondary sources. Please note that despite some obvious differences citizens/consumers/users will be used interchangeably throughout this chapter.

Fostering engagement via politicization

This chapter considers the particularities of the policymaking process in the financial services sector as well as the ways by which to encourage, via politicization, citizen engagement. We also discuss the appropriate balance between opacity and transparency in policymaking and regulation.

The current state of policymaking in finance makes citizen participation difficult. Policymaking in this field is decentred, which favors a more opaque process. There are five central characteristics to consider: complexity, fragmentation, interdependencies, ungovernability, and the rejection of a clear public/private dichotomy (Andenas and Chiu 2014; Black 2002, 2008). We look at each in turn.

First, the rise of modern scientific finance exemplifies complexity, putting a great deal of emphasis on modeling for all financial activities (de Goede 2001). Policymakers must confront this highly technical field. Finance's complexity is often the main reason used to exclude outsiders from decision-making. Policymaking requires expertise that few citizens possess. As an example, there are few efforts at consultation in the EU using plain language (McKeen-Edwards and Roberge 2007).

Second, the financial services sector is not a single entity; rather, the industry is fragmented into banking, securities, and insurance. There is a great deal of diversity even between these sub-sectors – retail banking and investment banking, stock market operation and over-the-counter trading, insurance and re-insurance, etc. In devising policy, governments must account for the multiplicity of actors, perspectives, and interests that are inherent to fragmented policy fields. There is no single actor, or group of actors, that can speak to the sector as a whole, and each sub-sector has its own interests, specificities, and challenges. The fragmentation of the field could facilitate, in theory, the inclusion of non-experts in policymaking. In practice, fragmentation makes it even harder to include and account for citizens' input into decision-making, again due to the complexity and number of issues to be considered in each sub-sector. Admittedly, consumer groups tend to have greater access to retail banking than they do to other parts of the industry.

Third, departments of finance, regulatory agencies, and private sector actors are interdependent. Global banking regulation (Basel I, II, and III), for instance, provides large banks with the opportunity to operate according to in-house risk models; the Basel Accords represent global standards that national governments adopt in the supervision and regulation of their financial services sector firms. The interdependence between government and industry creates a community of experts, but leaves little room for other voices in the process.

Fourth, finance is ungovernable. The concept of ungovernability does not mean that governments should not elaborate policy, or regulate the sector. The concept refers, instead, to the idea that the very best policy or regulation may not be sufficient to prevent or contain a financial crisis. Financial crises have taken place, in fact, with increased frequency since the fall of the Bretton Woods system. The high-stake nature of the field is another often-used argument for minimizing the participation of non-experts.

Finally, there is no clear public/private divide. Private authority is well-established in finance, and there is much rule-making that takes place out of the reach of the state. This is not to argue that governments could not regulate further if they so intended, but rather that private sector actors – professional associations, for example – often act as policymakers (McKeen-Edwards and Porter 2013). Professional associations represent their members, primarily, and there is almost no place for citizen input in private policymaking (Porter and Ronit 2006).

How is participation to be facilitated in a decentred policymaking environment? The practices of policymaking in finance make it hard to see who accounts for the public good. Government officials are likely to argue that it is part of their mandate, but without broader popular participation, they may well be far removed from the range of perspectives that exist across society. Politicization provides the means by which citizens can participate, deliberate, or, at the very least, be represented in the policymaking process. Politicization also strikes the right equilibrium between the need to increase transparency, to disseminate information, while keeping some required opacity. Politicization provides the means for mediated participation, within an institutionalized setting, to permit constructive dialogue. The concept of politicization, as applied here, does not refer to a government-dominated process, or a partisan-type exercise that could generate further polarization. Rather, politicization provides a stable mechanism institutionally by which to accommodate various perspectives into policymaking, even within a decentred environment. In the second section of this chapter, we present a practical proposal for the politicization of finance in Canada by creating a users' committee to give citizens a voice in the policymaking and regulatory process.

For politicization to be effective, policymakers, especially in finance, must strike a balance between opacity and transparency. Too much opacity makes participation difficult, while too much transparency can lead to disillusionment. There are, at the very least, three good reasons for increased transparency in policymaking in general, and more specifically in finance. The drawbacks are addressed further below. The first is that transparency is necessary to facilitate a democratic dialogue. Without access to information, citizens are hard-pressed to organize themselves and participate in the decision-making process, or even gain a voice as a legitimate interlocutor. Opacity, thus, at the very least, makes it difficult for citizens to engage since they do not possess enough information to participate effectively in the process. The second reason to favour transparency is that it is needed for purposes of accountability. Without information, there are few opportunities to hold actors to account for sub-optimal performance. This is a particularly important issue in finance where assessing performance, especially of regulatory agencies, is difficult (Roberge and Dunea 2015). Third, transparency is also needed to safeguard the legitimacy of the policymaking process and of the actors. Governments and private sector actors will often use output legitimacy, rather than input legitimacy, to protect from further scrutiny. Reliance on output legitimacy, of course, is problematic when there is a policy failure – like the global financial crisis – that shows the limits of existing policies.

There are, however, also very good reasons to protect opacity, especially in the financial services sector. For instance, the decision-making process is more efficient when opaque. In a fast-paced environment like finance, public authorities will find themselves under pressure to act quickly, most notably if it is to help prevent or contain a crisis. The effectiveness of policies and decisions made under pressure in an opaque environment is contestable; too often, there is a lack of available information to properly assess performance. Another reason to prefer opacity is that government officials handle confidential market information and disclosure can negatively affect market behavior. Regulators act as a 'referee' (Dickson 2012) in the marketplace and divulging information can make it appear as if they are taking sides. The final consideration relates to regulatory effectiveness. Transparency, it is argued, will lead regulators to use standardized instruments that generate one size fits all solutions making it difficult, in some circumstances, to reach desired policy and regulatory objectives (Ericson et al. 2003). Regulation is as much art as science, and relies on the good judgement and experience of regulators (Snider 2009). Transparency, thus, risks undermining regulators' ability to use their common sense.

There are other considerations, as well, in this debate. A more open policy process could encourage polarization. Transparency risks greater tension in the policymaking process. Politicization, in this case, provides an answer to polarization since the mediated nature of the engagement ensures that opposing perspectives are accounted for while minimizing the risk of destructive conflicts. The institutionalized nature of the engagement, and its inclusiveness, is expected to minimize the threats from polarization. That being said, there might well be reasons in finance to favour some conflict to break-up the seemingly all too cozy relationship between government and business. There is also the possibility that too much information can lead to a decline in trust (Grimmelikhuijsen et al. 2013). Citizens need to trust government and their financial firms since confidence is at the heart of the financial system. Lack of trust among consumers can lead to a serious market breakdown. Another consideration is: Which is most likely to lead to regulatory capture, or regulatory arbitrage? There is a strong argument to be made that the policymaking process can be highjacked if overly transparent (Barkow 2010), or that debates can be rendered meaningless to accommodate the lowest common denominator. At the same time, opacity can serve to hide relationships that are too close and/or that pose an ethical risk. The debate on opacity vs. transparency highlights the fact that policymaking in finance is subject to an uneven playing field. Banks and other private sector actors enjoy much greater access than citizens do. The challenge, therefore, is to find the right balance between opacity and transparency that facilitates participation, still taking into account the need to keep some information confidential.

Why include users in financial services sector policymaking in the first place? To what extent is the balance tilted towards opacity in financial services sector policymaking? Should policymaking in this field not simply be left to experts? Can increased participation improve policymaking, and especially, policy outcomes? There have been many policy reforms at the supra-national level and by national governments after the 2007–2008 global financial crisis; as part of these reforms, there have been uneven efforts across countries to provide for greater transparency and accountability. For instance, Great Britain's massive post-crisis regulatory restructuring sought, among many objectives, to provide for greater transparency and accountability in policy and rulemaking. The government dissolved the Financial Services Authority and, instead, created three new regulators: the Financial Policy Committee (FPC) responsible for macro-supervision, the Prudential Regulation Authority (PRA), responsible for micro-supervision – both located in the Bank of England – and the Financial Conduct Authority. The Bank of England's PRA website lists as part of its three key initiatives, strengthening accountability (Bank of England 2015). In Canada, policymaking in finance remains generally closed and there does not appear to be a lot of interest in addressing the situation.

There is reason to believe, as the literature in public administration demonstrates, that participation in policymaking under certain conditions can be of use to governments and citizens alike (Irvin and Stansbury 2004). We know of no research that attempts to link user input, decision-making, implementation, and policy outcomes specifically in finance, or that provides a comparison of the role of users of financial services in the policymaking process across countries. There are some indications that despite its peculiarities, financial services sector policymaking would benefit from greater openness. McKeen-Edwards (2013), for instance, argues that the inclusion of consumers in the EU through a users' committee has affected, at the very least, the agenda of regulatory agencies. McKeen-Edwards' research is limited, though, and she does note that users had little influence in terms of decision-making.

There is a strong argument to be made for the inclusion of citizens into the policymaking process. Policies affect citizens as consumers of financial services sector firms, and via the sector's impact on the economy. Governments, as remarked earlier, will suggest that it is their responsibility to protect the public's interest; financial firms will also claim to speak on behalf of and for their customers. We should be wary, however, of the nature of the relationship between government departments/agencies and private sector actors. The significance of the Washington–Wall Street consensus is debatable, but the close connections between politicians and bankers cannot be completely ignored (Johnson and Kwak 2010). Governments have a public mandate, but they are under tremendous pressure from multiple outside actors. Consumer advocates, of course, are also self-interested. They are unlikely, though, to dominate a process that is so heavily tilted in favour of private sector actors. As such, financial services sector users are in a position to provide an alternative perspective that counters that which is often heard, and is dominant, from financial institutions. The argument, therefore, is that the meaningful inclusion of users within a mediated setting can enhance the prospects for evidence-based policymaking, and act as a counterweight to a powerful industry.

Admittedly, the inclusion of users in policymaking is no easy task, and there are many possible roadblocks. There is a divide between the financialization of the economy – the importance of the policy field – and, the public's interest. The public often seems content, especially in Canada, to let governments and even private sector actors make the big decisions. Governments could theoretically open the doors wide open, encourage direct democracy, but citizens might still be quite reluctant to engage. Getting users to buy-in and participate, and to do so effectively, is part of the challenge. Citizens may become particularly interested in finance policy during or immediately after a crisis, when they are worried about the impact of the crisis on their personal finance. Citizens are less likely to be engaged when finance and the economy appear to be functioning more normally. In addition, citizens may be interested in very select parts of the industry – for example, bank fees and credit card fees – but they may not be as interested in other policy questions. Finance may be central to an economy, and policy failure and market breakdown may have far-reaching consequences; citizens, though, may not always understand how more esoteric aspects of the industry affect their own personal prospects. Moreover, citizen engagement is no fail-safe against policy failures. From that perspective, citizens may be happy to leave matters in the hands of experts, to trust that there will be few errors and that when mistakes are made they will be contained. Greater transparency is a worthy objective, but it is no magic remedy.

Decentred financial services sector policymaking renders the process opaque, in turn, making it harder for citizens to participate. The creation of a users' committee to facilitate mediated participation, as proposed in the second section of this chapter, represents a practical way to include and account for users' interests in policymaking while minimizing the risks and pitfalls of excessive transparency.

Financial services sector policy and rulemaking in Canada

This section considers ways to facilitate citizen engagement in Canadian financial services sector policymaking via politicization. It is divided into three subsections. First, the opacity of the Canadian system is discussed. Second, we consider the Office of the Superintendent of Financial Institutions (OSFI – the country's prudential regulator) in reference to the debate on opacity and transparency. Finally, we make a proposal for a regulatory users' committee, as a form of mediated process, to attain greater citizen input into policymaking.

Decentred policymaking in Canada

Canadian policymaking in finance is decentred, as described above. The policymaking process here again favours opacity to the detriment of access. First, although the country's financial services sector is small, so that it does not appear as complex as that in other countries, Canada's "big five" banks nonetheless dominate the industry and are active across sub-sectors, especially in the banking, securities, and insurance fields. Second, the policy field is fragmented. Jurisdictional authority over finance is split between the federal government and the provinces: the latter is responsible for banks and the solvency of insurance firms; the former is responsible for the securities sector, trusts, and parts of market conduct in the insurance industry. Third, there is interdependence between governments at all levels and private sector actors. For instance, the federal government has traditionally had a very cozy relationship with the "big banks" (Coleman 1996). Fourth, the sector is ungovernable. The financial services sector in Canada is generally considered safe; the governability challenge, as such, should not be seen in isolation, but from a global perspective where contagion from a crisis elsewhere, especially the United States, can threaten the Canadian system. The 2007 asset-backed commercial paper crisis resulted, in part, from exposure to the US sub-prime market. The events pointed, as well, to supervisory and regulatory failures (Harris 2010). Finally, private authority in finance also exists in Canada. For instance, the Investment Industry Regulatory Association of Canada (IIRAC) regulates dealer firms and is responsible for market integrity rules in regard to trading activity on equity marketplaces. Canadian policymaking is opaque, and part of the challenge is how to allow for citizen engagement in this decentred environment.

There are three further observations that are worth considering as they relate specifically to opacity in Canadian policymaking. The first observation is that there are few avenues for popular participation. Despite Canada's federal system that technically provides the possibility for citizens to engage and put pressure at both levels of political authority – though it also blurs responsibility and accountability – there are few avenues for users to provide input. There is no permanent mechanism for citizens to participate in the policymaking process. Parliamentary procedures, obviously, allow for limited participation through the normal political channels, and there have been times in the past when the financial services sector had political salience. There were structural adjustments to the industry through the 1980s and 1990s that elicited participation. For example, the process that led to the adoption of Bill C8 in 2001 – the last major revision of the Bank Act – was the result of a five-year consultation exercise that was open and transparent (Roberge 2006). The legislation itself was concerned with consumer protection and created the Financial Consumer Agency of Canada (FCAC). During this process, the federal government rejected merger requests from four of Canada's "big five" banks. The government's decision partially reflected the pressure that was put on it by citizens. Since that time, though, and despite the global financial crisis, the financial services sector has lost a lot of its prominence.

The second obstacle is users' apathy. There are few advocates, and no organization or group dedicated to finance. The community is, thus, disorganized making it difficult to exert pressure on policymakers. This is, of course, notable since business is organized. The finance policy network in Canada is small, closed, and resembles a policy community (Roberge 2013). There is a close-knit relationship among recognized participants, including governments and private sector actors. The network might be effective in managing the sector, but there is little permanent outside participation. Canadian financial services sector users are only circumstantially engaged. In the debates leading to the 2001 policy reform referenced above, *Democracy Watch* was the most active consumer group. There are generalist consumer associations like *Option consommateurs*. There are also ad hoc groups of individuals that are dedicated to the protection of small investors. However, the more powerful consumer lobbies of the type that exist in the United States or in Europe are not present in Canada. Financial services sector users are disorganized which makes it difficult to get their voices heard in the policymaking process.

The last consideration is that there are few avenues for redress when a user has been injured. There are many instances when Canadian financial services sector users have been ill-served by the industry and regulators (Livesey 2012), but there are few recourse options. In the banking sector, there is a fractured ombudsperson system. There are two ombudspersons for banking, the Ombudsman for Banking Services and Investments and the ADR Chambers Banking Ombuds Office. Within the securities industry, provincial regulators, with the possible exception of *l'Autorité des marchés financiers* in Québec, have been very slow and are generally unresponsive to users' concerns. The IIRAC investigates customer complaints on dealers, but it is a private organization and its processes are obscure, especially for a small investor. From the perspective of Canadian citizens, there are few avenues for redress, and that interaction generally seems to be to the advantage of the industry.

The global financial crisis could have opened a window to allow for a re-examination of the sector in Canada. Yet there was no debate and little appetite for reform. Though most states saw fit to review in-depth their national policy, the Canadian federal government chose not to re-examine the sector and to make, instead, incremental changes. The fact that there has not been a re-appraisal means that there have been few opportunities in recent years for users to engage with policymakers in this area. Canada may have escaped the worst of the financial crisis, but it has not necessarily learned from it (Williams 2012). The major financial services sector reform initiated by the federal government in the post-crisis era is the plan for the creation of a national securities regulator. This is a significant development, but it is only peripherally related to the global financial crisis. Though users have generally been favourable to the idea of a national regulator, due largely to the weakness of current provincial authorities, it remains to be seen whether the new system, if and when operational, will be more "consumer-friendly." The challenge, of course, is to facilitate engagement beyond the broad circumstantial consultative processes. Decisions made at the supervisory and regulatory level also require popular input and oversight.

There are good reasons going forward to include users, via mediated means, in finance policymaking. Canadian policymakers, like their counterparts in other countries, will need to address in years to come transformative changes in the industry resulting from, among other factors, information technologies. For instance, the rise of virtual currencies creates a real challenge for policymakers and industry professionals – in Canada, as elsewhere. Users' may very well have a radically different view on these changes than insiders. It is, therefore, important to consider in practice how to include users in the policy and regulatory-making process.

The Office of the Superintendent of Financial Institutions (OSFI)

This sub-section provides a succinct overview of how financial services sector regulatory agencies function in Canada focusing specifically on OSFI. We tend to focus on citizen input into policymaking, but there are good reasons to study, as well, the regulatory process. Regulators make important decisions, and non-decisions, that have a direct impact on the health of the industry. The public, as such, has a direct stake in making sure that regulators perform strongly, and that regulatory shortcomings get addressed quickly. Regulators, though, tend to work opaquely. Again, because of the technical nature of the work, citizens are generally excluded from the process. There are, thus, good reasons to seek ways to increase citizen participation into regulatory affairs. As the prudential supervisor, OSFI is responsible for the supervision and regulation of financial services sector firms, e.g., the "big five" banks. The Department of Finance, the Bank of Canada, the Canada Deposit Insurance Corporation (CDIC) and the FCAC are the other key public sector actors at the federal level. There are also provincial regulators – e.g., the Ontario Securities Commission and the Financial Services Commission of Ontario. In the opacity–transparency continuum, OSFI remains a closed organization.

Canada's prudential regulator, OSFI, is an independent regulatory agency with the mandate to supervise and regulate federal financial institutions. The organization is minimally transparent, reporting annually to Parliament via the Minister of Finance. The regulator's mode of operation, however, is for the most part opaque. Most importantly, OSFI and private sector actors enjoy a close rapport. On the positive side, the regulator is able to solve issues quickly, often pre-emptively and without much difficulty, as a result of this good working relationship. There are risks, though, in the way that OSFI and private sector actors interact; most evidently, there is a lack of clarity with regard to compliance (IMF 2014). Savage (2014: 29) describes the process for intervention as follows:

> The first step would be for the regulator to bring the situation to the attention of management and to require a well thought-out plan to address the issue. If the plan is not effective or is not followed, the regulator would follow up, perhaps by meeting directly with the board, and insisting that steps be taken to get the problem under control. If there continues to be no effective action, the regulator might consider other possible interventions, such as requiring the institution to increase its capital base to offset the higher level of risk, or requiring that the institution bring in new management with respect to the area of concern.

The regulator does not publicly report on compliance measures. OSFI can effectively contact and work across Canada's small network to address problems before or when they occur. At the same time, the regulator's stealthy approach may not always be necessary. In contrast, the Office of the Comptroller of the Currency in the United States provides more information on its compliance operations. OSFI remains much more generic in its documentation.

The other issue is whether or not there is a link between OSFI's perceived effectiveness and its opacity (Anand and Green 2012). The regulator has been praised for the way it responded to the global financial crisis. Kelly et al. (2012), for instance, suggest that OSFI has been agile in terms of monitoring system-wide issues in the insurance industry. There are, however, problems with the claim, in this case, that the regulator's effectiveness is due to its opacity. First and as noted earlier, the evaluation of regulatory performance is not a straightforward exercise. The assessment of effectiveness is made even more difficult in a period of crisis. The fact that Canadian firms performed comparatively well during the global financial crisis is not a demonstration in and of itself that the regulator was effective. Canadian success is attributable to many factors, among others the structure of the industry, that are not necessarily related to the country's regulatory arrangement. The regulator can only claim partial credit for firms having avoided the worst of the crisis since so many other factors over which it had only limited control were also at play.

To link regulatory effectiveness to market performance equally provides for a circular argument. The regulator is effective because firms did well, or the opposite could be envisioned – the regulator performed poorly because firms are in trouble; the two are not obligatorily connected. When claiming that OSFI performed well because it was opaque, there is also an assumption that the regulator would have been less effective if it had been more open. Though there may be merit to such an assertion, it is also relatively hard to demonstrate or disprove. Anand and Green (2012) in particular do not give much credence to the possibility of regulatory capture in Canada; they simply suggest that it is very unlikely. The argument is not convincing. It could be argued that regulatory capture is quite possible in a small network due to the familiarity between actors and the fact that access is limited. The collapse of the Irish banking sector during the global financial crisis is a good example of regulatory capture within a small policy network (Ross 2009). The argument, again, is not that opacity should never be favored, but rather that its use should be limited and regulators should still have to report after the fact. Transparency, not opacity, should be the default option.

Proposal for a transparent financial services sector – a users' committee

The appropriate response to polarization, and the lack of popular participation, is the same: increased politicization. Citizens need to be brought into the policy and regulatory process using a mediated approach. Based on the specific

Canadian challenges noted above, what reforms are needed to ensure greater transparency and to provide more opportunities for user input? The Canadian government should create a financial services sector users' committee, similar to the one that exists in the EU, to account for the interests of consumers in policy and rulemaking. Similar committees as that proposed here have existed in other policy fields such as healthcare (Abelson et al. 2011), though admittedly too often in an ad hoc fashion. The creation of a users' committee is not a cure-all; however, it is a practical way in which to instill greater transparency, and for consumers to have an institutionalized voice within the system. The proposal is sketched out below.

There are two initial considerations that need to be thought about in terms of creating this new organization. The first consideration relates to the mandate of the users' committee. The role of the users' committee is to unequivocally represent and give a voice to the interests of citizens in the policy and rule-making process. The committee could also act as an oversight body for regulators, especially OSFI. The FCAC in Canada is responsible for financial literacy and consumer awareness. The FCAC's role, as a regulator, is to inform, but it does not necessarily provide a way for users to access the system and to influence decision-making directly. The CDIC has a delineated role, to provide deposit insurance to bank consumers. The users' committee should have a statutory mandate that allows for participation from within the system, giving it greater influence than the simple participation of citizens in any consultative endeavor. As such, and evidently, the committee must be a permanent fixture to allow for constant and regular input. By being permanent, the committee will develop the required expertise to be a credible interlocutor. It is important, as well, that the committee itself is accountable to the broader public. The committee will need to operate judiciously since it will have access to sensitive market information for which confidentiality will be important. The committee will need to strike its own balance between opacity and transparency. At the same time, the users' committee can report on its activities as precisely as possible to the public. The added value of the users' committee to policymaking is its emphasis on the interests of consumers.

The second consideration relates to membership and expertise. As noted above, civil society is not currently organized to provide input into financial services sector policy and regulatory affairs. How will the committee be formed and who will sit as members? How will they be trained? The users' committee can only be an effective voice for consumers if it is perceived as credible and non-partisan by policymakers and regulators – OSFI – and citizens alike. The committee needs to be representative of broader social interests, without becoming overly large and cumbersome. Members could include consumer advocates, university professors, small business owners, etc. The users' committee will need to have a small permanent staff to manage its affairs on a daily business, including the organization of meetings and correspondence. The challenge relating to knowledge, expertise, training, and information will also need to be addressed. To make a substantive contribution, committee members will have to develop a solid understanding of policy and regulatory processes and of the financial services sector as a whole.

The proposal has limitations that must be acknowledged. Most importantly, the users' committee will have to demonstrate that it can be effective and play a beneficial role in the policy and regulatory process, or it will just be seen as an unnecessary layer of bureaucracy. The credibility of the committee will depend, in fact, on its value proposition and its ability to meet it. The committee will need to cooperate closely with regulators, for which it will need to gain their trust, but it will also need to protect its autonomy in order to be a sound advocate for consumers. The expectation for this committee, especially from users, must also be reasonable. The committee will not radically transform policy, or policy-making, in the field. It can, however, act as a permanent fixture to present and address users' concerns, and to allow for citizen oversight over policy and rule-making.

The creation of a users' committee would be a step in the right direction, though it might not be sufficient to improve transparency and openness in financial services sector policymaking. There are other measures that can be considered in order to provide even more transparency, and to allow for some possible broader public debate. As identified when analyzing OSFI, part of the problem is the lack of detail about its operations, especially the way it obtains compliance. The Act governing OSFI could be amended to include a "duty to be transparent." The default option should be for OSFI to divulge as much information as possible, with due consideration of its impact on market activities. The onus, though, should be on OSFI to justify why information is kept secret rather than being made publicly available. The FCAC, as another option, could also be strengthened; it is little known and its role could be expanded. The FCAC could be given the means necessary to address financial literacy – an important consideration in light of the high debt load of the Canadian population – and to increase awareness about the financial services sector and the way it operates. Basic knowledge about how the system works may help consumers to be prudent in managing their financial affairs. The creation of a users' committee alongside these measures would go a long way in opening up the policy process in Canada.

Finally, governmental measures and the creation of a new committee can only go so far in creating a climate of transparency, accountability, confidence, and trust. There is a need for civil society itself to get more organized and to put pressure on the federal government to bring about change. In the aftermath of the global financial crisis, Canadians have been very trusting of their government and financial services sector firms. The government's self-congratulatory approach is good politics, and it has lulled Canadians into believing that the sector was well managed, supervised, and regulated. Canadians need and should trust public authorities, private sector actors, and experts on this sensitive topic, but that does not mean that they should not be informed, that they should not be active, and that they should not hold actors accountable when appropriate. Canadians certainly have the right to wonder how well the sector is prepared for the next crisis, which is sure to come.

Conclusion

Polarization is on one end of the spectrum of political participation, and the inability to participate, lack of interest or apathy, is at the other end. The solution to both problems, though, is the same: politicization. There must be a mediated political mechanism to resolve conflict, and/or to encourage citizen engagement. Participation, in turn, requires transparency. We addressed these issues by focusing specifically on financial services sector policymaking in Canada. The Canadian case is a good example of a well-supervized and regulated system that would, nonetheless, benefit from greater citizen input. In a decentred policymaking environment, there are many challenges to facilitating greater voice and access. Within Canada, the creation of a users' committee should be seriously considered as a way of creating a permanent avenue for citizens to engage in financial services sector policy and rule-making, and to encourage greater accountability on the part of authorities. The complex and technical nature of the field should not serve as an excuse preventing greater citizen participation. Financial services sector users can make a substantive contribution to policy debates. There is bound to be resistance to increased transparency and more participation in a field where the stakes are often considered very high. It is exactly because the sector is so central to economic growth, development, and prosperity that citizen input should be encouraged.

There are ample opportunities for future research. For instance, how does users' input affect financial services sector policymaking? How does it contribute to desired policy outcomes? There is also a need to further refine the model for a users' committee as sketched above for Canada. Fung's "Recipes for Public Spheres" (2003) may well provide the necessary guidance in order to elaborate an effective mechanism for participation. Among other considerations, particular attention will need to be paid to the mandate, membership, method of deliberation, and the overall operation of such a committee.

Financial crises have been coming with increasing speed in the post-Bretton Woods era. Proponents of a more inclusive, open, and transparent policy process in finance need to be heard; there is no reason why opacity should be the default option. Globally, there has been marginal progress in engaging citizens in financial services sector policymaking. Canadians, for their part, have been comforted that the threat was elsewhere, and that it could be handled by others. This is a case where a little noise might wake people up, foster a debate, and get citizens talking about the best way to make sure that the financial industry is ready and able to support tomorrow's economy. It's time to break the silence.

References

Abelson, Julia, François-Pierre Gauvin, and Élisabeth Martin. 2011. "Mettre en pratique la théorie de la deliberation publique: Études de cas du secteur de la santé en Ontario et au Québec." *Téléscope* 17 (1): 135–155.
Anand, Anita and Andrew Green. 2012. "Regulating Financial Institutions: The Value of Opacity." *McGill Law Journal* 57 (3): 399–427.

Andenas, Mads and Iris H.-Y Chiu. 2014. *The Foundations and Future of Financial Regulation: Governance for Responsibility*. Abingdon, UK: Routledge.

Bank of England. 2015. "Prudential Regulation Authority." Available at: www.bankofengland.co.uk/pra/pages/default.aspx# (accessed May 22, 2015).

Barkow, Rachel E. 2010. "Insulating Agencies: Avoiding Capture through Institutional Design." *Texas Law Review* 89: 15–79.

Black, Julia. 2002. "Critical Reflections on Regulation." *Australian Journal of Legal Philosophy* 27: 1–35.

Black, Julia. 2008. "Constructing and Contesting Legitimacy and Accountability in Polycentric Regulatory Regimes." *Regulation & Governance* 2: 137–164.

Coleman, William D. 1996. *Financial Services, Globalization and Domestic Policy Change: A Comparison of North America and the European Union*. Basingstoke, UK: Macmillan.

de Goede, Marieke. 2001. "Discourses of Scientific Finance and the Failure of Long-Term Capital Management." *New Political Economy* 6 (2): 149–170.

Dickson, Julie. 2012. "Remarks by Superintendent Julie Dickson to the International Institute of Finance." Office of the Superintendent of Financial Institutions, Government of Canada. Available at: www.osfi-bsif.gc.ca/Eng/osfi-bsif/med/sp-ds/Pages/jd20120522.aspx (accessed March 20, 2014).

Ericson, Richard V., Aaron Doyle, and Dean Barry. 2003. *Insurance as Governance*. Toronto: University of Toronto Press.

Fung, Archon. 2003. "Recipes for Public Spheres: Eight Institutional Design Choices and their Consequences." *The Journal of Political Philosophy* 11 (3): 338–367.

Funke, Manuel, Moritz Schularick, and Christoph Trebesch. 2015. "The Political Aftermath of Financial Crises: Going to Extremes." *Vox: CEPR's Policy Portal*. Available at: www.voxeu.org/article/political-aftermath-financial-crises-going-extremes#.Vmb8yS2NqO8.email (accessed December 22, 2015).

Grimmelikhuijsen, Stephan, Gregory Porumbescu, Boram Hong, and Tobin Im. 2013. "The Effect of Transparency on Trust in Government: A Cross-National Comparative Experiment." *Public Administration Review* 73 (4): 575–586.

Harris, Stephen. 2010. "The Global Financial Meltdown and Financial Regulation: Shirking and Learning – Canada in an International Context." In *How Ottawa Spends 2010–2011*, edited by G. Bruce Doern and Christopher Stoney. Montréal/Kingston: McGill-Queen's University Press.

IMF. 2014. "Intensity and Effectiveness of Federal Bank Supervision in Canada – Technical Note." Canada Financial Sector Assessment Program. Available at: www.imf.org/external/pubs/cat/longres.aspx?sk=41406.0 (accessed August 14, 2014).

Irvin, Renée A. and John Stansbury. 2004. "Citizen Participation in Decision Making: Is it Worth the Effort?" *Public Administration Review* 564 (1): 55–69.

Johnson, Simon and James Kwak. 2010. *Thirteen Bankers: The Wall Street Takeover and the Next Financial Meltdown*. New York: Pantheon Books.

Kelly, Mary, Anne Kleffner, and Darrell Leadbetter. 2012. "Structure, Principles and Effectiveness of Insurance Regulation in the 21st Century: Insights from Canada." *The Geneva Papers on Risk and Insurance - Issues and Practice* 37 (1): 155–174.

Livesey, Bruce. 2012. *Thieves of Bay Street: How Banks, Brokerages and the Wealthy Steal Billions from Canadians*. Mississauga: Random House.

Macdonald, David. 2012. "The Big Banks' Big Secret." Canadian Centre for Policy Alternatives, Ottawa. Available at: www.policyalternatives.ca/publications/reports/big-banks-big-secret (accessed May 22, 2015).

McKeen-Edwards, Heather. 2013. "Integrating User Voices into the European Financial Services Policy Process." In *Making Multilevel Public Management Work: Stories of Successes and Failures from Europe and North America*, edited by Denita Cepiku, David K. Jesuit, and Ian Roberge. Boca Raton: CRC Press, pp. 51–65.

McKeen-Edwards, Heather and Tony Porter. 2013. *Transnational Financial Associations and the Governance of Global Finance: Assembling Wealth and Power*. Abingdon, UK: Routledge.

McKeen-Edwards, Heather and Ian Roberge. 2007. "Progressing Towards Legitimacy: Financial Services Sector Policymaking in the EU After Lamfalussy." *Current Politics and Economics of Europe* 18 (2): 223–243.

Porter, Tony and Karsten Ronit. 2006. "Self-Regulation as Policy Process: The Multiple and Criss-Crossing Stages of Private Rule-Making." *Policy Sciences* 39 (1): 41–72.

Roberge, Ian. 2006. "Middle-Sized Powers in Global Finance: Internationalization and Domestic Policymaking." *Policy Studies* 27 (3): 253–270.

Roberge, Ian. 2013. "Canada and the Global Financial Crisis: A Model to Follow?" *Interfaces Brasil/Canada* 13 (16): 131–152.

Roberge, Ian and Dona M. Dunea. 2015. "Why Opacity is Just Not Good Enough: The Effectiveness and Accountability of Canada's Office of the Superintendent of Financial Institutions." In *Building Responsive and Responsible Financial Regulators in the Aftermath of the Global Financial Crisis*, edited by Pablo Iglesias-Rodriguez. Cambridge: Intersentia, pp. 255–273.

Ross, Shane. 2009. *The Bankers: How the Banks Brought Ireland to its Knees*. Dublin: Penguin Books.

Savage, Lawrie. 2014. "From Trial to Triumph: How Canada's Past Financial Crises Helped Shape a Superior Regulatory System." University of Calgary School of Public Policy Research Paper No. 7-15.

Snider, Laureen. 2009. "Accommodating Power: The 'Common Sense' of Regulators." *Social and Legal Studies* 18 (2): 179–197.

Williams, Russell Alan. 2012. "The Limits of Policy Analytical Capacity – Canadian Financial Regulatory Reform." *International Journal of Public Sector Management* 25 (6–7): 455–463.

Conclusion

Managing polarization to make governance work

David K. Jesuit and Russell Alan Williams

The dynamics driving polarization and increasingly irreconcilable policy stances are unlikely to change in the twenty-first century. Increasing economic uncertainty, inequality and globalization provide a potent environment for a hardening of partisan attitudes to core policy questions – vulnerability has always been good ground for simple-minded populist approaches to complex problems. This, in combination with social and mainstream media dynamics, has contributed not only to an increasingly hostile tone in modern politics, but also to a decreasing willingness to compromise and to accept policy relevant evidence essential to good governance and effective policymaking. We should not be surprised that some policy prescriptions have assumed a level of symbolic importance among both the public and members of government. In North America and in Europe, recent years have shown an increasing tendency to approach policy questions as "policy-based evidence making" rather than the "evidence-based policymaking" we should hope for. This, in combination with the increasing challenges of multilevel governance, will complicate policymaking.

Indeed, the kind of political polarization already well identified in the United States, polarization operating at both the level of public opinion and within the formal institutions of governance, makes it harder to deal with some of the most pressing policy challenges confronting states. Whether the issue is climate change, migration, economic inequality, economic restructuring or deindustrialization, or basic questions about economic governance, the extent to which both political elites and the public have taken increasingly hardened and irreconcilable views raises serious questions about the future effectiveness of government policy. Without specific strategies and institutional responses, polarization has broadly predictable impacts.

First, we can expect, in some instances, to see radical oscillations in policy as the balance of power shifts between partisan alignments – think, for example, of the radical "flip flops" in presidential orders regarding abortion policy (discussed in the Introduction to this volume). While Chapter 10 offers the caution that this kind of partisan politicization is not inherently bad, the point here is that some of the most pressing policy challenges (inequality, climate change, etc.) will not be effectively managed by reversing course every few years. Hyper-partisan struggles involving completely antithetical policy prescriptions will produce a level of incoherence. The kind of "wicked problems" many governments face will not be managed by incoherence.

Second, we can expect a great deal of inaction on core policy questions. The popular way to understand this in the United States is through the lens of "gridlock," but the dynamic can be seen elsewhere. Essentially, whether a product of the division of powers between government institutions or of multilevel governance settings, in the absence of a culture of compromise and processes designed to pursue solutions to policy problems rather than simply preferred policies, multiple points of access can impede any potential action. Politics becomes a symbolic game of simply blocking all action to sustain cherished views of the "wrongness" of the other side's solutions.

Third, we can expect only further decline in the public's faith in government more broadly. If polarization undermines policy coherence and action in response to perceived policy problems, the result can only be growing frustration that government does not "work." Ironically, this feedback is particularly problematic, as it also tends to provide evidence that the other side is to blame for societal problems, which in turn increases polarization.

Public policy and governance

When the modern "policy science" movement began twenty-five years ago, it had two key purposes. On the one hand, it suggested that the study of public policy and governance had to pay more attention to "process." It was not good enough for policy scholars to simply argue about what governments *should* do to solve problems; instead we needed to help policymakers develop strategies for translating evidence and analysis into effective political action (Weiss 1990; Sabatier 1991). On the other hand, policy scholarship adopted a healthy skepticism about the difficulties governments would face in trying to pursue evidence-based policymaking; the literature has always highlighted the importance of successfully managing the political arena in order to accomplish policy objectives (Kingdon 1995; Cairney 2014) and the interests of governments were never solely to provide "good" policy. No one familiar with the development of the comparative policy and governance field could be optimistic that increasing evidence of political polarization would not pose at least some additional risks to making governance work.

As such, in this volume we have attempted to further our understanding of the impact of political polarization on policymaking and to try to identify some strategies and recommendations for overcoming the risks it poses. While the preceding chapters adopted various methods and offered a variety of perspectives, there are three overarching conclusions.

First, political polarization is an increasing problem for policymakers around the world. Globalization and the transformation of the world's economy into a knowledge-driven economy have led to a wedge between economic and social interests, which creates competing economic and social policy demands that foster polarization. Recent decades have also witnessed a steady increase in wealth and income inequality in most states around the world. This trend promotes polarization to the extent that voters' economic circumstances shape their partisan identities and votes. In addition, demographic trends have emerged in which like-minded people sort themselves into ideologically homogeneous neighborhoods. These citizens also engage in self-selected exposure to partisan media, heightening the ideological distance between neighborhoods. Finally, decentralized decision-making structures, such as those found in the United States, Canada and the European Union, also promote polarization. Such economic, demographic and institutional factors are not readily changed.

The reality of these developments "on the ground" can be seen in several of our chapters. For example, Lindsay Flynn and Piotr Paradowski (Chapter 3) highlight the role of inequality in redirecting political preferences across countries – a timely argument in light of the combined lessons of Brexit and the 2016 US General Election. Likewise, Lawrence Sych and Marcy Taylor (Chapter 9) provide considerable evidence of how broader financial problems associated with these economic and social changes contribute to competing ideas about the role of public universities.

The second major conclusion emerging from our chapters is that polarization does have the broadly predictable impacts on policymaking identified above. While Robert Bartlett and Walter F. Baber (Chapter 4) highlight the extent to which many public policies require better mechanisms of dialogue and compromise, based on their data from the United States, Michael R. Wolf, J. Cherie Strachan and Daniel M. Shea (Chapter 2) conclude, "many Americans explicitly reject compromise." Indeed, Chapter 2 paints a distressing picture for those who think effective governance involves a level of pragmatism.

Likewise, increased economic hardship has hardened bargaining positions in the EU. According to Raffael Hanschmann (Chapter 6), this "prevents policy change beyond lowest-common-denominator compromises." Self-interested provincial "neighborhoods" with fundamentally different economies pursue diametrically opposed environmental policies, according to Russell Williams and Susan Morrissey Wyse (Chapter 5), creating institutional incentives for environmental "dialogues of the deaf" between communities. While both of these chapters highlight the need for cooperation across jurisdictions in managing complex environmental problems, economic vulnerability promotes parochialism.

This brings us to our third and most important point: polarization can be managed. Bartlett and Baber (Chapter 4), for example, emphasize the importance of process in redefining what we mean when we seek political consensus, arguing that consensus "does not need to have a reach that is either wide or deep to merit our approbation as a source of democratic legitimacy." Though Williams and Wyse (Chapter 5) find that Canadian federalism inhibited effective national solutions to climate change, it did lead to a "wide range of policy innovation, learning, and bold attempts by individual provinces to reduce emissions."

While in some circumstances federalism and multilevel governance may promote polarization, careful attention to process can reverse that dynamic.

Grasse et al. (Chapter 8) find that reformed institutional structures that depoliticize issues in cities can reduce conflict in potentially polarized municipalities. They also conclude that administrative tools such as strategic planning "help to influence, and perhaps even ultimately moderate, political conflicts in polarized communities." Charles Conteh (Chapter 1) makes a similar argument about the resilience of urban governance even in cities challenged by significant economic restructuring. In a similar vein, Sych and Taylor (Chapter 9) argue that leaders in higher education should adopt "the practice of foresight and strategic thinking" in an effort to blunt the effects of political polarization in their communities. Finally, Thomas Rohrer and Pamela S. Gates (Chapter 7) call for a new pedagogy aimed at environmental issues to be implemented at primary and secondary school levels. Thus, progress towards developing solutions even in polarized environments can, and must, be made.

In conclusion, despite the polarizing elections of 2016, including Donald Trump's surprising "populist" victory in the United States and the unexpected "Brexit" vote in the United Kingdom, there is no reason to assume that a rising tide of simplistic, diametrically opposed policy positions, backed by hardening partisan identification, necessarily undermines effective governance. At the very least, as Roberge reminds us, polarization is an aspect of democratic governance. While heightened levels of ideological conflict almost certainly inhibit optimal solutions to substantial policy challenges from being advanced, we are, arguably, better for it. As our title implies, we find many areas of agreement with Putnam et al. (1993): making governance work is part and parcel of making democracy work. The trick, based on our observations, is fostering institutional environments in which competing views need not lead to incoherence and inaction.

Bibliography

Cairney, Paul. 2014. "How Can Policy Theory Have an Impact on Policymaking? The Role of the Theory-Led Academic-Practitioner Discussions." *Teaching Public Administration*, May: 1–18.

Kingdon, John W. 1995. *Agendas, Alternatives, and Public Policies*. New York: Harper-Collins.

Putnam, Robert, R. Leonardi and R. Nonetti. 1993. *Making Democracy Work: Civic Traditions in Modern Italy*. Princeton, NJ: Princeton University Press.

Sabatier, Paul A. 1991. "Toward Better Theories of the Policy Process." *PS: Political Science and Politics*, 24, no. 2: 144–156.

Weiss, Carol H. 1990. "The Uneasy Partnership Endures: Social Science and Government," in Stephen Brooks and Alain-G. Gagnon (eds.), *Social Scientists, Policy and the State*, pp. 97–112. New York: Praeger.

Index

Page numbers in *italics* denote tables, those in **bold** denote figures.

Ihrke, Douglas 178
Independents: compromise, view of 43–4, *43*; compromise vs. standing firm 44–5, *45*; disagreement in political discussion and worldview 46–7, *46*; economic development governance arrangements 48–9, *49*
industrial restructuring 15–35; implementation, as a concept 17–18; multi-actor implementation framework 17–20
industrial restructuring study: bridge organizations 28; "compassionate" and "ecologically responsible" region narrative 22; competition for resource allocation 28; economic development governance arrangements 22–4; economic growth strategies 21–2, 28; education problems 26; Finger Lakes Region, New York 25–8, 28–9; governance literature 18–19, 20; government management of crisis and change 28–9; integrating perspectives 19–20; Niagara, Ontario 20–5, 28–9; non-state actors 23, 26–7; organization theory 18, 19–20, 29; public transport 23–4; regional economic reinvention 27
institutions' mediating effects on polarization 174–85; community influences 175–6; conflict 179, *179*, 180–1, 182; dependent variables 179; fiscal stress 176, 178, 180; independent variables 178–9; leadership 176, 178; literature review 174–7; managerial paradoxes 176–7; models and data 177; municipal government, forms of 174–5; partisan competition at elections 178–9; path model of polarized municipalities **181**; strategic planning 175, 176, 178, 180–1, 182; study results 179–82, *180*, *182*
International Monetary Fund (IMF) 162

Jesuit, David K. 1–12, 174–85, 224–7
Jones, Michael D. 191
Jreisat, J.E. 18
judiciary 4–5

Kelly, Mary 218
Kettl, Donald F. 18
Klinsky, Sonja 113
Knill, C. 127
KPMG LLP 189
Kyoto Protocol 8, 106, 108, 109–10, 112, 115, 117–18, 163, 167

Labaree, David F. 193–4, 196
leadership 176, 178, 204
Lee, Dong-Wook 187, 191
Levine, Charles H. 176
Livesey, Bruce 209
Luxembourg Wealth Study (LWS) 69

McBeth, Mark K. 191
McKeen-Edwards, Heather 213
Martin, Susan 199
Mead, D. M. 189
Meckling, J. 129
Mintzberg, Henry 175
Morphew, Christopher C. 192

Nagoya Protocol on Access to Genetic Resources and the Fair and Equitable Sharing of Benefits Arising from their Utilization 99–101
"Negotiating Agreement in Politics" (American Political Science Association) 36
net worth concept 61, 72–3, 76, 81
New York 25–8, 28–9
Niagara Economic Development Corporation (NEDC) 22
Niagara Economic Development Department (NEDD) 22–5, 28, 29
Niagara, Ontario 20–5, 28–9
NOMINATE 4
non-authoritarians *see* authoritarian/non-authoritarian views

Office of the Superintendent of Financial Institutions (OSFI) (Canada) 217–18, 220
open-systems analysis 18
organization theory 18, 19–20, 29
originalism 4–5

Page, Dorian 189
Pandey, Sanjay K. 176–7
Paradowski, Piotr R. 60–84, 226
partisanship 62, 73–5, *74*, 81; partisan polarization 37–8, 70, 71, 224–5
People's Republic of China, energy policies and climate change 159, 164–6
Pew Research Center 1, 5–6, 38, 45, *45*, 166
polarization: belief systems 126; challenges to policy making 1–2, 15–16; consequences of 6–7; definition of 2–3, 63; governance and public policy 225–7; and inequality 60–1, 63; and institutions

wealth distribution and voting behavior
60–84, 73; age groups 76, 80; class 62;
discussion of findings 80–2; economic
resources: wealth versus income 64–8;
economic voting: wealth, income and
employment, Germany and the US
75–8, *75*; economic vs. non-economic
factors: the case of Sweden 78–80;
Germany, 2002 election 70; Lorenz
curves in the United States and
Sweden 66–7, **67**; most salient issue
areas 78–80, *79*; net worth 72–3, 76,
81; net worth concept 61; partisanship
62, 73–5, *74*, 81; policy preferences
62–3, 81; political affiliation by wealth
level **71**; relationship between
economic resources and vote choice
60–1; share of income and wealth held
by households 64–5, **65**; small
business owners 76–7; study findings
73–82; study methods and case
selection 69–73; Sweden, 2002

election 70; US political affiliation by
wealth level 70; vote choice 70, 72, *72*,
73, *74*, 81; vote choice in Germany
77–8, **78**; wealth and income
distributions by country 65–6, **66**;
wealth portfolios by country 67, *68*;
wealth, vote choice and political
polarization 61–3
Weaver, Andrew 115
Weiler, Jonathan 38, 39, 42, 47
Western Climate Initiative (WCI) 113, 114
Wilfrid Laurier University (WLU), Ontario
199–201
Williams, Russell Alan 1–12, 106–25,
224–7, 226
Wilson, Woodrow 2
Wiseman, Hannah J. 163
Wolf, Michael R. 36–59, 226
World Resource Initiative 107
Wyse, Susan Morrissey 106–25, 226

young people 169

Taylor & Francis eBooks

Helping you to choose the right eBooks for your Library

Add Routledge titles to your library's digital collection today. Taylor and Francis ebooks contains over 50,000 titles in the Humanities, Social Sciences, Behavioural Sciences, Built Environment and Law.

Choose from a range of subject packages or create your own!

Benefits for you

>> Free MARC records
>> COUNTER-compliant usage statistics
>> Flexible purchase and pricing options
>> All titles DRM-free.

Benefits for your user

>> Off-site, anytime access via Athens or referring URL
>> Print or copy pages or chapters
>> Full content search
>> Bookmark, highlight and annotate text
>> Access to thousands of pages of quality research at the click of a button.

REQUEST YOUR **FREE** INSTITUTIONAL TRIAL TODAY

Free Trials Available
We offer free trials to qualifying academic, corporate and government customers.

eCollections – Choose from over 30 subject eCollections, including:

Archaeology	Language Learning
Architecture	Law
Asian Studies	Literature
Business & Management	Media & Communication
Classical Studies	Middle East Studies
Construction	Music
Creative & Media Arts	Philosophy
Criminology & Criminal Justice	Planning
Economics	Politics
Education	Psychology & Mental Health
Energy	Religion
Engineering	Security
English Language & Linguistics	Social Work
Environment & Sustainability	Sociology
Geography	Sport
Health Studies	Theatre & Performance
History	Tourism, Hospitality & Events

For more information, pricing enquiries or to order a free trial, please contact your local sales team:
www.tandfebooks.com/page/sales